JUST JOEY

JUST JOEY

The Joey Dunlop Story

Jimmy Walker

CollinsWillow

An Imprint of HarperCollins*Publishers*

First published in 2001
by CollinsWillow
an imprint of HarperCollins*Publishers*

© Jimmy Walker 2001

9 8 7 6 5 4 3 2 1

A CIP catalogue record for this book is
available from the British Library

ISBN 0 00 711546 6

Typeset by Rowland Phototypesetting Ltd,
Bury St Edmunds, Suffolk

Printed and bound in Great Britain by
Clays Ltd, St Ives plc

Photographic acknowledgements
Belfast Telegraph p 2 (centre), 6 (bottom), 8;
Gavan Caldwell/Pacemaker p 2 (bottom), 7 (top);
Stephen Davison/Pacemaker p 9 (top left), 14 (top
right), 15 (bottom); **Alex Dunlop/Pacemaker** 13 (top);
Helen Louden p 1 (all), 12 (top); **EMAP Automotive
Library** p 11 (top), 16; **Roy Harris** p 3 (top), 6 (top and
centre), 15 (top right); **Paul Lindsay/Pacemaker** p 14
(bottom); **Clifford McClean/Pacemaker** p 4 (bottom),
5 (top); **Don Morley** p 7 (bottom), 9 (bottom);
Original Double Red Ltd p 5 (bottom), 14 (top left);
Mike Proudfoot/Isle of Man Newspapers p 12
(centre); **John Smyth/Pacemaker** p 10 (all), 11 (centre),
12 (bottom), 13 (bottom), **John Watterson** p 11
(bottom); **John Watterson/Isle of Man
Newspapers** p 9 (top right).

ACKNOWLEDGEMENTS

I would like to thank the following for the help they provided in bringing out this book. Firstly my wife Iris for her inspiration and encouragement without which I would never have begun the project. My good friend and broadcaster Harold Crooks for his painstaking work on the early part of Joey's career. Elaine Magill for putting up with my many tantrums when typing the manuscript – mostly during unsociable hours. My daughter Shelley for not putting up with my tantrums when she deputised for Elaine. The Dunlop family, especially Joey's eldest sister Helen, for her unfailing courtesy and kindness and Joey's brother Robert for his memorable foreword. *Belfast Telegraph* Librarian, Walter Macauley, for providing so much information so quickly. Hector Neill for wasting no time in providing me with enough anecdotes to write a book on Hector himself! Brian Reid for the same. Memory man Harry Havelin for his superb supply of statistics which were always made available at a moment's notice. 'Mr TT' Peter Kneale for his painstaking research into Joey's Isle of Man career. Samantha Tompkins, Librarian at *Motorcycle News*. Wallace Rollins, publisher of *Road Racing Ireland*. Photographers Stephen Davidson, Roy Harris, Trevor Armstrong and Gavin Caldwell.

Jimmy Walker
May 2001

CONTENTS

FOREWORD

THE JOEY I KNEW BY ROBERT DUNLOP

Most people saw Joey for his brilliance on a motorcycle but to me he was just a brother, no different from my other brother Jim, but with a different personality and, after all, that's what makes us what we are.

Joey and I shared the same blood group but we also had a similar passion for racing and this was what drove Joey on. I am grateful that he had this special passion and that is why he would never have stopped racing; it's also the reason I can't either. I am glad my father understands and recognises this, for it's this passion which makes a man great.

On that devastating day, Sunday 2 July, when Joey was killed, Jim and I arrived at a small house in Union Street, which we call home, in the town of Ballymoney along with my four sisters to break the news about Joey.

Mum was just coming home with her little dog after a walk when I met her just outside the front door. I couldn't tell Mum. How could I? I just said: 'I've a bit of bad news' and Mum replied heartily: 'What's wrong with you now?' But it became devastatingly clear what was up as we entered the living room and she saw the looks on the faces of her family. I will never forget my mother's weeping at the loss of her son. I wept for my mother that day for I was chilled to the bone.

Joey was a very deep person at times but also a happy-go-lucky old fashioned type who loved to laugh and fool with people. When I was a teenager I looked up to him as my big brother and I suppose I tried hard to impress him. Joey knew this so he would dare me to do anything and talk me into going first. Then he would have a good laugh when I would fall on my face.

I miss the fun and the craic. I miss his stories of his adventures all over the world. I miss the great battles we had on the track but I do have my memories and they will go on forever. I can no longer look beside me in a race and see Joey's yellow helmet and his piercing eyes inside. I just talk to him now and I'm sure he can still hear me.

INTRODUCTION

All the way down to the most famous finishing line in motorcycle road racing they were cheering him, wishing him on, willing him to land that elusive treble which would put Joey Dunlop, living legend, at the top of the sport's most famous pantheon.

Could the pint-sized speed star with the world famous yellow helmet and the luminous number three on his front racing plate make it 26 TT wins at a time of life when most men his age were putting their feet up or at best nipping out to the garden to watch the roses grow.

But retirement was never Joey's scene. The 48-year-old Dunlop had lived with excitement as his goal throughout his 30-year racing career. He wasn't going to let his thousands of fans down, and that Wednesday afternoon, 7 June 2000, saw him race into history by grabbing his third TT treble and his 26th win in all. It was an awe-inspiring achievement and one which put the sport on to the front page yet again.

Yet within a few short weeks of his memorable Isle of Man treble, during which time the enigmatic Ulsterman had been treated like a film star, Dunlop, the man who threatened to live forever, was dead.

It was the most stunning blow – not only felt by motorcycle sport in Ulster and Ireland but throughout the sporting world. The attitude of a shell-shocked Ulster public when the news came through on that fateful day, 2 July, that Dunlop had been killed in far off Estonia was one of disbelief.

I suppose everyone remembers where they were at the time of a famous person's death. President Kennedy in 1963, John Lennon in 1980 and Princess Diana in 1997 come quickly to mind. Well, as one Dunlop fan put it: 'Joey was our Princess Diana. We will never get over his death.'

So what made Joey Dunlop MBE and OBE such a charismatic character when in fact he was the most unassuming person you could ever have wished to meet? It wasn't just that he was a survivor in this high speed, and at times brutal, sport of road racing. It wasn't because he was simply the greatest in his field, a man whose uncanny skills on board a racing motorcycle were allied to a warmth of personality and an innate shyness which made him special. It wasn't even the anecdotes which are inextricably part of the Joey legend and which made him a folk hero. It was something indefinable. Even weeks after his death nobody could put a finger on it; it was like a death in the family. Nothing would ever be the same again.

Joey Dunlop was simply known everywhere, even by those to whom motorcycling is a remote sport which rarely enters their ordered and regulated world. To many Ulster folk road racers are 'bikers', those harum scarum individuals who invade seaside resorts on their high speed machines. But Joey Dunlop was never one of this breed. He was never a part of the crowd. I suppose you could say he was a loner who took perhaps one lone walk too many . . .

The circumstances behind his untimely crash in Estonia are like something out of a Greek tragedy. In many ways he went out as he had lived – on a race track leaving everyone mystified as to why he was there in the first place. In the days which followed there was an aura of disbelief in Ulster and it brought home the fact that Joey Dunlop was a bigger name even than George Best among the Province's sportsmen in recent history.

No one could really explain why this was so, for Joey rarely gave interviews yet wasn't offhand. He never disputed a result and in many ways he was typical of the sort of sporting competitor who let their performances speak for themselves. He was a sportsman more in tune with the 'obedient' Twenties and Thirties rather than the tempestuous Seventies, Eighties and Nineties. He always played according to the rules and what you saw was what you got. In short, Joey Dunlop could always say: 'I did it my way.'

CHAPTER 1

YEAR OF YER MAN

It was the week of the long distance loner. Seven days in June 2000 when time stood still and the seemingly eternal Joey Dunlop proved once again that you can turn back the clock if you still have the hunger to do something you know you do best of all.

It was TT week ... the circus had arrived and Joey Dunlop was the star performer. It was like Frank Sinatra arriving in Las Vegas. Douglas, Isle of Man, was Joey's kind of town.

The media swarmed around him as they had done for 20 years – twenty years during which Dunlop had become a living legend, the man who would go on forever and just keep winning and winning those torturous TTs. He was, in many ways, the quintessential TT rider. The man who rode against the clock better than anyone else in history. The Isle of Man Tourist Trophy, to give it its full title, is essentially a high speed time trial, with riders starting at intervals, and there was no one better than Joey at judging the pace of the opposition. He had a clock built inside his mind which advised him of every trick in the book ... every nuance ... everything which would give him an advantage of vital seconds over a perennially demanding, and often cruel, thirty seven and three quarter mile Mountain circuit.

Steve Hislop, who won 11 TT races between 1987 and 1994, was one of Joey's greatest admirers. 'He was my hero,' he told me. 'I remember going to the TT having read about Joey over the years. My brother Gary had won the Manx GP in 1982 and in 1983. I visited the Isle of Man for a holiday although I was intent on racing. My family of course were dead against it so I spent that week watching from the 11th Milestone. I watched Joey Dunlop and Norman Brown flash past me and I immediately got the bug. At the end of the day, I thought I would like to have a crack at this race. They were all heroes in my eyes but Joey was 'the man'.'

According to Hislop, Dunlop's invaluable quality was that he appeared to be born for the TT. 'It was just his style,' he said. 'He could read the conditions better than anyone and he was a really smooth rider. His appearance was really outstanding and worth going miles to see. Phillip McCallen was brave in the wet but a bit wild. Joey was canny and cool. He always knew what he was doing. I remember his winning a 250cc TT in 1998 in horrible conditions. Joey chose the right tyre, the rest dithered and floundered accordingly. By Ramsey Joey was so far in front the race was over.'

Dunlop was given the title of 'Yer Man' by his avid followers in the Isle of Man. The term is of Ulster extraction but nobody in Joey's home country ever used it. To his fellow Ulstermen he was always Joey. Just Joey. His thousands of fans and even those who didn't know anything about motorcycle sport would always ask after a big meeting – especially the TT – those simple words: 'How did Joey do?' This was self explanatory. Anything else was superfluous.

Despite his age – he was 48 when competing in what proved to be his final TT in June 2000 – his hordes of followers thought he would go on forever and that no disaster would ever come along to stem the flow of successes. To many in Ulster he was the embodiment of immortality. I remember one occasion in 1998 when Joey suffered a bad accident at the Tandragee 100, an Irish national road race held near a tiny Co Armagh village. The word came through that Joey Dunlop had been killed. As the crowds clustered round the paddock area desperate for news, someone blurted out: 'He can't be dead. He's Joey Dunlop!' This was an indication of the awe in which he was held. In the eyes of the motorcycle fraternity he was a god.

The rumours that day proved to be false of course, but Joey had suffered severe injuries in the crash, including a badly broken wedding ring finger which had to be amputated. Despite this he still went on to ride in all the major races including his annual pilgrimage to the TT.

The Tandragee race was the unlikely starting point for Joey's Isle of Man odyssey in 2000. Normally, the North West 200, which is held on a seaside triangular course in Counties Londonderry and Antrim, is the traditional warm up race for the island. But because of a change of dates the North West was held in early May and the Tandragee staged the week before TT practice began.

Joey – unusually for him – was involved in some controversy in Tandragee. A new chicane had been put in place at the paddock area on the instructions of the safety committee of the Ulster Centre of the Motor Cycle Union of Ireland. The riders didn't like it and the place erupted. Safety officer Harris Healey was besieged by competitors led by Joey, who maintained that in his view officials had gone 'over the top' in their strict interpretation of safety guidelines

'There will soon be no road racing if this goes on,' Joey fumed. 'I'm certainly not going to race with this chicane placed the way it is.' With that, he departed the scene and returned to his van, no doubt to have a quiet nap – as was sometimes the case.

Eventually the problem was resolved and Joey turned up on the line to lead from start to finish and win the 125cc race. Tragically, it was to be his last success on an Irish road.

The TT now loomed and the year 2000 had a very special meaning for Joey. During the 1990s his star had waned in the superbike races, the highest performance events during TT fortnight. Although he won the senior in 1995, you had to go back to 1988 to find his most recent victory in the Formula One class, a type of racing which he had dominated in the 1980s when five times world champion. Joey thought it was time for a change. He wanted another Formula One win and he wanted it badly.

At the beginning of the year Honda decided to bring out a new Fireblade model which Joey would ride at the North West 200 and the TT. But the whole plan went horribly wrong. By March it was obvious that the Fireblade would not be all that it had seemed. Development was slow and there was unrest within the Honda camp. I remember an irate Jim Moodie, who also raced for Honda, ringing me to tell me that there would be no up to date factory machines for the North West. He was miffed to say the least.

According to Roger Harvey, Honda UK race co-ordinator, when Dunlop heard of the problems surrounding the new Fireblade he asked for one of the new SP-1 machines. While less powerful, it was the best on offer. It was agreed that Joey would ride this at the North West 200 in preparation for the TT.

If Joey was disappointed he didn't show it. But then he never showed his emotions, at least not in public. He usually got on with the job and in this case the SP-1 came in the form of a kit bike which had been ridden by Englishman James Tosland in the British Supercup.

Dunlop was set to ride this machine for the Vimto team owned by Cumbrian millionaire Paul Bird who had already achieved success at the North West 200 with the Scotsman Callum Ramsey. The North West would be only Dunlop's second ride in the Vimto colours. Roger Harvey said, 'He had virtually no practice on it before the North West. He went to Cadwell Park one day but it poured down and the whole session was a waste of time. He also rode at the Cookstown 100 in Ulster.'

But Honda's main objective was to get a competitive bike for the TT. Harvey, who is a man who believes in thinking long and deliberately before making any observation, was of the opinion that the SP-1 was good enough but perhaps not as quick as the Fireblade which was still in the process of development. So Joey went into the North West with a machine which was arguably not as quick as the Yamahas ridden by David Jefferies and Michael Rutter.

The first practice session for the North West was beset by thick mist, which gave the riders great difficulty as they tried to work their way round the coastal road part of the track from Portrush to Portstewart. Despite the poor visibility and the fact that he was riding what for him was a virtually untested machine, Dunlop headed the practice leaderboard with a speed of 114.72mph which put him in front of Welshman Ian Lougher and Scot Iain Duffus.

But Joey was realistic. It was his first major outing on the new Honda, apart from a run at the previous Saturday's Cookstown 100, and with such meagre race practice he didn't give himself any real chance of setting the North West coast on fire. 'I don't know what I'm doing here,' he confessed. 'The engine is just not quick enough, I may as well use an ordinary road bike.' Given that Joey tended towards exaggeration at times, this was still a thought-provoking remark and although he had the fastest practice lap, he was no certainty to win either of the superbike races on the Saturday.

Joey was not alone in his criticism of the bike. After that night's practice John McGuinness, Dunlop's Vimto team-mate, came in to complain about the handling of the Honda he was riding. 'These superbikes are hard work,' said McGuinness. 'My machine was shaking all over the place on the way to Metropole Corner.' He sought Joey's advice. Should he change the suspension or was there some other alternative? Joey, poker-faced, gave his reply: 'My advice is grit your teeth and hang on!'

There would be no more practice at that year's North West. The following night the mist came down again with a vengeance and practice was wiped out, leaving Dunlop in pole position for the race itself.

With practice aborted Joey decided to revert to his old tactic of racing on open roads near his home. It wasn't long before it attracted the attentions of the police and they paid a visit to his home. Joey's wife Linda answered the door.

'Where is he?' the policeman asked her.

'He's out,' she replied.

'Yes, we know that,' said the policeman, 'he's just passed us at 150mph!'

'What are you going to do?' enquired Linda.

'We just wanted to wish him the best of luck for tomorrow,' came the reply.

This is a typical Joey story which illustrates just how well he was thought of; but tragically, as his sister Helen told me shortly after his untimely death: 'I don't think Joey ever appreciated how popular he was. He just couldn't take that in.'

Joey had never been a big fan of the North West 200. Although he lived near the track and the North West could be called his home race, he told me once, 'I have no time for it. There is too much close scratching among the riders and you have to depend too much on the guy in front of you. It can become quite hairy. It is certainly not my scene any more.'

Dunlop hadn't scored a win at the North West since 1988 and circumstances didn't change in his favour. He finished fifth in the first superbike race behind Michael Rutter and his best placing on the day was fourth in the 125cc race behind Ian Lougher. He also suffered the ignominy of being black flagged for the first time in his career. This was in the final race of the day when Paul Bird thought that Joey was burning up the rear tyre and causing danger to other competitors.

With the North West over, it was time to get down to the serious business of the TT. Dunlop's SP-1 had been found wanting and what Joey urgently required was something special in the way of heavy artillery for the Isle of Man. It came about when he had a word with his long time friend Bob McMillan, general manger of Honda racing. McMillan made suggestions to Honda in Japan and requested a new and very special engine for Dunlop. In a brilliant coup for Joey the Japanese top brass allowed Dunlop use of the engine which was being used by New Zealander Aaron Slight in the world superbike championship. So the engine was flown from Germany where it had been in action, and ended up at the TT shortly before practice. Three Japanese engineers accompanied this valuable piece of machinery along with mechanic Simon Greer and Neil Tuxworth whose responsibility it was to ensure that the engine was returned safely.

'We had a lot of work to do,' said Roger Harvey. 'In fact, we were operating from scratch. We had no information to check back on the same as we had in the old days of the RC 45 machine. This was entirely new ground and the first time we had been in the Isle of Man with this type of bike. We got to work during practice and were pleased with the way in which everything slotted together. We were a little concerned that Joey's age would not be in his favour when it came to winning the Formula One race but he was adamant that he could do it. He had the experience and on his day he was a class act as everyone knew.'

Joey's age was seen as a negative factor by many. As for Joey himself, he was slightly amused by the attitude of the top Japanese technician which appeared to convey the opinion: 'What am I doing in the Isle of Man giving this old man my pride and joy engine?' But, 48 years old or not, Joey always insisted that he was capable of winning and the looks he was getting made him more determined than ever.

Right from the start of TT practice Dunlop felt under pressure with very little time to set up the new bike, but the engine appeared to him to be perfect with loads of power although the handling was terrible. After making a lot of chassis and suspension changes, Honda came to the conclusion that the tyres were the problem and this was remedied by Tuesday night's practice. Prior to this the bike had been weaving all over the road and was almost impossible to keep in a straight line through the fast sections. This was where Dunlop was hoping to make up time.

On the Wednesday of practice week the Honda entourage flew back to Germany for the world superbike round and Joey was left with his machine for the Formula One TT. He enrolled his own pit crew. Ernie Coates would do the fuel as usual, Davy Wood the visors and one of the Vimto team, Graham Parker, was there to change the wheels.

Before the race Joey walked down the Glencrutchery Road under immense media attention to start third on the road behind Lougher and Nigel Davies. When he reached his machine a mechanic was still taping up wires below the seat!

Starting 10 seconds behind him was the other Vimto machine ridden by McGuinness. Next was Duffus on the first of the special Honda Fireblades with Rutter starting at Number 7 and Jefferies 20 seconds after that. Moodie on his Fireblade was the 12th rider away, followed by Ulsterman Adrian Archibald from Dunlop's home town of Ballymoney.

So who would set the pace on the opening lap? By the bottom of Bray Hill, Dunlop knew the handling problem wasn't cured but it wasn't as bad as in practice. At Glen Helen, Lougher still led on the road from Davies but Dunlop was right up behind and going well. Everyone wanted to know who was leading on corrected time and when the timekeeper had finished its calculations Manx listeners heard that Dunlop led Jefferies by two seconds with Rutter third, a further second behind. Joint fourth were Lougher, McGuinness and Moodie, three seconds down on Rutter. Dunlop outbraked Davies at the end of Cronk-y-Voddy straight and pushed on towards the wet roads around Ramsey.

At Ramsey Hairpin it was announced that he had increased his lead to six seconds over Jefferies with Rutter only one second behind his Yamaha team-mate. Dunlop caught Lougher on the Mountain and led him across the line to complete the opening lap. McGuinness was third on the road followed by Davies, Rutter, Duffus and Jefferies. Joey's opening lap was 121.31mph but his lead was only 0.3 seconds over Rutter.

With a clear road ahead of him Dunlop pushed on but still at a comfortable pace similar to his opening lap. He led Rutter by two seconds at Glen Helen on lap two, and at Ramsey Joey pointed to the rear wheel indicating he wanted a tyre change at the end of the lap. He had stretched his lead over Rutter to eight seconds but Jefferies was making a charge, moving back up to second place from fourth and only six seconds behind.

Dunlop's green light came on, indicating that he was nearing the end of the lap and the air crackled with tension as everyone waited for Joey to come in. Unknown to Joey, Jefferies was in the process of lapping at 122.66mph on the second lap and had closed Joey's lead down to just half a second as Dunlop came in to pit. The pit stop had often been Joey's Achilles heel, he had thrown away leads in the opening laps of several Formula One races in the pits. Now, more than ever, it was crucial he made a seamless stop.

The buzzer went and Dunlop approached the pits very slowly, carefully changing down gears. He said later, 'I was trying to keep the engine revving as it cuts out when it is not ticking over.' His three pit attendants worked slickly to get Joey moving again. Davy Wood had the new visor ready, Ernie Coates had sorted out the fuel and Graham Parker had the new rear tyre. Thirty seconds later Dunlop was on his way; the crowd in the grandstand cheered him on down the pit lane as many others breathed a huge sigh of relief. Nothing had gone wrong. More than that, he had gained a crucial six seconds on Jefferies on corrected time.

At Glen Helen on lap three Dunlop still led by seven seconds from Jefferies and they had pulled away from third and fourth placed Rutter and McGuinness. It was now a straight head to head between the old and ageing maestro on the red Honda, and the precocious new 'Golden Bear' on the yellow Yamaha machine. Dunlop versus Jefferies. The young pretender further reduced Dunlop's lead to four seconds at Ramsey but Joey got the message and regained another second before the end of the lap. Dunlop crossed the line at 171mph; one minute later Jefferies did the same at 170mph – awesome speeds as the two high flyers approached the top of Bray Hill to start their fourth lap. Rutter was still third but some 26 seconds behind and only five ahead of McGuinness. Moodie was fifth ahead of Lougher, Jason Griffiths, Davies and Richard Britton.

At Glen Helen, Jefferies had gained another second and then another 2.5 at Ramsey. Joey's lead was only 1.5 seconds as they charged down the Mountain towards their second pit stop.

The pit stop is the very essence of the TT. That's where all the action takes place and where races are won and lost. Some unkind souls might say that there is no drama at the TT except when the riders come in to refuel. I am inclined to agree with this view for I have always found it difficult to understand why so many thousands of fans get such pleasure lining this thirty seven and three quarter mile circuit to see their favourite rider only on six occasions, in the sum of two hours, as is the case in the Formula One race. It's even worse in the smaller classes where the 250cc and 125cc riders circulate only four times.

In many cases there must surely be spectators round the more distant parts of the track who haven't a clue who is winning the race. That was certainly the case back in the 1950s when I first went to the TT. But thanks to the excellence and professionalism of Manx Radio and their timekeepers, everyone is kept up to date if they have a radio with them or if they are near a loudspeaker.

Manx Radio certainly piled on the drama when Dunlop was coming in for his second stop. It was nail-biting stuff. Dunlop was first in and his approach to the 'stop box' was a lot quicker than the first time; as he put his foot down there was an unexpected silence. His engine had cut out. Unbelievably, Dunlop was now in trouble. Or was he? The crowd were in silence, willing Joey to get going again and wipe away the nightmare vision of another Formula One disaster. Then, as the crowd stared in disbelief, through the eerie silence came what seemed the death rattle of an electric starter motor and then the roar of the powerful twin engine.

The 'death rattle' proved to be the kiss of life as far as Dunlop was concerned. He had hit the starter button and got the engine going again to the relief of his pit crew. 'I came in to the stop box harder than usual and the engine stalled,' a wistful Dunlop said afterwards. 'Luckily my team had told me beforehand about the electric starter below my left thumb. Once I got going again I felt a wave of relief.'

If the first stop was good, this one was quicker still by five seconds. The crowd got to their feet and cheered Joey on. As he left the pits, McGuinness and Jefferies arrived together, with Jefferies' fourth lap speed of 123.18mph giving him the overall lead by a wafer-thin half a second. Jefferies' pit stop was slower than Dunlop's and Joey gained six seconds on corrected time as the riders left to start their penultimate lap.

Moments later and David Jefferies' challenge was over. At Doran's Bend the clutch basket on his machine exploded and he toured to a halt. The great race had ended prematurely and we will never know if Jefferies, on that big Yahama, could have caught and beaten Joey over the final lap. The first Dunlop knew about Jefferies' disaster was when he started to get +50 signals from his crew and he knew something must have happened to his nearest challenger, but as he said afterwards: 'I was ready for the last lap battle. I had my mind made up that it would go to the wire. Obviously Jefferies' exit made it easier for me but I still had to finish the race.'

How true. No lap, whatever the circumstances, is ever easy on the snaking Isle of Man circuit. Dunlop was 50 seconds ahead of Rutter at Glen Helen, with McGuinness a further 12 seconds in arrears. By the end of the lap he crossed the line to start his final circuit with a 52 second advantage over the triple North West 200 winner Rutter. McGuinness had dropped further behind in third, 22 seconds behind Rutter.

Dunlop didn't have to go any faster on his sixth and final lap. It didn't matter about times. Everyone wanted to see Joey win that exclusive Formula One title again; he had always said it would come his way but very few had believed him. Still, the style and pride of the man had to be admired – with another smooth lap of 122mph he won by almost a minute.

Joey was never one for giving on the spot interviews after races. The instant quip never was his scene as Manx Radio commentator Geoff Cannell knows only too well. Cannell spends his time in the pit lane interviewing riders throughout the race. His location is known as 'gasoline alley' for obvious reasons. He has a thick skin, as he needs to have, for his job is to shove a microphone into a rider's face as soon as he comes in and virtually demand an explanation of what has happened. You can understand some riders' reaction. They would like to tell Cannell where he could stick his mike!

Joey Dunlop would never have been so rude but, at the same time, eloquent descriptions of his race were not something he specialised in. Even so, when Cannell approached him and shouted excitedly in his ear: 'Twenty four TT wins . . . a Formula One victory after 12 years . . . surely Joey, this has to be one of your most memorable races?' he might have expected an enthusiastic reaction. But no.

Joey, as understated as they come, replied succinctly: 'Och, it was alright.'

Poor Cannell. He must have felt like the comedian who died on stage and wanted the ground to open up beneath him. What was he expecting? Chapter and verse? Not from 'Yer Man'.

Typically, Joey was more forthcoming when he spoke to *Road Racing Ireland* at some length after the race. He said: 'It was a relief to finish but very satisfying to prove that I was worth all the support and effort some people had given me. I couldn't start to explain the pressure I was under. It felt as if everything rested on my shoulders. But I did it. Just as last year when I finished second and other years when I didn't finish at all, I went to the beer tent for a drink with my family and friends.'

Whatever Joey's feelings in public or private, there can be no doubt that this victory was one of the high points of his career. Steve Hislop spoke for many when he said: 'Winning that Formula One race was a major achievement. It established Joey Dunlop as a genuine superbike rider again. Perhaps some would say that Carl Fogarty and I would have beaten Joey's TT total had we continued to race. But that is debatable. You have got to hand it to the man, he produced the goods when it mattered.'

In the immediate aftermath of the race Joey phoned the Honda world superbike team in Germany, alerting them to his success. Then, for the 24th time, he took his place proudly on the top of the podium. 'Honda gave me the best bike possible and I didn't let them down,' he said.

As for the unfortunate Jefferies, he had sensed the aura of occasion, especially in the grandstand area at that time. With Joey's followers howling their approval he was asked over the PA system what could have been a dangerous question. Would he have beaten Joey but for that broken clutch? Jefferies is no fool. He wasn't going to commit himself. He just said: 'Don't ask me. There are too many Joey Dunlop fans around.'

For the thousands of Dunlop fans who were there, Joey's Formula One victory was just the start. With a day's rest on Sunday it was back to business for Joey in Monday's 250cc race. This was the class which Joey had dominated during the 1990s and he wasn't going to let another one slip away. He had failed the previous year but this time he was up for the job.

Unfortunately, given the unpredictable weather, the Isle of Man is not the sort of place where a rider can fully psyche himself up knowing that a race will start on time. Mist on the mountain is the old bugbear, and once again it struck in time for the 250cc race. The 10.15am start was put back to 1.00pm because of the conditions. Some riders fretted and fumed but the calmest man around was Joey Dunlop. He had seen it all before and he was reflecting on the fact that he had only cured the problems with his Honda on the very last practice lap on Friday evening.

Making the most of the delay, Joey asked Leslie Moore, a reporter from *Road Racing Ireland*, to ask the Suzuki parade lap riders what the conditions were like when they returned. The message passed onto him from Barry Woodland and Mick Grant was: damp in all the usual places but no lying water except running water across the road at the campsite at Glen Vine. The mist however was still a big problem. At 1.15pm it was announced that the race would start in 15 minutes but Dunlop was by no means ready. He was still standing beside his machine which had no front wheel. He had sent one of his mechanics back to the paddock to have his slick tyre slightly cut and was waiting for his return. With the rest of the riders already lining up on the road for the start, Joey was running out of time. With only five minutes left, he got a spare wheel fitted with an intermediate tyre ready to put in – a tyre choice he didn't want to have. Fortunately, the intermediate wheel was never tightened for the original wheel arrived a minute later and Joey was quickly on his knees fitting it. That was his style.

Whether he would have made it to the line on time no one knows, but with a minute to go it was announced that there would be another 15 minute delay. The organisers were still announcing delays an hour later – by which time most of the riders had gone for a cup of tea and a lie down. At 2.45pm it was announced that the race would be cut to three laps and would hopefully start at 3.00pm. Eventually it started at 3.15pm.

The delays didn't bother Joey. He was a cut above the other riders, especially in the 250cc class, and aboard a machine which he later revealed was the best 250cc he had ever ridden at the TT, his superiority showed. Following the first pit stops, Joey led by nine seconds from second-placed John McGuinness, whose cause was not helped by a big slide at Creg-ny-Baa. McGuinness retired with water in the engine at Quarter Bridge on lap three and the race was more or less over at that point.

At Glen Helen on lap three after corrected time, Dunlop led by 72 seconds from Bruce Anstey. The signal boards went out to Joey and he said later: 'I slowed down over the Mountain aware of the fact that I might run out of fuel and I had a couple of scary slides.' Despite slowing he won the race by 67 seconds from Anstey who in turn pulled out nine seconds on Lougher.

So it was double delight for Dunlop and he was quick to inform Honda's Neil Tuxworth: 'I had to work hard preparing that bike. Next year I might come back as a mechanic!'

At the prizegiving in Douglas that night the crowd went wild. To a huge ovation Joey Dunlop, champion of Ulster, was made an unofficial Knight of the Isle of Man. The big moment came when the prizes were given out for the 250cc race and David Cretney, Isle of Man Minister for Tourism and Leisure, presented the wily veteran with a gold replica of the Manx Sword of State. 'You have done so much for tourism on this island that I now present you with this honour,' he said. 'Not only are you king of the mountains but you are now a knight of the Isle of Man.'

Dunlop and his family were naturally thrilled by the occasion although Joey had a somewhat embarrassed look on his face as he knelt down before the Manx minister to receive the accolade. The picture went round the world and the Mayor of Dunlop's home town of Ballymoney, Councillor William Logan, said: 'Joey is a wonderful ambassador for our country. The people of the island love to see him coming over. I take the view that without him the TT would never be the same.' How prophetic those words may turn out to be.

Dunlop was only the third road racer to be presented with the replica of the Sword of State. The previous riders were Mitsuoh Ito, the only Japanese rider to win a TT race, and Stanley Woods, 10 times a TT winner in the 1930s. The main part of the inscription read: 'Presented to Joey Dunlop OBE MBE on behalf of all his Isle of Man supporters TT 2000.'

Dunlop now had the chance to win four TTs in one week and his next target was the 125cc race which had happy memories for him for it was back in 1992 that he beat his brother Robert in this class to equal Mike Hailwood's long-standing record of 14 TT wins. The 125cc race had been Joey's speciality in recent years and there were very few who would oppose his chances. But once again the mist on the mountain struck with a vengeance. Another delay . . . the riders were out on the road with only a minute to go when it was announced that the start would be held back for 15 minutes.

Twelve minutes later they all returned and at last Paul Williams led them away followed by Darran Lindsay, Joey and Robert Dunlop, Ian Lougher, Denis McCullough and Gary Dynes. At Glen Helen, Lindsay had overtaken Williams and led on the road as the rest came through in numerical order. But when times were calculated it was Joey again. He led by four seconds from Lindsay and Robert Dunlop and by seven seconds from Lougher.

People have often said that Joey went well when he had his 'race face' on. This was the case in the Isle of Man on that Wednesday. Before the start most of the riders were feeling confident of winning but that man Joey Dunlop was going for his 26th victory. He quickly passed Williams and then Lindsay at Sulby Bridge and made sure those following him never saw him after the start. At Ramsey he had a 10 second advantage over Lindsay and Robert; 11 seconds over McCullough and 14 over Dynes.

At the end of the lap Joey on corrected time had pulled out a lead of 18 seconds over his nearest rivals with a speed of 108.56mph. Joey wasn't relaxing the pace and by the time he reached Ramsey again at the second lap his lead had grown to 22 seconds.

Joey said later: 'I took it easy over the Mountain as I was starting to worry about running out of petrol again. I am always thinking about that and it probably ruined a good lap speed.' Even with Joey reducing the pace no one gained any time on him. His pit stop took only 17 seconds as he pulled the fuel pipe out himself such was his eagerness to get away quickly. At Glen Helen on lap three, Joey was now 28 seconds ahead of McCullough and the race was as good as over. At the end of the lap Joey's lead was a comfortable 25 seconds with one lap to go. Joey had just enough fuel to cross the line with a 16 second advantage over McCullough with Robert Dunlop 28 seconds further behind in third place.

'This was the hardest win physically and mentally of the week,' Joey reflected in the post-race press conference. 'You have to concentrate so hard on keeping your speed up and being tucked in on a 125cc machine.'

At the age of 48 Joey had completed a remarkable treble with the Senior race still to come on the Friday. Joey hadn't won this race since 1995. However it was a race where everything went wrong because of the atrocious weather. In fact Dunlop had to wait until the Saturday before getting out on to the line.

Earlier there had been drama when the rumour flew around the paddock that Joey Dunlop was not going to start. Where did this come from? No one really knew. Eventually it was revealed that Jim

Moodie had been the centre of a storm in the Honda camp. It was understood that Moodie wanted a quicker bike for the Senior. This was never confirmed and Moodie replied 'no comment' to everyone who asked him about the circumstances of the row. Honda team manager Harvey said 'Jim felt his bikes should have been quicker; we had a long discussion and eventually we decided it was in everyone's interest we should part company.' It appeared however that the Honda camp had been torn apart by this move and Moodie withdrew his bikes from the starting area shortly before the Production race in which he was also due to appear.

The senior, when it did come, was an anticlimax. Joey had already achieved his treble, fans had left the island in their thousands and really most of the spectators were just glad to see the meeting end. It had that air about it for Joey too. Speaking about his win in the 125cc on the Wednesday he had said: 'After the [125cc] I just wanted to relax and celebrate, but I knew the effort my sponsor John Harris had put in getting his machine prepared for the following 600cc race. I was off again but really I had given my best in the 125cc. I had achieved a treble, and to be honest fatigue set in near the end of the 600cc battle. I basically toured round for the last two laps to finish fourth.'

The Senior race was won by Yamaha's David Jefferies. He came into the pits for his final stop with a 28 second lead. After casually asking who was second – it was his team-mate Michael Rutter – he blasted away. He was out for a lap record on his final circuit – the only flying lap of the race – and he did it, becoming the first rider to lap the Mountain circuit at over 125mph and a fraction under 18 minutes.

Dunlop had to be content with third place behind Jefferies and Rutter. It was almost a repeat of The North West 200 races where the English pair have had the edge in recent years. Joey said: 'The handling wasn't as good as in the Formula One race and I hadn't the speed to pull out and pass the Yamahas. The last two laps were quick when I got caught up with Rutter on the road. But I overshot at Governor's trying to be first over the line.'

Jack Valentine, head of the V&M Yamaha team, couldn't contain himself at the finish. He bellowed into the microphone held by the ever present Geoff Cannell: 'We are the greatest. We proved today we can beat Honda.' He didn't say anything about Joey apart from referring to him as the world's best road racer. But we all knew that anyway.

As Joey made his weary way back to the paddock area he could reflect on the fact that Jefferies might be a new kid on the block who could go on to greater things, but it would take something else to beat his total of 26 TT victories. What a week. In those seven sizzling days 'Yer Man' had become everybody's man.

CHAPTER 2

A BOY FROM BALLYMONEY

The 1950s are looked upon by many as the glory days of motorcycle racing. It was the era of Geoff Duke, Harold Daniel, John Surtees, Les Graham, Bob McIntyre and Belfast rider Artie Bell, who was carrying on a great and well established tradition of Irish road racers, following in the wheel-tracks of the legendary Stanley Woods and Kildare's Ernie Lyons.

At this time, in Ballymoney on 25 February 1952, three weeks after Queen Elizabeth came to the throne, William Joseph Dunlop, the man they would call the 'King of the Roads' was born to parents Willie and May. He was the second of seven children. His elder sister was Helen and the others were Linda, Jim, Virginia, and twins Robert and Margaret.

Little did his parents realise that on that date a 'star was born', who would leave a legacy to motorcycling that had never been achieved before, not even by the greats already mentioned, and one that would never be equalled.

Like most sporting icons Joey's entry into this life was a humble one. At a time when the six-year-old George Best was starting to kick a football around the streets of a Belfast council estate, Joey Dunlop first saw the light of day in an old semi-detached stone cottage one mile from the little County Antrim hamlet of Dunloy. And, as was to prove the case in later years, Joey was quick on the draw. So quick in fact that he 'arrived' in the world before his time.

His parents had sent for the midwife but before she could arrive Joey was on his way and was delivered by his auntie Peggy and a neighbour, a Mrs Warnock. 'How can I ever forget that day in view of what has happened in later years,' said Joey's mother. 'He was a straightforward birth and was born at home because that was the custom in those days. Very few children in remote rural areas of Northern Ireland were born in hospital.'

According to his mother Joey was 'a great wee lad who gave no trouble. In fact he never cried unless he was hungry.' How many other parents would wish the same in the case of their own offspring!

Joey's sister Helen was six years older than Joey and she took the latest Dunlop under her wing. Helen, who later married Mervyn Robinson, a road racing genius who was to provide the spark which would ignite Joey's meteoric road racing career, told me: 'I was very close to Joey from the start. But then I could say that about all the rest of my brothers and sisters. It's just that when they arrived 'girl boy, girl boy' I became 'paired' with Joey just as my brother Jim and Linda were together and of course Robert and Margaret were twins. We had another sister Shirley but she died when she was only seven months old.'

The Dunlop family didn't remain long in that tiny cottage and soon moved to a place called The Leck, three miles from where Joey was born. They took up residence in a house owned by Joey's grandmother which was situated on a farm. By a quirk of fate this same farmhouse was occupied temporarily over 30 years later by Joey's brother Robert, his wife Louise and their family.

Joey quickly grew up and attended Garryduff Primary School, and it was at that time that he was first introduced to the motor-cycle. In those days very few people had cars and getting to school could be a tough task. Said Helen Dunlop: 'Our school was about two and a half miles away from where we lived, and my dad took Joey and me to and from the schoolhouse on his motorbike. I still have memories of me sitting on the pillion and Joey propped up on the petrol tank! Those were happy days and I wish I had a picture to remind me of them.'

As time went on Joey, like most other kids, developed an interest in toys – especially those with wheels. Helen passed on a tricycle which kept Joey occupied in his early years. Following that Joey graduated to a bicycle with stabilizers and Helen remembers her father teaching Joey to ride it and promptly running into trouble. 'I looked out the window and Dad was pushing Joey on the bike which was now minus the stabilizers,' she said. 'Dad was trying to give him confidence but they both lost control and headed straight into a barbed wire fence. They were a sorry sight!'

The family later moved to Culduff which, by another stroke of coincidence, was just behind the bungalow which Joey many years later built for his wife Linda and his own family. This home, along with Garryduff Presbyterian Church where Joey is buried just two miles away, has become a shrine for motorcycling fans since his death.

The move to Culduff meant a change of school and Joey attended Lislagan Primary School for a short time but it wasn't long before the Dunlops were on the move again. When Joey was 14 the new family home became a bungalow in a council estate at Killyrammar, still in the Ballymoney area. By then Joey was attending Ballymoney Secondary Intermediate School and a whole new world was opening up to him.

Also attending that school, but at different times, were Mervyn Robinson, Frank Kennedy and Joey's brother Jim. All three along with Joey would in the 1970s become known in the motorcycle road racing world as the 'Armoy Armada'. They resembled the 'four horsemen' as they charged their way through the Ulster short circuit scene and as Bill Kennedy, Frank's brother, later to become Mayor of Ballymoney, put it: 'We became life long friends in our teenage years and saw some tremendous achievements as well as many tragedies. But through it all we enjoyed ourselves in a way that the modern racers don't seem to do. Mervyn, Joey, Jim and

Frank started something in the Ballymoney area that eventually had a major effect on road racing in Northern Ireland. They gave the sport a new image and lifted it to marvellous heights. So much so that at one time there were about fourteen riders in the Ballymoney District Council area racing motorbikes.

'Joey Dunlop was in my view the greatest ambassador for the sport that I have ever known and I'm not just talking about the glory years. Joey helped to raise the interest at our national meetings and he never neglected them. It should be remembered that he cut his teeth on Ulster short circuits at Kirkistown and Maghaberry, both in Co Down, Aghadowey in Co Londonderry and St Angelo in Co Fermanagh. At the same time he was also competing on public roads. Joey in fact raced at every meeting he could physically attend and he was up against some pretty hot competition. There was no such thing as a clubman. In those days you were thrown in at the deep end and you either sank or swam. Riders like Joey, Mervyn and Frank soon came to the top for they had unique ability.'

Strangely for such a small area, Joey didn't know either Frank or Mervyn in his school days at Ballymoney Secondary. But according to Helen: 'This was not unusual for we all attended school at different years. In fact, I didn't even know Mervyn Robinson when I was at school and yet I later married him.'

Helen's meeting with Mervyn was the launch pad for Joey Dunlop's career. She met Mervyn in 1967 at a fish and chip shop called 'The Pop In' in Ballymoney. 'It was a place where we all hung out and Mervyn and I hit it off immediately,' she said. 'Some time later I brought Mervyn home to meet the folks and he was introduced to Joey.'

This was a meeting which, in motorcycling terms, resembled that of Lennon and McCartney. The two clicked immediately and Mervyn excitedly told Joey about the prospects which could lie ahead as a road racer. The young Dunlop at that stage hadn't shown a great deal of interest in motorcycling but Robinson had been racing for about a year and he was consumed with enthusiasm. This was transmitted to Joey and in many ways it could be said that Mervyn Robinson was the Svengali who manipulated the early Dunlop career. As Helen told me: 'I think it would be fair to say if there hadn't been Mervyn Robinson there would have been no Joey Dunlop.'

Joey's career began when he was 16. He bought a 250 BSA road bike and set out on a day trip to Portrush on the Co Antrim coast. His mother remembers that day well. 'I told Joey not to forget his insurance, his road tax and his helmet, but he forgot to put up 'L' plates and he was stopped by the police at Coleraine on the way back from Portrush. Shortly afterwards he appeared in court and lost his licence for three months.'

Joey later bought an Ariel Arrow from Robinson but his interest in a touring road bike lapsed for 20 years, before Joey applied again for a licence and did the test as part of the Department of Environment road safety promotion.

But it was road racing which he had on his mind in 1968 and that year Robinson sold him his first competitive machine. It was a 199cc Triumph Cub and Willie Dunlop remembers it well. 'It was no ordinary Cub for Joey was forever wanting to change or improve things,' he said. 'He never seemed to be happy unless he was working out something different. With Joey's help I floored the loft at our house at Killyrammer so that Joey could work at the bike and it was there that he learned the first rudiments of racing bike preparation. I suppose you could say that these were lessons he never forgot and which he built upon right to the end of his career.'

Helen also has memories of her brother working in the loft. 'It was like a small house on its own,' she told me. 'Joey had spanners, and other tools lying about the place as well as a motorcycle engine. He and Mervyn used to spend the night up there discussing their plans and in fact there were times when Mervyn came to see me and promptly disappeared up into the loft and I never saw him again that night!'

However all this work on motorcycles required income and Joey, like everyone else, had to have a job. His father Willie worked as a mechanic for Jim Wallace, a car dealer in Ballymoney and, in 1968, Joey joined the company as an apprentice. He stayed two years before moving to Danny McCooke's coal yard in Ballymoney where he began an apprenticeship as a diesel fitter. This was when he was 18 and you had to be an all-rounder in those days as Joey's dad explained. 'Apart from working on engines, Joey had to deliver coal,' he said. 'It was pretty tough going and there were times when the lorry he was driving would break down and Joey had to get it started again. But he was a good wee boy who just loved engines.'

The folks around the Ballymoney area could vouch for that for many of them were amazed with the aptitude which the young Dunlop showed for motorcycle and car engines. It was obvious, even at that early age, that he had a rare gift which nobody else around could match.

You have to bear in mind that in those days there were many excellent mechanics working in big garages in Ballymoney and nearby Ballymena and in smaller rural businesses who were very good at their job. Mechanics were not specialists; they had to work out what was wrong with a car, lorry or bike then fix it and if they did not have the part they probably had to make it. In this type of competitive scene Joey was unique.

Few people have the talent to tackle any problem and solve it. Joey could put his hand to anything and nobody had to instruct him. He could have been working on a gearbox with a book in front of him and turned round and asked for a small chisel. After a few taps he would say, 'That's it now.' Most times he did not put into words what he had done.

Joey did not just fix engines; he pulled them down, took them out, and put in bigger ones. He took gearboxes apart and changed the sprockets, all in his own quiet way. When he was working in this way he preferred to do it in peace, free from distractions and people observing him at work. At times he would be sitting on his knees working away and would turn his head and give an onlooker a glare as if to say 'I'm busy go away and let me get on with it.' This was a trait which he maintained throughout his career. In short he didn't suffer fools or intruders gladly.

Danny McCooke, in addition to being Joey's first employer, was also his first sponsor and it was while at McCooke's that Joey met up with Mervyn 'Curly' Scott who was also serving his time as a fitter and who was later to become Dunlop's long term mechanic. The two apprentices soon struck up a friendship and a great common interest in motorcycles. This was not always in the best interest of McCooke's business, but Danny was an understanding type. 'Joey was not an ordinary mechanic,' he said. 'He did things his way. It was obvious early on that he had a special feel for the job. It was demanding at times and the job was dirty but that never worried him. He had started racing when he joined me. Sometimes he might have been working on his bikes all night and then fail to turn up for work the next morning. But when he did, he gave his very best and he was such a good man at the job it was easy for me to overlook those little flaws in his timekeeping.'

Curly Scott remembers Joey coming to work driving a yellow Austin Mini. 'He was racing bikes at the time and he couldn't wait to join Mervyn and Frank riding round the roads at night,' he said.

When Joey had made his racing debut he was under-age according to the rules of the Motor Cycle Union of Ireland and he had to receive parental consent in order to race. 'I remember signing the forms which started Joey on his career,' said Willie. 'I never thought at the time that anything would come of it but look where road racing took him eventually.'

The date of Joey Dunlop's first appearance was April 1969, he was 17 and the venue was a disused airfield at Maghaberry. The young Dunlop did not cut much ice that day but Robinson encouraged him to keep going and Joey persisted. Robinson had a goal that both of them would make it to the top and they pursued a grand plan which nearly came adrift in dramatic circumstances on Easter Monday, 1970, a date which Helen remembers well:

'Joey and Mervyn had been racing at Kirkistown,' she told me. 'It was one of the biggest days of the year and the place was packed.

Joey had no luck and we left the track and headed for home. Joey was driving the Mini, with his then girlfriend Linda Patterson in the passenger seat. I was in the back seat with Mervyn and we had a trailer hooked on to the Mini which carried the bikes and a huge amount of accessories.

'On our way home we decided to turn right at the Fort Royal Restaurant between Ballymena and Ballymoney but as we did so a car hit us from behind and careered over the top of us. Fortunately no one was seriously injured and the bikes weren't badly damaged but one of the tools flew out of the trailer and smashed the windscreen of an oncoming car. Again nobody was hurt but it was a close call. A few cuts and bruises and we were home safely.'

The following year, 1971, Helen married Mervyn and moved to the village of Bushside two miles from Armoy – a town which, in later years, became synonymous with Joey. In 1972 Joey married Linda, who also lived in Killyrammer, and they also settled in Bushside. Mervyn and Helen eventually moved to Armoy but Joey and Linda remained in Bushside. As Helen points out: 'Fans throughout the world believe that Joey lived in Armoy but this was never the case. It was Mervyn and I who lived there. Joey and Linda stayed in Bushside until Joey decided to build a new bungalow at Garryduff and that was where he was living when he was killed.'

After the Triumph Cub, Joey bought a 200 Suzuki which was basically a road bike but which he and Mervyn 'breathed upon', as they say, and converted it into a racing bike; still it was no match for the genuine racing machinery that he was competing against. Something had to be done!

In Armoy, Mervyn and Joey met up with garage owner Hugh O'Kane, another motorcycle fanatic, who was to later sponsor Mervyn. It came to the attention of Messrs Dunlop and Robinson that O'Kane had a very special racing bike in his possession, a 350 7R AJS, known in the early days as the 'Boy Racer'.

The pair approached Hugh to see if he would give Joey a ride on the bike, which was granted of course. 'Joey took it up the road, which was the normal thing to do in those days,' explained Hugh.

'When he came back he was breathless with excitement. He told me that it was so quick a bike compared to his, that he would love to get a ride on it at Kirkistown. Joey only rode the bike two or three races at the most, but Mervyn rode it quite a bit. He took it to the Manx Grand Prix in 1972, where he broke the frame in six places and then ran out of fuel.

'When Joey got a ride on the bike, it was well past its sell by date, but it was still a lot faster than the wee Suzuki. This was just before the Aermacchi era, when the whole scene was changed from the AJSes, Nortons and Matchlesses to the Italian machines.

'In 1973 I bought Robbo the 350 Aermacchi on which Gerry Mateer had finished in sixth place at the TT. About the same time Danny McCooke bought Joey a similar one, but I don't think Joey's was as fast as Mervyn's.'

Before Danny bought the bike, Joey invited him to come and see him ride on the open roads around Armoy. 'The boys worked at their bikes at an old derelict farmhouse, using the roads to test them,' Danny said. 'Joey went away up the mountain road out of the village at a normal rate, but then would come down at racing speed. When I saw him do this for the first time I was impressed, if that is the right word. The way he rode and the riding style made me realise that he had something very special and with the proper machinery would be a winner, so along came the Aermacchi.'

Even in those days, the first thing the boys did when they got a new bike was to pull it apart and rebuild it. Joey Dunlop learned a lot from his brother-in-law whom O'Kane described as another genius.

'Mervyn was extremely clever, and a really good mechanic,' said O'Kane. 'He could have done cranks, pistons, barrels, the lot. One of Mervyn's many characteristics which rubbed off on Joey was that he did not trust anyone else to do the job properly. In later years Joey was exactly the same.

'Joey, like Mervyn, learned a lot through experience and experimenting. Like Mervyn he was an honours graduate of the school of experience. Any knowledge they acquired they used and never forgot, but they kept very much to themselves. They and Frank Kennedy literally talked, ate and slept racing motorbikes . . . that is, when they *did* sleep!

'Most nights before a race, they would meet in my garage to put the finishing touches to the bikes. Joey preferred to work on the bikes the night before a race, rather than go to bed and lie awake thinking about the race.

'When they had them ready, it was not unusual for them to take them out for a practice run up and down the road, in the early hours of the morning, when the noise of the bikes was horrendous. Strangely nobody objected, at least nothing was said to them or to me.

'Another of Joey's favourite ploys was to learn the courses at night. If he was not working on his bikes the night before a race such as the Cookstown, the Mid-Antrim or the Carrowdore, he thought nothing of driving to the course and doing a few laps in the dark. He always said that what you saw by the lights of the car was what you saw when you were racing.

'I know of quite a few people whom he 'entertained' to a racing lap before a meeting, especially around the TT course, which nobody took more care in learning, or of which nobody had greater knowledge.'

Joey was truly dedicated to road racing to the point of single-mindedness but that in itself would not prevent injury. Joey had his fair share of problems in this respect in the early days for there were no such things in the late Sixties and early Seventies as knee-sliders or protectors, so like many others he suffered from knee and ankle injuries. But, unlike others, he was fortunate to meet green-grocer Matt Gibson who was also a physio and who had other more mystic attributes which were later to prove invaluable to Joey.

It is not generally known that Joey Dunlop suffered greatly from nerves in his stomach before a race. He especially disliked massed starts and that was one of the reasons why he came to love the TT and the Isle of Man, for only rarely would there be another rider racing alongside him.

When he told Gibson about his nerves he was advised to get a bottle of Lucozade, keep it and refill the same bottle during the season. Joey did this religiously and never had pains of tension again. It was pure psychology, but it worked. However, there was a never to be forgotten day much later in Joey's career when he discovered that one of his children had drunk the Lucozade. A panic phone call to Gibson solved the matter. Joey was told that as long as he had the bottle and filled it with any sort of beverage it would work. Joey did this and that's what he believed right up until the end. He had tremendous faith.

As Gibson put it: 'Joey had a mind of his own and a character unlike anyone else but was very easy to work with. He was looked upon as a self healing man. Even if the medical advice was not to race for a certain time, Joey put his own timetable on things. If he felt it was time for a plaster to come off so he could ride again, he took it off and in all instances he never seemed to suffer any ill effects. In fact he seemed to get better more quickly.'

Joey was a loner right from day one and his lifelong friend and founder of the Armoy Armada Supporters Club, Andy English, knew him better than anyone. 'When people would come along and see Joey working at his bikes in a paddock or garage, they would stand back, look at him working and admire his skill for a little while,' he said.

'After some time they would edge a little bit closer, and try to move into a position where they thought he would notice them and maybe say something. Sometimes they would have an autograph book, or programme for Joey to sign and it was clear that they were becoming impatient, as he kept his head down and just went on working, until he had the job completed.

'Then he would greet them and happily sign, but he would then return to his work just as quickly as he had stopped. It used to amuse me that folk were not happy at being kept waiting for a minute or two. It was obvious that they did not know Joey, as I knew him.

'If they had been with me in the garage at home, or at the TT, or anywhere, they would soon have learned how he operated. He was completely committed to whatever task he had taken on, and nothing was in his head but that job.

'On many occasions I recall us going into the garage at home early in the morning and working right through the day, with nothing but the odd cup of tea and at five o'clock or six he would utter his first words, 'I think it is time for a pint.' Many folk could not have put up with that, but I understood how he thought, how he stuck at the job in hand and knew that he was grateful for the help I was giving.

'I never looked upon his attitude as an insult, or that he was ignoring me for he wasn't. He was totally engrossed in what he was doing. He was a perfectionist, who did not want to be distracted. I looked upon it as a privilege to work with him and see him use his skills. It wasn't a social occasion, although we had plenty of those, but that is another story.'

Joey's long hours and almost monk-like dedication to the preparation of his bikes was underlined by Billy Kennedy. 'Before Joey was married but going out with Linda, he would come over to the garage in Armoy in the wee Mini. He would go in and work at the bikes for hours, into the early hours of the morning, while Linda would sit in the car, playing tapes.

'In those days it was the big broad four-track tapes which were all the go. They were mostly American Country and Western, which Joey and Linda liked. This did not happen just one night in the week, but almost every night. Linda was certainly dedicated to Joey right from the start, sharing his interests as well as his life.'

Dunlop's unique combination of rider and engineer was not always appreciated by his later long time employers Honda. On numerous occasions it was a bone of contention as he preferred to work on his own bikes rather than have a designated 'works' mechanic to do it for him. This practical interest in things mechanical was to develop as he grew older. It was one of Joey's great natural attributes, knowing what was happening to an engine or a chassis, analysing it and then being able to communicate exactly what was happening to the development engineers.

This was best illustrated by a unique occasion at the memorable 2000 TT. On the final Friday of practice week the media were invited to the Honda garage for a presentation of riders and their machines. When they arrived Joey and his personal 250cc sponsor Bertie Payne were working on the bike. Unexpectedly, Joey invited my friend and colleague Harold Crooks to come behind the barrier and see what he was doing. It was one of those times when a reporter feels very special at witnessing something unique.

First he told Harold that he was cleaning the ports of the cylinder head with a piece of emery paper, something which he did every time the engine was run. Once satisfied that it was perfect, he put it on the engine and started to tighten it down with a torque wrench.

Crooks asked him how he knew what tension to apply to each nut or bolt. His reply was amazing. 'I could tell you the torque needed for every nut and bolt on every bike I have ridden without looking at a manual,' Joey said. 'In fact I could lie in bed and change an engine, or gearbox or anything in my head I have done it so many times, it comes naturally.'

He then went on to plan a new exhaust pipe bracket, as the original did not fit the special engine from Honda. With an artistic stroke of genius, he fashioned a bracket out of a piece of metal from an oil can. 'That will do as a template until I get a proper bit of steel to make one for the race, for that one would never last the distance,' he said.

After he won the race, Crooks asked him about the bracket. 'Do you know,' he said. 'I never changed the thing, and when I finished it was just hanging on. That could have cost me the race but then luck was on my side today.'

Another close friend who was amazed at, but also understood, Joey's character was his early sponsor Brian Coll, who was a professional musician and had a band called Brian Coll and The Buccaroos. 'I would only try to imagine how Joey's mind and body worked,' he said. 'I was performing all over Ireland, in Britain including London. I was therefore used to long, late nights one evening, and then getting into a van and driving hundreds of miles to the next concert.

'However, if we did not get some sleep at night we tried to make up for it the next day. But what about Joey? He would work all day, at least half the night, get up the next morning, go out and win a race, and then party until the early hours again. The man had a unique constitution. It was once said that they broke the mould when they made Joey Dunlop. This was surely true, not only when applied to his riding and engineering ability, but just to the man himself.

'His quietness and cat-like concentration on the job in hand also intrigued me. On many occasions I spent many very enjoyable hours in his company, especially in his bar in Ballymoney. But once when I was helping him out a little bit, I went to see him in the garage in Douglas during TT week.

'True to form he was working away at the bikes and it was obvious that he was trying to sort out a problem, which was demanding his full attention. After some considerable time, I knew that it was time to get off-side and leave him to it. On the way out I met Davy Wood, his manager, and said to him that I been in to see Joey for about an hour, but that he had not spoken to me.

'Davy, in his own immutable style and lingo said, "Don't be annoyed or put out by that pal. I have been here for three or four days, working with him, and he hasn't spoken to me yet. What are a few minutes?"'

Joey Dunlop's unique characteristics were the hallmarks of a man who never changed. These were the things that endeared him to so many people all over the world. In any other person the same traits would have been seen and treated as flaws, but in the life of Joey Dunlop, they were accepted as attributes, by his family, his friends and by his millions of fans who were more than happy to watch him at work off the bike, as well as on it.

As well as being an early sponsor of Joey, Brian Coll was also a huge fan and keen motorcyclist who purchased and rode quite a number of Joey's bikes after their racing days were over. A story of one such purchase began with a unique and memorable tale, in the Isle of Man many years later in 1983.

That year, Honda Britain had decided to supply Joey, Ron Haslam and Wayne Gardner with special CBR 1100R machines for a 'Street Bike' class. Coll had tried to buy one of these machines from his local dealer before going to the TT, but the deal was not completed.

While in the Isle of Man, he agreed to buy Joey's bike at the end of the season. He was therefore taking more than a passing interest in Joey's performances on the bike, and a keen insight into how it was performing, with the result that he went to Jurby Airfield, near Ramsey, where it was being tested.

Impressed with everything he saw, at the end of the test session, he admitted: 'I got carried away a bit, and passed the remark that I wouldn't mind a lift back to Douglas on the back of the bike. Immediately Davy Wood conveyed my request to Joey.'

Joey replied: 'I dinnae mind in the least. It is up to Brian. If he really wants a sail back, I'll take him. It is entirely up to him.'

When Wood heard this, he asked Brian: 'Are you serious pal or have you gone completely mad? Do you know what you are letting yourself in for?'

The late Hubert Gibson, who was a legend in his own right in the racing world, an organiser of trips to race meetings all over the world, and the man who managed the great Raymond McCullough during the Armoy Armada v Dromara Destroyer days, was present at Jurby. He too questioned Coll's sanity.

Coll went on: 'Hubert looked at me with the strangest of looks and said: "I know that you ride your own bikes on the road, and that this one will be yours at the end of season, but do you realise what you are doing? You may be grey in the hair at the moment, but by the time you reach Douglas you will be as white as Santa Claus!"

'At this point the first tinge of doubt started to come into my mind, but I had total confidence in Joey,' continued Coll. 'I had seen him perform on so many occasions, talked about his skill, how safe he looked and how I admired all these qualities. My faith was about to be put to the test, and I could not chicken out.

'I was wearing a light Honda T-shirt and a pair of jeans, as the weather was nice. They very kindly supplied me with one of Joey's helmets. By this time the bike was running and Joey was waiting for me to get on to the dual seat behind him. With unforgettable looks and a sympathetic pat on the back from Messrs Wood, Gibson and company we left Jurby and headed back towards the TT course.

'I expected Joey to turn right and head back to Douglas via Glen Helen and Ballacraine. Instead, he turned left towards Ramsay. At this stage I was surprised that I was enjoying the trip as we had been going at a reasonable speed, sixty or seventy miles per hour, along the wee roads out to the course and even the first part through Ginger Hall.

'Then everything changed when two or three guys passed us, lighting up the competitive fire in the wee man's bones. It was back to his natural instincts from then on. He took a handful of the throttle and inside a couple of miles or probably less we were back past them in no uncertain style.

'At this point I was beginning to understand the meaning of Davy Wood's and Hubert Gibson's questions about my sanity. In fact I was wondering if there was any way I could stop this roller coaster ride without losing face.

'On the way into Ramsey the speed had certainly increased, and I was now scared and prepared to admit it. Coming towards Parliament Square, in Ramsey, I thought my prayers were going to be answered, for praying hard I was. I saw a policeman on traffic duty and was sure he would stop us, at which I planned to step off the bike, and get a bus, a taxi or even a train back to Douglas. It was not to be, as we approached the constable, he waved us on and as Joey acknowledged him with a wave he accelerated towards the Ramsay Hairpin and the Mountain.

'With this in prospect all kinds of doubts filled my mind. At the same time, as I was holding on for grim death, I did not want to grab Joey, much as I wanted to, as we went up through the Water

Works and the Gooseneck, with the footrests scraping the ground at times because of the extra weight.

'Over the Mountain it was at times a dream in the bits that I enjoyed, but at others it was more like a nightmare. To be honest there are parts of the trip that I can't recall, but on the way down from Kate's Cottage to Creg-ny-Baa, I chanced to look over his shoulder and could see the rev counter was reading eleven thousand, the equivalent of about 145 miles per hour.

'As I pulled my head back, my neck froze, and my heartbeat increased as I anticipated what it would be like down to Hillberry. I said to myself that this is serious, and if I ever get off this thing that is it, I'll congratulate Joey, thank him and if I have any breath left, I'll run away as quickly as possible.

'I honestly don't remember where he stopped in Douglas, but I do remember that when I got off I was trembling from head to foot from a mixture of fear and cold. I was shaking so badly that I could not hold the lighter steady enough to light a cigarette which I needed more then than at any other time in my life, before or since.

'As I scrambled off the bike a number of fans shouted at me, telling me how lucky a guy I was to have got a ride with Joey Dunlop. I know it was a privilege that very few have had the honour to experience. It was a revelation, but I would never do it again.

'That is not a criticism of Joey, but the biggest compliment I would pay him. I had the best seat in the house to see the master at work, and it made me realise just how brilliant and outstanding a workman he was. Road racers are something else, but Joey Dunlop was indescribably special.'

The tale did not finish there, for five weeks after the TT, Brian went to see Joey riding the bike at Brands Hatch. The race had started when he arrived, and was into the third lap with Joey lying in third place when the commentator announced that Joey had crashed.

Brian finishes the story: 'I was standing with Linda, when a few minutes later Joey came walking back towards the paddock. On enquiring if he had done himself any damage he replied, "None at all, but your bike is wrecked."'

The machine was soon repaired and Brian picked it up in London at the end of the season, and rode it all the way to his home in Omagh where it continued to give him a lot of pleasure and vivid memories.

CHAPTER 3

THE ARMOY ARMADA

The achievements of Joey Dunlop, Mervyn Robinson, Frank Kennedy and Jim Dunlop, will live long in the memory of all those that knew them. But surprisingly for such a small community, they were not the first Armoy sportsmen to make history.

Four years before Joey Dunlop was born, a brilliant young athlete by the name of Steve McCooke had represented Great Britain in the 10,000 metres at the 1948 Olympic Games in London. As was later the case with Joey, McCooke was honoured with an official letter from the monarch. McCooke's bore the words: 'As patron of the British Olympic Association I send you my best wishes for your success in the Olympiad of 1948. Signed George R.' In the race, which was won by the great Emil Zatopek, McCooke led for one and a half laps, but then retired on the sixth lap. The amazing Zatopek went on to win three gold medals in the 5,000 metres, the 10,000 metres and the Marathon at the next Games in Helsinki in 1952.

So, even in the year in which Joey was born, the village of Armoy was already on the Buckingham Palace mailing list. It was to be used on at least three further occasions for its most famous resident.

The fame of Joey and his fellow competitors soon grew locally and then further afield. Their names and exploits were beginning to be revered in the Armoy and Ballymoney districts, but feared by their rivals from other parts of the island, especially in the County Down area of Dromara, where future stars Ray McCullough, Trevor Steele, Ian McGregor and Brian Reid were making their own headlines.

The desire to win was an integral part of the make-up of the Armoy men; the keenness of the rivalry among them intense. At the beginning there was no doubt that Robinson was a better rider than any of the other three, but that did not stop them trying to outdo one another at every opportunity. Off the track they were the best of friends, but on it they took no prisoners. Their drive to beat one another was only surpassed by their open desire to beat everyone else, especially the County Down men, who were becoming known collectively as the Dromara Destroyers.

The Armoy Armada riders played as hard as they raced as a young Brian Reid – later to become World Formula 2 Champion – was to discover. Reid, who started racing in 1976, told me about the first day he met Joey Dunlop.

'It was in 1975. I had gone up to Aghadowey along with some friends to see a day's racing. Joey's brother Jim fell off that day and broke his collar bone. We were driving up the road after the meeting and we met Joey coming the opposite way in his van. We waved out through the window and he stopped and said: "Come on with us for a drink." I was driving so I couldn't indulge, but I took the rest of the boys and we joined Joey for what I thought were a few drinks. How wrong can you be!

'Joey and the lads soon went on the rounds before ending up in Joey's mother's house where we saw Jim lying with his broken collar bone. Then at the end of the night we went back to Joey's place at Bushside to have a few more drinks. Just as we were about to leave, Robbo popped in and said: "Where's the Gurk [Joey's nickname]?" Needless to say, we weren't home until all hours. Joey always enjoyed the 'craic' and I thought a lot of him for I had never met him before and he was something of a hero. I must say that despite his partying I never saw him any the worse for wear.

'He was hard to talk to at first, but he warmed up when the drink began to flow and was in the right sort of mood. He was going well that day and it was a great night. But there were other times when you just knew to look at him that there was no point in trying to start up a conversation. He was in another world. And sometimes he was such a deep thinker that he appeared to be miles away. That was just Joey.'

The rivalry between the Dromara Destroyers grew as the careers of the Armoy riders developed; and with it grew their popularity and fan base. Most of their supporters were regular patrons of a hostelry in Ballymoney known as the Railway Tavern, later to become known as 'Joey's Bar' after Joey bought it. In the lounge of the Tavern, as the ale flowed, many races were run and re-run; the exploits and achievements of the local riders were a regular topic of conversation.

Naturally, it was not too long before these supporters felt that they should be doing something for the local men who had brought the sport of road racing to life in their own area and throughout Northern Ireland. It was decided to form a club, with the main aim of helping Joey Dunlop, Robinson and Kennedy as much as possible. It was also strongly felt at the time that if Jim Dunlop was given the chance and suitable machinery provided, he too could be as good as the others.

The Armoy Armada Supporters' Club, as it was named, was born with the object of raising funds to be divided equally among the four riders, plus a guarantee for the following season. It was also a goal of the club to raise the profile of the motorcycling and improve the sport by whatever means were available to them. To raise the funds for their riders, the officials of the Armoy Armada struck a membership fee of two pounds plus dues of one pound per month. Talk-ins, quizzes, film shows and other fund raising events were also planned.

But who were the men behind the riders? Among the many backers was Laurence Kelly, owner of the Railway Tavern; another was Andy English. He acted as treasurer of the club, responsible for club membership, selling tickets for functions, and arranging many of the social occasions which were so important to them all.

Thirty years later, when Joey took his collection of bikes, trophies, leathers, helmets and other memorabilia to put on display in the Isle of Man during the Millennium TT fortnight, it was English who took responsibility for most of the arrangements. It was also Andy who was on the door, collecting the money, and acting as security guard. As they say, some things never change. During that time on the island, Andy enthused about the display, which was very impressive. Prophetically he expressed a real hope that some kind of permanent 'shop window' would be established in Joey's native Ballymoney, where all of Joey's treasures could be put on display.

Naturally Joey and Jim's father, Willie, was their greatest supporter during the early days along with Tom Louden, Mel Murphy, club chairman, photographer Billy Gillan, Desmond Shirley, Alaister Patrick, the one-time secretary, and Maurice McCaughan, a civil servant, who had a long association with the riders.

Among the early sponsors of the Armada riders were Hugh O'Kane who backed Robinson, Danny McCooke who backed Joey, and Sam Taggart who looked after Kennedy. Portglenone rider Con Law, who later acted as a travelling marshal at Irish road races, once described Robinson as 'completely mad' but with great ability.

Mervyn's career began in 1968, on a twin cylinder Villiers-engined FKS Special, which he had borrowed from Kennedy. This early attempt at racing did not last very long, owing not only to the poor performance of the bike but, more likely, to a lack of finance or sponsorship. In his first season, Mervyn competed in three meetings at Cookstown, Killinchy and Mid-Antrim, before being forced into temporary retirement until 1970, when he came back to race a Triumph Tiger Cub in the very strong 200cc class.

Mervyn was an excellent engineer as well as being a class rider. This mechanical ability was not lost on local garage owner O'Kane, who asked him to build up a 350 7R AJS which he had purchased some time earlier. As payment for the work carried out on the bike, Hugh allowed Mervyn to race the bike at Kirkistown. It was on this AJS that Joey had impressed McCooke, and it was on it that Mervyn gained his first trophy, a fifth place in the Mid-Antrim 150.

In 1973 the AJS was replaced by a 350 Aermacchi and at that year's North West 200 he was the first placed four-stroke rider in a class dominated by two-strokes. Mervyn's performance at the North West and at other meetings, especially the Temple 100, so impressed a potential buyer that Hugh sold the Aermacchi. As a replacement, O'Kane bought Ballymena rider Billy McCosh's Yamaha for the rest of the season, during which Robinson's best placing was third at the Carrowdore 100, a race held at the end of the Ulster season through a tiny Co Down village near Strangford Lough.

Another McCosh machine, a water-cooled Yamaha, was bought for the 1974 season, during which Robinson scored his first win plus two others at the Jurby road races in the Isle of Man. Mervyn may have been on a learning curve, racing-wise, but when it came to celebrating, no tuition was needed, especially when Joey was barman! In June 1974, he had his first Irish race win at Kirkistown in the Embassy Championship race. The breakthrough had been made, and at Fore in the Irish Republic it was reported that 'he brought home a bagful of silverware' in addition to a rising reputation.

At this stage O'Kane recognised that Mervyn was in need of a second bike. He was riding the 350 in his own class and in the 500, when he was permitted. This was taking a toll on the machinery, so he bought back the old air-cooled Yamaha previously ridden by Mervyn and converted it into a 500. This gave Robinson two bikes to race, and made life for everyone that much easier.

It was around this time that Mervyn, a relentless practical joker and prankster, coined the phrase 'fablon cranks'. As today, the decals for the side number plates of the bikes were different colours for different classes, and were made from a material called fablon. Instead of changing engines, or barrels, or anything mechanical on the bike to alter its capacity to make it legal for another race, Mervyn simply changed the fablon number plate on the side in the hope of fooling the race organisers, and this introduced into the language the phrase 'fablon cranks'. It was a typical 'Robbo' ploy.

In August 1975, his career reached a new peak when he beat the best of the British in the 500cc race at the Ulster Grand Prix. Tony Rutter was second and the calibre of Robinson's win can be gauged from the fact that Rutter had done the double in the 350 and 500 at the Ulster, the previous year. Rutter, the Brierly Hill rider, was full of praise for Robinson, commenting: 'There was no doubt that he was the best rider on the day. In the terrible weather, he was battling against the conditions as well as his rivals. He deserved his win.'

Mervyn finished off the season with one of the most memorable races of the year, and of his tragically short career, in the Embassy Championship final at Kirkistown. The rivalry between the Armada and the Destroyers was now reaching unprecedented levels; everyone expected a showdown whenever they met and they were rarely disappointed.

The Embassy race was one occasion when the supporters could have no complaints. For the entire race they were at it hammer and tongs with Ray McCullough often sandwiched between Mervyn and Joey. 'I knew at times that they were trying to chop me up a bit,' admitted McCullough. 'I had been leading and then they both passed me with one going up one side and the other up the other. It was like this the whole way through the race, right to the last lap. I knew where they were as we all came down to the hairpin. Mervyn was on the inside, Joey was on the outside and I was in the middle. I left my braking as late as I could, Joey left his too late and ran wide, while Mervyn was going too fast and went straight on and I went on to win the race and the title.'

The first race in the new 1976 season was the Cookstown 100, where Robinson was still suffering from damaged nerves in his right arm, the result of a crash at Aghadowey at the end of the previous year. He still finished third in the 350 race, but slipped back to fifth in the 500 race when he lost his front brake. Still, he kept going to get the points in the road racing championship. It was a bad year for Mervyn. He came off at Skerries and then broke a collar bone at Mondello Park near Dublin. Never one to be outdone, he came back to the Mid-Antrim and blasted the opposition to bits in the 500 race, winning by the proverbial mile. The Armada were sailing high again, or so they thought.

There was further bad luck at Carrowdore, where his 500cc engine blew to pieces, when a conrod went through the side of the engine, depriving him of the 500 road race championship, for which he needed at least a second place. A catalogue of disasters befell him during the 1977 season, riding both the O'Kane Motors' 350 Seeley Yamaha and Sam Taggart's Sparton.

While practising on the Sparton at the St Angelo airfield circuit near Enniskillen, Mervyn hit a post and crashed heavily. He sustained severe concussion which badly affected his balance. It kept him out of racing for the most of the season. When he did return to action he collided with another rider during practice at Kirkistown, sustaining a serious leg injury.

It was a serious blow and his career and life were brought to a sudden halt not long after, but not before he made a remarkable comeback, taking the title of 'Monarch of Mondello' at Mondello Park and the '50 Mile Champion' at Carrowdore. He crashed and died in the 1980 North West 200.

The second member of the Armoy brigade, the man who was seen by everyone as the Admiral of the Armada, was of course Joey. According to his mother, Joey was a fan of the late Bill Ivy who was World 125cc Champion in 1967. The battles between Ivy and Phil Read were legendary in the late 1960s and caught Joey's imagination. He wanted to emulate Ivy so much that he decided to have an ivy leaf similar to Bill's painted on his yellow helmet. 'Joey picked an ivy leaf out of a hedge and drew around the outline on the helmet,' his mother said. 'He was 19 at the time and Robert, who was 10, coloured it in. Joey wore this helmet with the ivy insignia in all his early road races.'

As we have seen, his racing career began in 1969 on the Triumph Cub at a disused airfield called Maghaberry, a site which is now a maximum security prison! The following year, 1970, Joey was involved in that road accident returning home from Kirkistown on Easter Monday. Joey recovered by the end of July in time to compete in the Temple road races in Co Down but he crashed out. His bike stood on its end in the middle of a corner as Joey experienced his first wheelie, before going through a hedge!

For the 1971 season, Joey purchased a Suzuki. In the first race of the year at Tandragee he finished second in the 200cc class but the race was not without incident. The skills of his team were quickly required just before the off when Joey bent a conrod while trying to start the bike. At this point the inventiveness of Joey and his father, a talent which became the hallmark of his career, came into play. Willie Dunlop and Mervyn Robinson used two ring spanners to straighten the conrod, put it back in the piston, and assembled the engine. Joey went out to finish second!

The podium place at Tandragee was the highlight of Joey's season aboard the Suzuki. The bike simply wasn't competitive enough or consistent on a regular basis. Something needed to change; in 1972 Joey got a big break.

After watching Joey ride the Hugh O'Kane 7R AJS on the open roads around Armoy, Danny McCooke realised that 'Yer Man' had a lot of potential. For the 1973 season Danny bought a 350 four-stroke Aermacchi to compete against the mighty two-stroke Yamahas which had dominated the class, and which were looked upon in those days as probably the fastest and most competitive machines in the business.

Joey suffered a major disappointment at the North West 200, when he broke the chain going off the starting line, but at the Ulster Grand Prix, things went much better. Although he did not win, he scored a personal victory, as his bike was the first four-stroke home. During the season he had a second and two third places at the Jurby road races, an event which was very popular with the Armoy men and where they gained a great deal of vital road experience.

Back home Joey finished fourth behind three Yamahas at the Carrowdore 100.

As the result at Carrowdore proved, although the Aermacchis were very good bikes, they were not a match for the Yamahas. As the saying goes, 'If you can't beat them, join them,' and this is exactly what McCooke and Dunlop did for the 1974 season. An air-cooled 350 Yamaha was purchased and competition began in earnest.

Among those with whom Joey began to battle on a more level playing field, in addition to Robinson, were Abe Alexander, known as the 'White Tornado' as he wore white leathers, and Ian McGregor, one of the most experienced 350 riders on the scene. Usually it was Alexander or McGregor who filled the front two places as Joey and Mervyn fought with each other for the third place on the podium.

The Road Racing Club of Ireland, which catered mainly for the riders, ran at Maghaberry, and for the 1974 season the one and a half mile course had been altered considerably. It had been changed from a figure 8 configuration to a new-look L-shape. The club's first meeting of the season, the Embassy Championship race, was a major event on the programme, with Abe Alexander, Campbell Gorman, Mervyn Robinson, Frank Kennedy and Joey Dunlop all in the line up. During the 12 lap race, Gorman, Robinson, Alexander and Dunlop were involved in a hectic battle. Alexander had a slight advantage over Gorman with Robinson and Dunlop arguing fiercely over third. Having got ahead of Robinson, Joey went after Gorman who was now losing contact with the leader Alexander.

Joey overdid things and came off, sustaining hand injuries and breaking his collarbone. He ended up in hospital, as Alexander took the win from Gorman and Gordon Bell, with Mervyn Robinson in fourth and Frank Kennedy in ninth. Another Ballymoney man, George McQuitty, completed the top ten on his 500 Suzuki.

At the second meeting at Maghaberry that year Joey scored his first win, when he beat Sam McClements and Bobby Wylie. Mervyn Robinson had been the early leader but a broken pipe forced his retirement, promoting Gordon Bell to first place. Bell was then side-lined when his chain broke, which left Dunlop well clear of the field and on his way to a famous win. It was part of a double Armada celebration as Mervyn Robinson won both the 500cc race and the Embassy Championship round.

The Road Racing Club's tenure at Maghaberry ended with their third meeting there in 1974. Both Kennedy and Robinson figured on the podium. Frank finished second to Gordon Bell in the 500 race and Mervyn came home in third place in the 350 race behind Stanley Junk and Bell.

The RR Club moved their racing to their present location at Aghadowey in Co Londonderry for the 1975 season, where the Armada moved up a gear at the opening meeting. Unlike some of the other riders, the Armada took to the Aghadowey circuit like a duck to water and dominated the day's racing.

Robinson won the Embassy Championship race which was unique in that the Armada members filled the first three places with Kennedy in second and Joey in third. Robbo had taken over the lead from Joey on the second lap and underlining the fact that the rivalry among the Armoy men was very keen, Kennedy snatched second place from under Joey's nose on the last lap.

With the Armada now growing in strength and with it Dunlop's profile, it wasn't long before Joey attracted the attention of a new sponsor or team of sponsors. Three brothers, John, Martin and Noel Rea were racing fanatics always on the lookout for up and coming new talent. Their interest in, and eventual signing of, Joey began one of the greatest sponsor-rider relationships in the history of road racing.

John Rea, or 'Stormy' as he was known to his friends, had made his fortune in America. In time he became like a second father to Joey, who in return held John in the highest regard. At John's funeral service in 1993 in Larne, the hitherto quiet and shy Joey amazed everyone when he stepped into the pulpit and paid an emotional tribute to John, underlining the bond that existed between them.

The origins of John and Joey's relationship can be traced to 1975; they were introduced by Hector Neill, one of the great personalities of the Ulster road racing scene. Neill was a larger than life Pat Jennings lookalike who ran a car salvage business near Belfast. His first love, however, was in sponsoring and promoting road racers. Hector was a long time friend of Tom Herron, one of the great Ulster racers of the 1970s and along with his 'sidekick' Stanley 'Mouse' Morrow, Hector rarely missed a meeting in the hope of spotting new talent.

In around 1974, Neill came across the up and coming Dunlop; he knew instantly that this unknown rider would eventually go to the top. All the rider needed, Hector mused, was the proper machinery and backing.

'I remember the first time I saw Dunlop racing,' Hector recalled. 'It was on a short circuit somewhere. The Mouse and I were looking at this guy and nobody seemed to know who he was. I checked the programme and saw 'W J Dunlop from Armoy'. So I started to watch him race for he seemed to have a bit of flair.'

Neill could tell that Joey's biggest handicap was his bikes. Without the financial clout to afford a higher specification machine Joey just plodded on as best he could. But all that changed one day after a race in the Irish Republic.

'I was chatting with John Rea who was sponsoring Gordon Bell. Gordon rode in the odd race for John and I got the impression that John was going to pull the plug on road racing because he needed something to spark his interest. Another rider who was a close friend of mine, Norman Dunn, was there at the time and he mentioned to John that there was a rider called Joe Dunlop [not Joey in those days] whom he thought could fit the bill. John said: "Get him for me", and that was the start of the John Rea-Joey Dunlop partnership.'

Joey's first ride in the Rea Racing colours was in the 350cc race at the Tandragee 100 in 1975 where he finished second to Ray McCullough. Joey then returned to Aghadowey for the second meeting at the County Londonderry circuit, where he scored easy wins in both the 350 and 500 races and finished second to Mervyn Robinson in the Embassy Championship race. In wet conditions Joey won the 350 race by half a lap from Gordon Bell. In the 500 race, Joey was again the master, this time beating his friend and fellow Armada rider, Robinson.

Delighted with their new recruit, the Rea brothers provided Joey with a 500 machine but initially things did not go well. The 500 blew up in practice at the North West 200; to make matters worse the 350 seized on the first lap at Portrush. It was a similar sorry saga at the Cookstown 100. The necessary parts for the 500 could not be got in time, so Joey had only the 350, which seized again during the race.

The Rea brothers, very unhappy with the service that their man was getting from the 350, purchased a new motor and a Seeley frame in which to house it. Joey prepared the bike himself, and rewarded his backers by winning the 'King of Kirkistown' title on the debut of the bike. Another step forward had been taken, and with a clutch of wins at Mondello Park, and a record breaking win at the Temple 100, his first road success, Joey was on the up and up.

At the Mid-Antrim event he won the 500 race again breaking the lap record and in the third and final Aghadowey meeting, Joey again won the 350 and 500 races with Mervyn taking the honours in the Embassy race where he found a way past McCullough at half distance. McCullough held on to second ahead of Joey and Kennedy, who was still playing a strong supporting role in Armada ranks.

At Carrowdore, Joey won both the 350 and 500 races, but then lost out to McCullough in the Embassy Final at Kirkistown.

Joey retained the same machinery for the 1976 season, during which he made his debut in English racing at Oulton Park. Here he made the acquaintance of TT winner Charlie Williams, who in recent years has commentated upon Joey's unbeatable TT record, as a main presenter with Radio TT. The rest of the 1976 season was a catalogue of successes, both on the roads and in short circuits. He was unbeaten at Mondello Park and practically unbeatable in the

500 Irish short circuit championship, winning all the races in which he finished.

As the 1976 season went on, support for the 'Armada' became legendary. So many locals from the Ballymoney area wanted to attend the meetings that John Rea purchased a bus to transport them to all the races. Dozens of members of the Armoy Armada's Supporters' Club would meet down at the Railway Tavern on the morning of a race, sometimes at an unearthly hour. Stocks of refreshments, both liquid and solid, but mainly liquid, were put on board and John took the wheel. Then they would start the journey to Kirkistown, Tandragee or wherever the race was; it was traditional for one of the members to stand up front with John to engage him in chat, while the others discussed the prospects for the day, and argued about how the boys might do.

Billy Kennedy told me of those heady days. 'At the meeting everybody went their own way, as John usually went to join Joey in the paddock, or some of his many friends. He also spent quite a bit of time going round the paddock, talking to other riders, and in many instances slipping them some money to help buy tyres or other parts. He always did this in the quietest of ways, so that nobody would know what he was doing.

'After the meeting was over, everyone returned to the bus for the journey home. If the boys did well, it was celebration time, and if they didn't, it was an excuse to drown the sorrows. No matter what had happened the return journeys to Ballymoney were always memorable – for some at least!'

The season ended with Joey winning a new trophy for the 'Best Road Racer of the Year' as he finished up with lap records at almost every circuit he had raced at including the Irish road meetings, the Southern 100, Mondello Park, and the Jurby races. By the close of 1976 Joey was on the threshold of his first mammoth season.

John Rea was now his exclusive sponsor, as Martin and Noel had found riders of their own. A change in the set-up signalled another step up in horsepower for Joey – John bought Pat O'Mahoney's

750cc Yamaha, which had been increased in capacity from its original 700. Joey first tested the bike at Oulton Park, following which he decided to retain its engine but install it in a Suzuki frame. It was pretty crude, but very effective. In addition to this Suzuki/Yamaha hybrid, Joey had a 350cc cantilever Yamaha, and a 250 Yamaha, all of which he prepared himself.

Whilst Joey and Mervyn undeniably spearheaded the challenge of the Armada, both Kennedy and Joey's brother, Jim Dunlop, nevertheless played major supporting roles.

Frank was a giant of man in both stature and nature who ran a car sales business on the edge of Armoy village after serving his time as a motor mechanic. His first foray into racing was aboard the now famous AJS of Hugh O'Kane. On it he had a number of minor successes, mainly at short circuits.

After several seasons of mixed fortunes – seventh placed finishes at the Tandragee 100 and North West 200 in 1973 were tempered by several serious crashes – his career probably peaked in 1976. Sam Taggart, seeing Frank's potential, decided to give him full sponsorship backing with a new 500cc Sparton. Frank was overwhelmed with the arrival of the Sparton, late on a Saturday evening. He immediately phoned Harold Crooks who went to Armoy on the Sunday morning to see the unique machine, report on it and have the first pictures taken of it.

On the Sparton at the North West 200, Frank was leading by almost 20 seconds from English rider Martin Sharpe when the ignition broke and the engine went on to one cylinder. This unfortunate failure robbed Frank of certain victory at a race which he so dearly wanted to win. Later that season at the Mid-Antrim 150, he crashed while battling with Mervyn Robinson. The Sparton developed a mechanical fault on the second lap and the bike went from under him. Frank was flung off, breaking his collarbone.

Returning to action in 1977 at Aghadowey, riding a new 351 Yamaha, Frank's bike sucked a stone into the carburettor, jamming the slides and pitching Frank off at high speed. He broke both arms, and badly damaged his left hand, on which he had to have a special cage fitted. These injuries kept him out of racing for the rest of the year. His incredible resolve signalled a return to action the following year and capped an amazing return with wins at the Cookstown and Carrowdore and victory in the Ulster and Irish road racing championships.

The Armada fever was at its height when Jim Dunlop, Joey's brother, started racing in 1975, on Joey's 200 Suzuki. Curiously, Jim had more success on it than Joey. On his first visit to Mondello Park, he finished second to established expert Sammy Dempster. A trip to Knockhill in Scotland ensured that he had a road racing licence which allowed him to ride at Cookstown where he won Group C. In order to race the Suzuki, Jim usually took the barrels off his father's bike for the Saturday and then replaced them so that Willie could get to work on Monday morning!

During the 1976 season, breakdowns were the order of the day for the 350 air-cooled Yamaha that he had acquired. It was the same story with a TR3 Yamaha that he built up during the season. Joey then loaned him his water-cooled Yamaha for the races at Fore, where he finished fifth in the 500 race.

In order to accumulate funds for the 1977 season Jim went to work in England. When he came home, he discovered that Martin Rea had bought Joey's water-cooled 350, and wanted Jim to ride it, in what was really his first serious season in racing with a good sponsor backing him.

That year Jim went to the Manx Grand Prix, and was lying in sixth place, and the leading newcomer, when his clutch broke with just over a lap to go, putting him out of the race and depriving him of the coveted Newcomer's Award. It had been a hard season for Jim, but his riding skills had improved greatly, and he was rewarded with the trophy for the Best Up and Coming Rider. Like his brother Joey, Jim was on his way up and starting to contribute to the pool of success being enjoyed by the Armoy Armada.

When all their achievements are collated, it makes for amazing reading – produced by a group of four young sportsmen from a small rural community whose enthusiasm, guts, bravery and determination took them to great heights in their chosen sport. We weren't to know it at the time but for Joey Dunlop these were preliminary skirmishes to the great battles which he dominated over the next two decades.

CHAPTER 4

DAYS IN THE FAST LANE

They were poles apart. In looks, attitude and ambition. Yet they were the closest of friends. And they shared one timeless and priceless quality – superb and enviable talent on a racing motorcycle. They were Tom Herron and Joey Dunlop.

Tom Herron was the hero of the late 1970s, in an era when Joey was still fighting to forge a hard-earned corner in the hearts of a thrill-thirsty public.

They both suffered violent deaths following the sport they loved. And for one moment in time their careers fused. This was on a never-to-be-forgotten day – some might say the worst in the history of Ulster road racing – when Herron crashed and was killed in the 1979 North West 200. In contrast, Dunlop took the first steps to glory by winning the race unaware that his close pal was lying on the road with his life blood ebbing away. It was said at the time – and with hindsight I suppose it's true – that Herron passed on the baton of his greatness to Dunlop on that terrible afternoon.

With his swarthy skin, deep set brown eyes and volatile temperament, Herron was more like an Italian than an Irishman. The son of a wealthy businessman from Newcastle in Co Down, Herron appeared to have everything going for him – as opposed to Dunlop who sprang from humble beginnings. Herron was good and he knew it. In fact he was convinced he was the best and he had a temper to go with his talent.

Hector Neill, one of his closest friends and the man who guided him in his early years, told me once of an incident while Tom and Hector were spectating at the Carrowdore 100. As Herron and Neill were walking along the pavement beside the track and passing one of the many pubs which festooned the area, someone called out to Herron, 'So you think you are a racer – some hope,' or words to that effect. According to Hector, Herron immediately grabbed the offending fan and pushed him against a wall. Hector had to rescue the unfortunate bystander and Tom was quickly cooled down.

But that was Tom's way. He lived in the spotlight, he loved the glory but his life was on a razor's edge. He was a chain smoker – at least he seemed to be for he was always asking for a cigarette after every race. But he was a winner, no doubt about that.

In 1976 he completed a memorable TT double when he won the Lightweight 250cc and the Senior. Very few Irish riders had been successful in the TT at this period and Herron was rightly hailed as a hero. He flew home the day after his Senior triumph in a private plane which landed at Ards Airport, seven miles from Belfast near Strangford Lough. I remember the occasion well because I went down to the airport to greet him.

After the plane landed the first person to emerge from the pilot's seat was none other than fellow road racer Ivor Greenwood, who was to become another piece in the jigsaw which formed the early years of Joey Dunlop. Greenwood looked like an extra from a First World War film as he jumped from the aircraft complete with flying helmet and jacket. Greenwood, a close friend of Tom, was a man of many talents, another of which, I learnt that day, was having a pilot's licence. In addition to racing motorcycles, he was also a marvellous raconteur and wit – on many occasions at a social function he could at a moment's notice climb on to the stage and regale the audience with stories and songs all put over with a unique charm. He was also a stock car driver. In fact, he seemed to be everything!

The second figure to climb from the plane was Tom. He was pictured holding the coveted TT trophies aloft. It was a memorable moment.

But still there was a shock in store. From out of the back of the plane tumbled a third, crumpled figure. It was Joey Dunlop! He had asked Greenwood for a lift home from the Manx races and, it being only a two-seated plane, Ivor had stuffed him in with the luggage at the back!

Following his TT successes, Herron decided to have a break and attended, as a spectator, one of Ulster's top road races on the summer calendar, the Killinchy 150, over the world championship Dundrod circuit. Competing that day was the young Joey Dunlop who had yet to score a win over the course which in time was to be inextricably linked with his name.

However, in 1976 he was still making his way and fighting out those nail-biting battles with Mervyn Robinson. They were an act worth going a long way to see, like two bull terriers on the rampage and they had an ever closing vice-like grip on the Ulster racing scene.

The Killinchy 150, which is now run under the name of the Dundrod 150, was organised by the Killinchy motorcycle club in Co Down. It was usually a trial race for the Ulster Grand Prix and in those years attracted many English performers eager to have a run round this unique track. The Killinchy club were mainly a moto-cross outfit, but they had a man in their midst, Billy Gibson, who virtually ran the show single-handedly, along with his son Alan.

At the 1976 event Dunlop was on a revenge mission – Robinson had the previous year won the 500cc class at the Ulster Grand Prix and in so doing became the first home based rider to win this race since Dick Creith from Bushmills, Co Antrim in 1965. Dunlop had a troubled time at the 1975 Ulster, for he fell off at the hairpin during the 350cc race breaking his collarbone. He was a sad picture as he trudged back to the paddock.

Meanwhile, the race was won by a rider whom many would

claim was the greatest Ulster ever produced – and that includes Dunlop and Herron. Ray McCullough won that 1975 350cc race, smashing the lap record on four occasions and beating Herron in the process. To enthusiastic cheering McCullough crossed the line with 42 seconds in hand. In my view it was one of his greatest victories.

McCullough was a class act. In fact, there used to be a photo-graph in a Douglas, Isle of Man hotel showing McCullough hacking around Dundrod in the mid 1970s on a Yamaha on treaded tyres pulling a lean angle which few have seen surpassed. 'He would do that with both wheels a foot in the air,' recalled Mick Grant, one of his opponents in those days. 'The way he rode seemed to defy the laws of physics.'

McCullough was Dunlop's idol in the Seventies. And no wonder. Personally, I thought he was breathtaking, but the problem with Ray was that he was unadventurous and didn't like travelling. He preferred to do all his racing at home, where he was virtually unbeatable, and very rarely raced in England or the Isle of Man. With such an insular approach to competition it would be difficult to describe him as Ulster's best ever road racer, but those who saw him in his heyday will never forget his smooth and sophisticated style of racing which was years ahead of its time.

Another of his many achievements was that he beat on the track one of the greatest promoters of the sport of motorcycling in the 1970s – the inimitable Barry Sheene. This was in 1971 at Bishopscourt in Co Down but it must be admitted that Sheene was very much in the early stages of a career which later blossomed with staggering effect.

Like Dunlop, McCullough had a slightly uneasy relationship with the media. I remember when Ray had beaten the mighty Phil Read in the world championship 250cc Ulster Grand Prix in 1971, he was brought into the Press tent for a live broadcast by the team representing Radio Telefise Eireann. They sat the embar-rassed Ray down before a microphone and asked for his reaction to the race.

'So Ray,' the interviewer began, 'how does it feel to beat Phil Read a world champion in a race round Dundrod?'

Silence. Ray just sat there sporting a nervous grin and said nothing.

The panic stricken interviewer stared in disbelief – remember this was live – and said, 'Go on say something' at which McCullough still appeared stage struck. The unfortunate RTE man didn't know what to do and the rest of us in the Press tent burst out laughing. Eventually some sort of interview was arrived at, but obviously not according to plan.

So in 1976 and 1977 Joey not only had his brother-in-law Robinson as a major adversary but also McCullough and he handled everything with class and courage. He was nothing if not a fighter and Joey's first Dundrod win in 1976 saw him beat Robinson into second place in the 500cc class and make his first inroads on the public's imagination.

The year 1977 saw major changes in world road racing, changes which were to eventually elevate Dunlop into a major sporting hero – although he didn't know this at the time. Following a well orchestrated campaign by a few top class riders to have the Isle of Man mountain circuit banned from the existing world championship set-up because of its hazardous nature, the FIM eventually requested that the Auto-Cycle Union devise a completely new formula suitable for TT racing to be in place for the 1977 season.

Consequently, the 1976 races were the last to be staged under the old banner. The ACU, who had been given precious little time for the job, were involved in months of soul searching, eventually launching a new world road racing championship for TT Formula One, TT Formula Two and TT Formula Three machines. The new formula basically catered for production motorcycles, namely those available to the public, and each year evidence had to be produced to show that at least 200 units of a certain model had been sold in order for it to be eligible. Every machine had to be supplied with complete electrical equipment in working order; be fitted with a starting device and generator and the engine run on pump fuel. The classes were devised as follows:

TT Formula One - over 350cc up to 500cc (two strokes) and over 600cc up to 1000cc (four strokes).
TT Formula Two - over 250cc up to 350cc (two strokes) and over 400cc up to 600cc (four strokes).
TT Formula Three - over 125cc up to 250cc (two strokes) and over 200cc up to 400cc (four strokes).

This restructuring meant that the TT was saved as a world championship race. Admittedly it was a new world title the riders were going for, but it had the backing of a major factory – Honda. They came up with the ideal rider in Phil Read to compete in the only round of the championship in that 1977 season – the TT itself.

So the Formula One world championship was born and, in pouring rain, Read powered his Honda round the famous old circuit to become the inaugural winner of a series which was, in later years, to be totally monopolised not only by Honda but by Joey Dunlop.

Also that year Read won the Senior TT on a Suzuki, while Joey finished fourth in that race thanks to his pal Herron who, the night before, had taken him round the course in a car showing Joey every inch of the thirty seven and three quarter mile mountain circuit and the tactics required to navigate it as quickly as possible. Herron showed Joey the places to go fast and also where to take things easily. 'If it hadn't been for Tom I would never have been able to reach such a high placing,' Joey told me afterwards. 'I will always be grateful to him because he showed me how to get among the quick boys round this track. It was only my second visit here and now I feel ready for many more.'

Joey didn't say so but, buoyed by his showing in the Senior, he already had his eyes on the last race of the meeting. This was the Jubilee TT which was staged to mark the 25th anniversary of the Queen ascending to the throne. Somewhat at odds with the momentous occasion it was honouring, the Jubilee race was hurriedly added to the programme at the last minute. I remember talking to Vernon Cooper, then head of the ACU, and he told me that, with the programme rearranged to accommodate Formula One on the opening Saturday, they were left with a gap to fill the following Friday.

The main race of the meeting – after Formula One – was the Classic 1000cc which featured all the top riders. The Jubilee, in comparison, was really an afterthought. This became obvious when, after Wednesday's Classic had been won by Mick Grant, riders began to leave the island to fulfil prior commitments. As a result the Jubilee race was significantly devalued, ultimately attracting a field which could be described as the 'scrapings' of those who were left on the island.

One of those entrants was a still unknown Joey Dunlop, and under-strength field or not, he had a point to prove. He knew the opposition wasn't hot but the course itself was the challenge and he set about taming it in a way which not only transformed the race into an exciting spectacle, but ensured its place in motorcycling's Hall of Fame – for this was the first of Joey's 26 TT wins.

To add icing to the cake, Dunlop also became the third fastest man around the TT course that Friday afternoon when he recorded a scaring lap of 110.93mph. His fastest lap was on the second circuit as he ground out what, by the end of the race, was a 52 second lead over nearest rival George Fogarty, father of future world superbike champion Carl. Joey cruised to victory and a £1,000 cheque.

Dunlop led from start to finish and was five seconds ahead of the field as they hit Ballacraine. By the time he had completed his first lap he was almost 17 seconds clear of Fogarty thanks to a superb standing start lap of 110.80mph. It was thought that Dunlop might really threaten Mick Grant's outright lap record but the lack of pressure on the rider, coupled with a worn rear tyre, took away an incentive for record breaking. Behind Fogarty came TT veteran Bill Smith who was heading for yet another silver replica on his 500cc Suzuki; Derek Chatterton, riding well despite severe pain in his back was fourth, and Steve Tonkin fifth.

Dunlop's lead kept increasing all the time and with another lap completed and the fastest lap for the race at 110.93mph Joey came into the pits with a handsome 31 second advantage over Fogarty. The leaderboard men – Dunlop, Fogarty, Chatterton and Smith, but not Tonkin – called for fuel at the end of lap two which enabled non-stop Tonkin to move into third sport ahead of Smith. Dunlop was 34 seconds up as he jumped Ballaugh Bridge for the third time with Fogarty and Tomkin now separated by only three seconds. Smith was a further 44 seconds adrift and on to the leaderboard came Derek Huxley in fifth spot ahead of Chatterton, Roger Nicholls, Dennis Casement and Neil Tuxworth, who was to become Honda race manager in later years.

Still Dunlop kept going, covering the seven miles between the Grandstand and Ballacraine at an average of 119mph. His lead was widening . . . 37 seconds at Ramsey . . . 44 at the Bungalow. The race was now only for the minor positions. Joey had it all wrapped up! With enough fuel to see him through the remaining thirty seven and three quarter miles, Dunlop screamed past the grandstand for the last time obviously easing off with his healthy margin clearly relayed to him by his pit crew.

After the race Joey explained that even though he was lapping at a speed which would have been very respectable in the previous Wednesday's Classic race, incredibly he still had a few miles per hour to spare. 'I had a few tyre problems at the start but pulled out a big enough gap to avoid too many problems under pressure. I didn't think I was lapping at such a high speed for I still had something in reserve,' he confided.

Mechanically, his 750 Yamaha, which was housed in a Seeley frame originally built for a Suzuki, was perfect, apart from fuel that had leaked from the filler cap on to the rear tyre.

Irish listeners to Manx Radio were soon phoning in their congratulations after Joey's most prestigious victory to date. It was great to be on the island at that time. I remember feeling that we had seen a new star emerge on to the firmament. But like so many others, I had no idea how brightly he was to shine, especially when sparked off by a rider of similar talent and outlook, Ron Haslam.

The arch rivalry between the young Dunlop and Nottingham's Haslam in the late 1970s and the early 1980s resembled the Muhammad Ali–Joe Frazier boxing matches of a few years earlier. The only difference was that while Ali and Frazier looked as if they could stop trains such was their bulk and power, Dunlop and Haslam gave every appearance of being a pair of competitors for whom a good square meal would not go amiss.

To say they looked pale, pinched and gaunt would be to understate the point. They had that hang-dog expression, a lean and hungry look, common to riders who live on the edge.

Dunlop, especially in the Seventies, had the appearance of a drifter. He had long, black, greasy hair which virtually covered his face; he always walked about with a far away look in his eyes and that inevitable cigarette dangling from his lips. In addition, he developed a stooped look about the shoulders, giving the impression that he carried the cares of the world on his lean frame.

But really all Joey cared about was the motorcycle which he happened to be racing at the time. He devoted all his attention to it before racing. No one dared to come near him except someone who had vital information which Joey needed. In much later years Steve Hislop was to say to me:

'You got nothing from Joey when it came to knowledge of a racing bike. When Roger Burnett and I were with Honda, Joey used to set himself up elsewhere and we never saw him except when he came in to ask where we were and to look around him. We knew he was quizzing us about the preparation of our machines to see if there was something he had missed, but we never told him anything. It's not that we didn't want to communicate but Joey was a very distant type. He took what information he could from others but to the best of my knowledge very rarely imparted any in return. That was his way and no one took exception to it.'

In the summers of 1977 and 1979 Dunlop and Haslam put on a show in the 'Killinchy' meetings Dundrod the like of which had not been seen for many years. Haslam was an English rider on the verge of major success in England while it could be argued that Dunlop was in the same category at home. They were evenly matched head to head and although there were scores of other big name riders on the track, the spotlight was always on Joey and Ron.

Both riders had a lot in common on the track and it was the same off it. I always felt that both were protected from outsiders by the women who guided their affairs. Haslam's wife Anne seldom let the Press speak to Ron. She always answered the phone and to the best of my knowledge still does so today, even when Ron has long since stopped racing. She was protective – perhaps overprotective – but that's the way she saw it and I have no doubt she felt she was doing the right thing.

The same could be said of Joey, for Linda usually answered the phone. In fact during the 30 years in which I covered Dunlop's career, only on one occasion did I get to speak to him in this way, following a crash at Brands Hatch in 1989 which almost ended his career. That sounds amazing, but totally accurate. On every occasion but that one time, it was Linda who answered the phone, and when I asked for Joey he was never there. The only answer I ever got was, 'He's sleeping' or 'He has gone out' or 'He is fixing the bikes.'

There was the air of a certain lack of communication between the pair which may not have been true, but that was the feeling which came across. Even right up to the time of his death, on his last journey which proved to end up in fatal circumstances, there was apparent confusion as to where he was going. When I phoned Linda on the night he left, she told me: 'He's gone to Latvia.' In fact he had gone to Estonia. Admittedly, the countries are side by side but it's a bit like saying 'I'm going to France' when in fact I'm going to Germany.

It was Joey's habit of suddenly taking off and disappearing into the middle of Europe or even Australia which added to the myth of this really unique rider. Fans would regularly turn out expecting to see Joey riding at a local road race in Ulster and find that he wasn't among the starters. But no one ever took exception to this, they seemed to accept it as part of the Joey mystique. I could never understand why, but that was the way it was and Joey lost no friends as a result of his frequent 'disappearing acts'.

Off the track he was never one for the instant soundbite. Former road racer and world champion Brian Reid confirmed this when he told me: 'You had to be in Joey's company for at least an hour before he warmed up and began to have what you could call a serious conversation. Up until then, he was always very shy and withdrawn and never discussed his thoughts. He was difficult to get to know but to be in his company for any length of time usually turned out to be rewarding.'

As far as Dunlop and Haslam were concerned there was always a close rivalry and friendship. Fans of Dunlop probably don't want to remember the fact but Haslam had by far the better of the exchanges especially when it came to the TT and the Ulster Grand Prix in the early 1980s. If you go back to the 1977 Killinchy 150, Dunlop beat Haslam in the 500cc class but Haslam turned the tables in the 1000cc race which ended the day, a race in which Dunlop finished third. Then, at the 1979 races, Dunlop won the 500cc class again with Haslam down the field in fourth place; Joey also won the 1000cc race at the end of the meeting when Haslam fell off and Joey turned out an easy victor.

But it was a different story at the start of the decade that followed, as Joey moved into the Formula One TT discipline. Haslam won the 1981 TT but, as motorcycle fans know, the result was reshuffled and Graeme Crosby ended up as the winner because the international jury decided there had been a timing discrepancy. Then in the only other round of the world championship, the Ulster Grand Prix, Haslam won again. In effect, Haslam won two world championship Formula One races out of two, and still didn't win the title. A rather unusual set of circumstances.

Going on to 1982, and Haslam's presence remains, although bizarrely this was the year of Joey's first world championship success. The Formula One TT was held over three rounds – the TT in the Isle of Man, Portugal (Vila Real) and of course the Ulster Grand Prix. Haslam won the Isle of Man with Joey second; Ron didn't ride in the Vila Real race in which Joey was again second, this time to Wayne Gardner, another Honda rider. At the Ulster Grand Prix Haslam won again with Joey second.

So, you can see, it certainly wasn't all Joey Dunlop in those early days of Formula One. Haslam was very much a star performer and a major player on the world championship scene. I would be prepared to say that had he not gone on to other types of racing – world Grand Prix and world superbikes – then he might have challenged Joey for that record total number of TT victories. But, as was the case with Herron, McCullough and Hislop, just when it looked as though another rider might go close to giving Dunlop a run for his money, they decided on alternative careers or, as was the sad case with Herron, their lives came to a tragic end.

Motorcycle road racing sadly has been plagued by fatal accidents and the Killinchy 150 of 1977 did not escape. One of the favourites for the race was Derbyshire rider Geoff Barry who had won the 1000cc class at the previous year's Ulster Grand Prix. Barry was a likeable character, a happy-go-lucky sort and I will always remember his win in 1976 at the Ulster, for the weather was scorching and that was certainly unusual for Dundrod as anyone who has attended there will tell you!

Anyway, in the 1977 Killinchy, Barry was disputing the lead in the final race of the day, the 1000cc class. Joining him at the front was Haslam when suddenly Barry clipped a grass bank and bounced down the road at Tournagrough near the Hairpin. This is a fast sweeping descent and although Barry was in the lead at the time, Haslam had room to pass and go on and win. Barry died from head injuries shortly after being admitted to hospital. His accident came with only two laps to go in the race and ironically on the previous circuit he had set up a new record of 111.68mph which stood until the end of the race.

Barry was a tremendous favourite with the Ulster crowds and especially in the North West 200 where he was a regular competitor for six years. He first came to the notice of the Ulster fans in the rain-wrecked North West 200 of 1971, the last on the old course which took the race through the town of Portstewart. On that occasion he finished second to his close friend John Cooper in the 500cc race.

There was no North West in 1972, but the following year when the race was moved to the present shortened version of the old course, Barry showed he had lots of class by winning the first ever 750cc race at the meeting. He also finished second in one of the superbike races won by Mick Grant at the 1976 North West 200. A modest man, but at the same time an intense road racer, he was always keen to get into the thick of things. He had a spectacular style and he was greatly missed.

Barry's fatal crash at Killinchy naturally took the gloss off Haslam's victory – he beat Ray McCullough into second place with Joey third. Earlier in the day Ron had been beaten by Dunlop in the 500cc class. And this first meeting of the two famous riders of that era is worth detailing.

The race was held in pouring rain with Dunlop in the lead all the way. Joe Lindsay, a Belfast rider who was later killed in the Skerries 100, finished in third place. Joey's average speed was 105.28mph which was just down on the record he established when winning the previous year. Joey took his chance with both hands and at the end of the first lap had established a lead of 10 yards over Trevor Steele – a member of the Dromara Destroyers – followed by Graham Young, Stephen Cull, Lindsay and Courtney Junk.

On the second lap Joey increased his advantage and in fact set a new 500cc lap record for the Killinchy race with a speed of 108.27mph. Haslam was in second place at the end of lap two but next time round he was fifth, then, with rain covering the circuit, he produced more power from his Suzuki to burst through into third place behind Dunlop and Junk at the end of the fourth lap, the halfway mark.

Haslam moved into second place on lap five after turning in a lap of 108.27mph on the fourth circuit. Lindsay, however, was pushing hard and passed Junk for third place which he held to the finish. Dunlop took the flag first, followed by Haslam with Junk fourth, and Frank Kennedy just edging out Steele for sixth place.

However, despite Joey's success over Haslam, the day belonged to 350cc hero McCullough and the main headline in the *Belfast Telegraph*'s sporting edition that evening was 'McCullough Still King of Dundrod'. That will give you some idea of the high esteem in which the Dromara rider was held. Times changed in years to come but in those days McCullough was the top rider grabbing all the attention.

Alan Gibson meanwhile was very much a Haslam fan and two years later when Alan's father Billy brought Ron back to Dundrod for a further crack at Dunlop in the Killinchy 150, Alan took up his post at the Hairpin bend beside Haslam's sponsor Mal Carter, a heavily set Halifax businessman who did not mince his words. Mal, whose son Alan Carter later became a top class rider on the world Grand Prix circuit and who had a marvellous race with Joey Dunlop at Kirkistown years later, had one of the new electrical timing devices from America at that 1979 Killinchy race. He and Alan Gibson timed Haslam and Dunlop as they scorched round the track in the final race of the day, the 1000cc class. This was quite simply an epic with Dunlop and Haslam side by side throughout most of the race until, with one lap to go, Haslam, who was just tucked in behind Joey at the time, lost it and fell off at the Hairpin.

Gibson recalls Carter's reaction when he saw Haslam falling off. 'He just said "pillock",' Alan told me. 'Mal did not take defeat easily.' Alan continued: 'Earlier we had timed Joey and Ron at over 120mph on a Hairpin to Hairpin basis. This made it, by our reckoning, the first ever 120mph lap around Dundrod. However, we had to go by the official timekeepers whose version of the speeds was slightly different. They gave the fastest lap to Joey at 118.70mph but they were clocking on a Grandstand to Grandstand basis. At the same time this was a big difference in speeds and I know that Mal Carter's digital timing machine was way ahead of its time.'

Alan also recalls the fact that when Haslam fell off, Joey was well aware what had happened. 'I saw Joey looking behind him once or twice and I know he saw Ron lying at the side of the road,' Alan said. 'Joey, I'm sure, realised at the time that the race was his and he eased off appropriately on the final lap. I was very disappointed because I wanted to see a flying finish as did everyone else, but Joey performed with his usual style and grace and ended up an easy winner.'

This win completed a treble for Dunlop on the day for he had also won the 500cc race beating Ian Richards and Donny Robinson, and the 250cc class beating Ian Richards and that man Ray McCullough. Dunlop's hat trick was the first ever in the 23-year history of the Killinchy race and coming as it did on top of his double at the North West 200 three weeks earlier it made Dunlop a much talked about rider. He wasn't quite a hero but he was beginning to get there.

It was at this time too that the legend of Joey Dunlop off the course began to be built up. This involved more and more his quaint and unworldly travelling habits which sat awkwardly with his high speed sophisticated style on the track. Joey was never one to worry about hotel accommodation or, come to that, accommodation of any kind, while as far as money was concerned, it didn't seem to bother him at all. He certainly didn't have an obsession about safeguarding it as Alan Gibson once discovered.

'My Dad and I were at Donington Park in 1982,' said Alan, 'and we had been given tickets by Alan Carter to stay in the Carter caravan. We arrived at the track, saw the caravan and knocked on the door. To our surprise the door was open and my Dad said, "Good, they have made the bed and everything seems ready for us to stay here." There was a duvet over the bed and my dad tugged it. To my surprise, underneath was a snoring Joey Dunlop, rolled up like a hedgehog! "What are you doing here?" said dad. "Hello Billy, what are you doing here?" said Joey. Dad shook his head in amazement. Joey just got up and walked out. I honestly don't know where he spent the night but I know Dad and I had the use of the caravan.'

But Alan's experience of Joey's eccentricities didn't end there. He continued: 'Joey had a Ford Capri which everyone used as a runabout during the meeting. The door was never locked, the windows were always down, if anybody wanted to go on an errand they used Joey's car. It was just like that. Joey didn't seem to mind at all.

'Then, after the meeting was over, he came over to our car which we had cared for lovingly and sat on the bonnet. He was about to get a telling off when my Dad engaged him in conversation and asked him was he coming home with us on the ferry from Stranraer. Joey replied that he was staying at Donington because there was a car auction and he was going to buy another car.

'Dad said to him: "Have you got the money with you?" and Joey replied, "Yes, I have it here in the car." To our amazement he leant in and produced a polythene bag which was stuffed with over £2,000 in readies! It was under the seat of the car and anyone could have stolen it.

'But that was Joey's way and he just didn't seem to mind. He lived a life which many other people must have envied. Carefree or careless? You can make up your own mind.'

But it wasn't only Alan Gibson and his father who had first-hand experience of Joey's cavalier attitude towards money. Victor Freeman, Joey's first manager from 1976 until 1980, had closer contact than most. It was his job to make sure that everything in Joey's sporting life, including his financial concerns, ran smoothly. Freeman, who came from Coleraine and was for 10 years race secretary of the North West 200, was a close friend of John Rea. Freeman told me: 'One day in 1976, I had a phone call from Rea to say that he had started sponsoring Joey Dunlop. According to John, "He is going to be something special." The only problem was that Joey fell down in the administrative side. You could give Joey a bike and he would ride it anywhere but other than that he wasn't interested.'

Freeman found Joey easy to work with but he added: 'You needed to know when to approach Joey and when not to. You had to pick your moment. He was usually involved with his bikes. I never had any real problem with him and he was one of the straightest fellows I ever met. He kept nothing hidden from you. If he didn't want to talk he wouldn't and he was as honest as the day is long.'

Freeman confirmed one of the many stories which circulated concerning Dunlop's lack of concern over money. In the early 1980s Joey won a substantial cheque at the North West 200. According to Victor, Clerk of the Course Billy Nutt signed the cheque and gave it to Joey at the end of race day which was in early May. Sometime later Billy noticed that the money hadn't gone through the bank and at the Ulster Grand Prix in August Billy approached Joey and asked him if he was satisfied with what he been paid. Joey replied that he was. Billy then asked him was he sure that he had received the money. Joey replied: 'I think so, but come into my van and we'll see.'

Joey then searched around the van and eventually came up with a crumbled ball of paper which he unfurled to show Billy that the cheque had still not been cashed!

Freeman's lasting memory came from 1978, two years after he had begun to manage Joey. 'We decided to go to Silverstone for the British Grand Prix for the first time,' said Freeman. 'We set out along with Joey's father Willie and Victor Boyd who worked on the bikes. We drove there in a Bedford van and parked in a tent which was in the paddock. Willie and I were sitting in the tent after the first practice in which Joey had failed to qualify for the 250cc and 350cc races.

'Then, into the tent came Tom Herron, who said to Willie "What's wrong with Joey, why did he not qualify?" Herron added that Joey was the most natural rider he had ever seen while Tom himself had to push hard to keep himself in the top bracket. Joey replied: "You boys are too quick for me." Herron consoled him by saying: "You just don't know the course. Tuck in behind me and you'll qualify."

'This is just what happened. Joey went on to finish 14th in one of the races!'

CHAPTER 5

MASTER OF DUNDROD

Joey Dunlop's TT career didn't immediately flourish after his first Isle of Man win. But then no one expected that it would, for Dunlop, when all is said and done, was still a relative unknown and the field of riders he had beaten was not top class.

Tom Herron was still the number one Ulster name and in 1978 he had the game virtually to himself. He scored a double win at a never-to-be-forgotten North West 200 in which he set the fastest lap in the British Isles with a speed of 127.63mph – figures which have never been beaten on any course to date. In addition, the charismatic Herron also won the Senior TT on a Suzuki and ended the year in blazing triumph at home when he scored a treble in the Ulster Grand Prix. He was also beaten by a whisker in the 250cc British Grand Prix at Silverstone. Anton Mang edged out Tom by two one-hundredths of a second.

Three moves were made in 1978 which were to have a vital bearing on Dunlop's career. As far as racing was concerned he may have appeared to be stuck in gear, but behind the scenes the wheels were turning rapidly. In 1978 the Ulster Grand Prix promoters decided to go for the Formula One class and included it in their programme. It wasn't a world championship round but no one had any doubt that it would become one the following year.

The second major straw in the wind was the fact that Honda

decided to compete at the Ulster in the Formula One race and they sent over the previous year's TT winner, Phil Read, to ride the factory bike. Read had a vast knowledge of the Dundrod course and had already captivated a major army of fans in the two Lightweight classes back in the late 1960s. He later competed successfully in the world 500cc championship but it would be fair to say that he was nearing the end of his career when he came to Dundrod in 1978.

The third strand which indirectly assisted the burgeoning Dunlop career was provided by the ever present Hector Neill, who produced a motorcycle which boosted Joey to a new level. It was an RG 500cc Suzuki, similar to the one ridden by Read in the 1977 Senior TT.

So, by mid 1978, Herron was on top of the heap, the Ulster Grand Prix was fighting its way back into world championship status – even though it was a second division type of series – and there was what turned out to be a famous Suzuki waiting on the sidelines to give Dunlop the kick start he was looking for.

Herron's name was on everyone's lips as the Ulster came round and he and Tony Rutter were entered on 'Mocheck' Hondas. Herron and Rutter were reckoned by some observers, including myself, to be better than Read on the works Honda but fate decided that we would never be able to find the answer to that question.

On the first practice night, which was a Wednesday, Read failed to turn up. No one thought any the worse of him because riders can become delayed and after all the final and most important practice was to come the following evening. However, when Read didn't appear again the media began to swarm like bees round the Honda HQ, which was manned by the stoic Honda team manager Barry Symmons – another figure who was to have a major influence on Joey in later years.

Symmons was a typical company man. A swarthy, thick set figure, he said nothing and blocked every question. 'Where's Read?' I asked. Barry dragged deeply on a cigarette and replied guardedly: 'I expect him to be here. There is no panic.'

But of course this was not the case. When a world class rider like

Phil Read fails to turn up for the number one team at a meeting like the Ulster Grand Prix, there has to be a certain amount of disbelief in the air. Was he coming at all? Symmons remained impassive, and when I asked him what would happen if Read didn't show, he replied: 'There is no one of Read's quality available here to ride this machine.' We were of course hoping that Barry would hint that the bike would go to Herron. But from his manner it was obvious that Barry's thoughts were elsewhere.

On the Friday morning – the day before the race – Read flew into Belfast and I rang him. He was in good spirits and didn't really expect any problems if he turned up the next day without having had any practice. But then Read wasn't aware of the formidable character and disposition of the official who held the post of clerk of the course. Kevin Martin took no nonsense from anybody. If Kevin decided you weren't racing, you could safely book the next plane home. I phoned Kevin and asked him what the position was regarding Read and he replied: 'He will not be racing.'

Later that evening, along with my wife Iris, I attended the annual Ulster Grand Prix stewards' dinner in Lisburn, just beside the course. We arrived too late to be in at the start of the function and as a result had a drink in the bar outside the main room before deciding when would be an appropriate time to enter. As we were sipping from our glasses the door opened and in came Kevin. 'I'm just slipping out,' he told me. 'It's a bit hot in there. Do you mind if I join you?'

With that Kevin, myself and my wife had a drink and we chatted about everything except Phil Read. In the meantime the door to the main function room kept opening from time to time with different heads popping out to ask why Kevin wasn't coming back. Well, he seemed to be enjoying the conversation and he stayed with us all evening and to the best of my knowledge never rejoined the dinner! At the end of the night, I tentatively put the question of Phil Read and Kevin replied: 'Nothing has changed, you will see tomorrow morning.'

The following day Read arrived with his girlfriend in the paddock looking in good humour and cracking jokes. I chatted to him and welcomed him back to Dundrod where he hadn't been for many years. We then strolled up to the clerk of the course's caravan to meet Kevin Martin. I stood outside as Read went in and shortly afterwards Phil reappeared looking rather bemused. 'I'm not being allowed to start,' he said. But he didn't seem to be too annoyed and wandered off to the other end of the pits to watch the racing.

During the meeting he apologised to the many fans who had come especially to see him but there was no real explanation as to why he hadn't turned up for practice in the first place.

Racing went ahead and Symmons decided that Cheshire rider John Williams should take over Read's Honda. He needn't have bothered for Herron produced an effortless performance, which was one of the greatest ever seen round the famous track, to win the Formula One race by almost 22 seconds from his team-mate Rutter. He also set a record lap of 113.96mph.

With this in the bag he went on to complete a treble – he had already won the 250cc race from South African Jon Ekerold. Herron's final success came in the last race of the day, the 1000cc, in which on a Yamaha he beat Rutter into second place with another lap record of 118.84mph. Third place was taken by Roger Marshall who would in later years become another of Joey Dunlop's arch rivals both in Formula One and in other superbike races.

But if Herron was the man who captured the imagination of Ulster fans that vintage year of 1978 there was another rider who returned from what seemed to be a bygone age to achieve something which was unique then and is still the case now. He came back after an 11-year absence to win a world crown.

Mike Hailwood, despite his age of 38 and his balding appearance, was able to take on the best including Read and make the Formula One TT of that year a race which will forever stand out as a benchmark, whenever the Isle of Man is discussed; quite rightly, commemorative plaques paying tribute to Hailwood and Joey Dunlop sit side by side in a place of honour at the TT Grandstand.

In 1967 Hailwood had retired when Honda decided to drop out

of Grand Prix competition. Hailwood had been their team leader on the 500cc machine and in my view there was no one better round the Isle of Man and Dundrod. He seemed locked in retirement in his New Zealand home until his good friend Ted Macauley, a *Daily Mirror* sports writer, contacted him and persuaded him to make a comeback. Ted argued that if Phil Read could win the previous year's Formula One TT then Hailwood could certainly win the 1978 version. According to Ted, Hailwood took a lot of persuading and felt he would be making a fool of himself.

I travelled to that year's TT full of enthusiasm because Hailwood was a name from the Sixties which, in my view, was the golden era of motorcycle road racing.

In many ways I envied Macauley for the closeness he had with riders like Hailwood and Jim Redman, another star of those far off years. Macauley was a cool, suave character who sported a moustache and he had the look of a man who would not be out of place no matter what the company. In those early days, I felt awkward at not knowing the big name riders as well as Ted or anyone else of Ted's era. As a result, I found there was a hidden 'wall' between myself and riders of the status of Hailwood and Redman which I would have to break down if I were to get anywhere in the business. To be honest, I held them in awe.

On one thoroughly wet night during an Ulster Grand Prix practice at Dundrod I had an embarrassing experience. I was wearing a hat to shield myself from the downpour and had occasion to speak to Hailwood. I nervously knocked on the door of his mobile home and entered. As I stooped down, the rain ran down the brim of my hat and on to his face! You can imagine my feelings – and his!

However, in later years as we matured and mellowed, we became close friends and his return in 1978 filled me with renewed enthusiasm for road racing. According to Macauley's excellent book *Mike*, which deals with the 1978 and 1979 TT races, Hailwood followed Mick Grant round in practice. Afterwards he spoke to Macauley over dinner. 'How the bloody hell Granty's ever won here I'll never know,' he said. 'I have followed him over the

Mountain and he was all over the place. Frightened the life out of me. He must have been nearly off on every corner. He's fast all right but he's got some of the strangest lines you have ever seen.'

Grant, for his part, was delighted to be riding with someone like Hailwood. 'The idea of taking him on at the Island was marvellous,' he said at the time. 'I knew Hailwood had a hard job in front of him. He was up against not only myself – and I held the lap record at that time – but Read, John Williams, Charlie Williams, and of course Tom Herron.'

On one of the practice days, Macauley and Hailwood were driving round the course in a Rover car trying to sort out the sequence of the 33rd Milestone. Mike was convinced he was racing among lunatics for Herron was riding alongside them to and fro on a borrowed motorbike sizing up the approach, the entry and the exit. Eventually Mike stopped and wound down the window. Herron dashed over, pushed his face in and said: 'Give us a clue Mike. How do you get through this bit so fast?' But there was no trick according to Mike. 'I just shut my eyes,' he said. 'That way I don't get scared.'

Hailwood went on to win the TT and wasn't replaced as 'King of the Island' until Joey came along and eventually fulfilled his early promise when taking the place by storm in the 1980s.

The major springboard for Joey's success, as already mentioned, was the RG 500cc Suzuki provided by Hector Neill. This first came into play back in 1977 when Ulster rider Billy Guthrie owned it. Billy blew the engine in it at the TT and Phil Read hired the bike from Billy; got the loan of an engine from Suzuki and won the Senior. The bike was bought shortly afterwards by Neill for Ivor Greenwood and Ivor competed on a few short circuits before Hector entered him for the Killinchy 150 of 1978. Many observers thought it an odd decision for Tom Herron was also in the race.

'They argued for nights about who would win,' said Hector. 'No one could imagine Ivor taking on Herron and being successful – not in a million years.'

The race itself was a strange affair. Tom was in the lead and then mysteriously he dropped back and Ivor took the chequered flag. The motorcycle world still doesn't know to this day whether Tom shut off and gave Ivor the race or whether he was genuinely beaten. So the bike was bought for Ivor, but not long after that he slid off, injuring his hip, so he wasn't keen to do much more racing. The bike had now become available for someone else to ride.

Hector picks up the story: 'One day at Kirkistown Joey Dunlop was having a bad afternoon. He had two or three small bikes and they were all going badly. I said to the Mouse: "Go over and ask Joey if he would he take a ride on that 500 Suzuki." Joey came over to it, sat on it, grabbed it and said, "Love it." He then immediately went out and won on it. I think he won two or three times at Kirkistown.

'We also had it at Aghadowey, and he won there but some of the best races were in the Isle of Man July meeting round the Southern 100 course. Joey rode it twice for me there and won both times. Just about then he was on his way to getting better bikes from John Rea but he rode the Suzuki for me again in 1979 at the North West 200 and also at the TT.

'I will always remember the Senior of that year for Ivor set the bike up for him because Ivor felt that as the Suzuki was bought for him to ride he should be doing all the work on it. But he set the jetting up completely wrong and Joey went out and came in again after just over a lap saying the bike just wouldn't go. Joey wasn't too pleased and after that he insisted on doing all the mechanical work himself.'

The 1979 TT races were not the most memorable from Joey's point of view. In addition to the fiasco with the Suzuki Dunlop was holding 11th place on his Yamaha on the second lap of the 250cc Junior race when he pulled in to retire.

Then in the Formula Two race Joey, who was riding a Benelli, finished 13th behind Alan Jackson. Dunlop also rode a Benelli in the Formula One race but this lasted only two laps. After holding 12th place, he retired on the second lap when the valve seat came away from the cylinder head and bent an inlet valve. His best performance was sixth in the 1000cc classic behind Alex George and Hailwood.

This was a bit of an anti-climax after what had happened only a fortnight earlier when Joey had set alight the Ulster public's imagination by scoring two superb superbike victories at the North West 200. These were his first international successes but they were quickly overshadowed by events which were to devastate the meeting.

The 1979 North West 200, the 50th anniversary of the race, should have been the best in modern times. Over the years, the North West had attracted riders of the calibre of Geoff Duke, Bob McIntyre, Read and Hailwood, and in 1979 Hailwood was there again – but to spectate, not to ride. He was to go on and win the Senior TT that year on a Suzuki but as far as the North West was concerned he had no entry and apparently little interest.

Brian Coll, one of Hailwood's closest friends, decided that the North West could not be run without Hailwood's presence, so he invited him to the meeting just to show the spectators that he was there. 'The idea was to add glamour to the occasion,' Coll said. 'I gave him £1,000 in an envelope and Mike said to me: "What are you giving me that for, I don't need the money." I replied: "I would pay you double that amount, Mike, just to have you here. This has made my day."'

As far as the riders on the track were concerned all the big names who dominated racing on public roads were there. Herron, George, Rutter, Steve Parrish, Grant and Haslam. And of course the up and coming Joey Dunlop. Joey was down to ride John Rea's Yamaha in the two superbike races. He had achieved some successes on this but never at international level. This Yamaha was another machine which was destined to go down in history, along with the Neill Suzuki, as a bike which helped to launch Joey's long and glittering career.

There is an interesting story about how Joey picked up the Yamaha in the first place. Apparently, Joey and his pal Ernie Coates, a motorcycle dealer from Belfast, were on the Continent collecting some parts. Joey came across a bike sitting for sale. It had done only one or two races and the bike was as good as new. As soon as Joey saw it he fell in love with it.

He phoned Rea immediately. 'I have spotted this 750 Yamaha,' said Joey. 'It's the bee's knees and I have to have it'. John said: 'Right. I'll buy it.' And so the big Yamaha arrived with Rea and Dunlop. John was head of a transport company and I have it on good authority that when he was putting the transaction through the books the 750cc Yamaha somehow appeared as a Volvo truck!

The hot favourite for the North West in 1979 was naturally Herron. A fortnight before the race he had moved into third place in the world 500cc championship ahead of the number one head-line grabber of the time, Barry Sheene, and his prospects appeared to be outstanding. I wrote when previewing the race: 'Tom could be forgiven for regarding next week's trip back home for the North West 200 as something of a semi-holiday before the rigours and stresses of the TT.' I wasn't to know at the time – nor was anyone else – that these words would come back to haunt me.

As holder of the lap record, Herron appeared to be head and shoulders above the rest. But Parrish, Grant, Haslam, John Newbold and Rutter were all riders with the capability to push Tom all the way. And what about Joey? Well we just didn't know. He looked good and sounded good in practice but the race would tell the tale.

However, the performances of the riders on the road during practice took second place to the news that Herron had damaged his thumb in the previous weekend's Spanish Grand Prix and that didn't do anything for his chances. In fact it looked very much as though Tom wouldn't be riding.

Herron was an unhappy looking figure as he walked about the paddock with most of his right arm swathed in a combination of bandages and plaster. He looked more like a man who had just sneaked out of hospital rather than a rider capable of setting lap records. He told me: 'The hand is painful and riding with it is uncomfortable but I intend to be out there on the line.' Even though he was taking an unexpected back seat as far as practising was concerned, Herron still had the fans swarming round him. And many of them, as well as asking for autographs, decided to sign Tom's plaster!

Practice was dominated by Haslam who appeared to be bang in form and was riding with great style and nerve. He ended up top of the heap in the superbike class with a speed of 119.89mph. But significantly Dunlop had squeezed into second place at 116.36mph and was beginning to make an impression. Marshall, a rider who was to provide Dunlop with relentless competition in the years that followed, was in third place on 116.26mph, but the other big names just failed to get it together.

Grant, for example, couldn't make up his mind which Suzuki he was going to ride and Rutter's mind was on long distance weather forecasts. I felt sorry for Tony for he kept looking at the number of black clouds which threatened from time to time. His uncertainty over whether it would be a wet or dry race clearly unsettled him.

Dunlop, on the other hand, had everything to play for. No one, except perhaps his inner circle, expected Joey to produce the fireworks with which he later became associated. Signs were not good when he ran into tyre trouble – an old North West bugbear because of the high speeds – and came in after only two laps with large chunks of rubber missing from his rear wheel. Still, at the end of the night, he had marked a few cards as to what was going to happen on the Saturday.

The format for that year's North West meant that the first race was scheduled as a Match event between two teams of riders, one of them captained by Herron and the other by Rutter. It was a novel idea which had been tried the previous year and appeared to work.

Race day dawned and the excitement mounted. With such a high class field of riders we had to expect something special. We weren't disappointed – but for all the wrong reasons. On the very first lap there was a major accident at the stretch of road near the New University of Coleraine. Frank Kennedy, Australian Waring Willing and Englishman Kevin Stowe were all involved in a spectacular pile up which ended with burning bikes strewn across the road. In addition, such was the blaze that a nearby hedge was set on fire.

Kennedy and Willing had been side by side when they approached Shell Hill Bridge. Their bikes collided and blew up; within seconds they had burst into flames. Stowe ploughed into the inferno and all three riders were immediately taken to hospital. Fire crews which had been placed strategically along the course were also called in. It was a nightmare but the race went on, unlike modern days when it would have been stopped immediately. The bikes and the riders were quickly cleared off the course and the race continued.

One rider who narrowly missed being involved was Herron. As I was standing at the side of the road listening with half an ear to the PA system which was recording details of the crash, Herron came walking along the footpath into the paddock area. He looked badly shaken and said to me: 'There's been a bad accident. I went under Frank's bike which was flying through the air. It was like riding into a wall of flame.'

Meanwhile Joey, who was totally unaware of what had happened, was fighting it out with Grant urged on by a crowd of something approaching 80,000 who were becoming more and more excited as the race continued. Only those who had seen the accident were aware of the seriousness of the crash. Everyone else was naturally glued to the local boy, Dunlop, who was pushing for victory. Joey lived only a few miles from the course and this was one race he was determined to win.

Grant set the pace and was leading the race until a dramatic last lap when Dunlop passed him on the stretch between Portstewart and Coleraine, not far from where the earlier accident had occurred. With the crowd at a high pitch of excitement, Dunlop swept into Portrush like a conquering hero and his thousands of fans, congregated at that popular vantage point, couldn't contain themselves.

It was going to be Joey. There was no doubt about it and that's just what happened. On the final run in over the Atlantic coast road between Portrush and Portstewart Dunlop asserted himself and the result was a formality. Fans spilled onto the track to embrace him as he crossed the line and Joey looked on cloud nine as he blurted: 'I can't believe it. This is a race I have always wanted to win before my home crowd but always something has gone wrong. Today I thought I would be jinxed again for the clutch was slipping when I was moving into top gear. But I've beaten Mick Grant. Tell me I'm not dreaming.'

A rueful Grant also recorded that he'd had problems as his Suzuki had started to 'miss' from halfway. 'It got worse over the final two laps,' he said. 'But I still thought I'd win and I can tell you I had a major shock when Joey passed me. I didn't think he was that close.' Meanwhile Herron, who had pulled out of the race on his 500cc Suzuki, said: 'My bike was wobbling all over the place. I don't know what was wrong but I felt at one stage that I was going to go over the edge of the coast road. I don't think I will go out again.'

Sadly Tom changed his mind and with it the course of Ulster road racing history.

Dunlop, in addition to winning, set a tremendous lap of 124.66mph to beat Grant and Jeff Sayle with Rutter fourth, George fifth and Alan Jackson sixth. Joey was obviously on a high. Later in the day Joey finished fifth on the Neill Suzuki and filled the same place in the 350cc class on a Yamaha. But these races while important in themselves were only a sideshow to the big event of the day – the final superbike.

The race was clouded however by the news that Scottish rider Brian Hamilton had been killed at a place appropriately called the Black Hill in the opening event and also that Kennedy and Stowe were critically ill following the inferno at Shell Hill Bridge. Kennedy was to die some weeks later in hospital.

The fans weren't to know this at the time, although I was aware of the great unease which existed among race officials. When covering motorcycle road racing I have always been conscious of wearing two hats – one to describe the action on the track and the other to pick up news of serious accidents. It's all part of the job but it's never easy. That day, while attempting to chart the progress of Joey Dunlop, I had a gut feeling that his close friend Frank Kennedy would not make it and the news about Hamilton and Stowe produced an air of gloom among those closest to what was going on.

Tom Steele was clerk of the course and Billy Nutt – later to become race promoter – was race secretary. Both held their nerve but it couldn't have been easy. The North West 200 was an enormously risky undertaking to run in the Seventies before major changes were made to the course which have made it a lot safer to race on.

Safe roads would have been the last thing on Joey's mind as he wheeled his bike to the line for the final battle of the day. To my amazement he was joined on the line by Herron whom I thought would have retired for the afternoon. I spoke to Tom at the time and he said: 'I'm just going out to do a few laps. I will be riding at the TT and I need the practice.' That was the last time I ever spoke to him.

The race went off at a cracking pace with George in the lead before having to retire when his rear tyre began to give him problems with oil spilling out over it. This left Dunlop in the lead and he surged on to his place in history. Joey broke away from the field and with a fastest lap of 123.81mph – slower than his best lap of the day – he romped to victory beating Rutter and Sayle into second and third places.

Sadly, the jubilation which greeted him was soon punctured by the news that Herron had crashed at Juniper Hill – one of the fastest bends on the track, not far from the finish – on the very last lap. Hector Neill told me afterwards: 'Steve Parrish came dashing in to tell me "Herron's fallen big time. You'd better get up there". I ran up the road and met Brian Coll coming down. Brian was in tears: "I think Tom's seriously injured," he said. "It's a sad day for the North West and for road racing."'

Tom was still alive after the crash but died in hospital later when blood entered his lungs. If there had been a helicopter, which is present at the meeting these days, Tom would likely still be alive. But back then, critically injured riders had to rely on ambulance

A young Joey with his father Willie. Joey's father recognised, at an early age, his son's talent for fixing and riding motorcycles.

Joey strikes a stylish pose on board one of his early bikes, an Aermacchi, in the early 1970s.

MOTOR CYCLE ROAD RACING CLUB OF IRELAND
LTD.

SHORT CIRCUIT

RACES

MAGHABERRY AIRFIELD, MOIRA

SATURDAY, 26th APRIL, 1969

First Race 1.30 p.m.

M.C.U.I. (U.C.) 265

OFFICIAL PROGRAMME 1/-

WARNING
MOTOR CYCLE RACING IS DANGEROUS
Persons attending this meeting do so entirely at their own risk.

It is a condition of admission that all persons having any
connection with the promotion and-or organisation conduct of the
meeting including the owner of land and the drivers and owners of
vehicles and passengers in the vehicles, are absolved from all lia
-bility arising out of accidents, howsoever caused resulting in damage and-or personal injury to spectators.

EVENT 3 — HEAT 2
200cc SCRATCH   6 LAPS

No.	Rider	Machine	
20	N. MAGILL	196cc BULTACO	....
21	J. DUNLOP	199cc TRIUMPH	....
22	G. McADOO	199cc TRIUMPH	....
23	W. PRICE	199cc TRIUMPH	....
24	J. REDMOND	200cc DUCATI	....
25	B. DAVIS	199cc ARIEL ARROW	....
26	S. P. DEMPSTER	199cc TRIUMPH	....
27	W. S. McKEE	199cc TRIUMPH	....
28	W. H. BLOOMER	196cc BULTACO	....
29	A. S. ROWAN	196cc BULTACO	....
30	P. NICOLETTI	199cc TRIUMPH	....
31	W. T. GRAHAM	175cc DUCATI	....
32	W. L. SMYTH	199cc TRIUMPH	....
33	T. TROUTAN	19cc TRIUMPH	....
34	D. THOMPSON	196cc BULTACO	....
35	J. LEWIS	199cc TRIUMPH	....
36	J. OWENS	175cc DUCATI	....

1 ....2 3

4 ....5 6

7 ....8 9

Rider No. 21 is
Joey Dunlop!
Here he feature
in the program
for his first
ever race, at
Maghaberry
Airfield, on
26 April 1969.

Joey was not the only star to
come from the Dunlop clan.
His brothers Jim (left) and
Robert (right) were acclaimed
riders in their own right.

Joey (No. 106) lines up on
the grid on a Yamaha at
one of his first ever races
at Maghaberry. Note the
Ballmoney Transport
Company sponsorship.

Opposite above Riding a
Yamaha in the colours of
John Rea, his lifelong friend
and sponsor, at the St Angelo
Airfield, Enniskillen, 1976.

Opposite Left to right:
Stanley Morrow, aka The
Mouse, Graeme Crosby, and
Hector Neill at the Ulster
Grand Prix in 1980.

Mervyn Robinson, Joey's brother-in-law and dear friend, celebrates victory at the 1975 Ulster Grand Prix. Tragically, five years later, he was killed while competing at the North West 200. His death almost led Joey to retire.

Tom Herron, one of the all-time great motorcycle racers and a hero to Joey, lost his life at the 1979 North West 200.

Although he will always be
remembered as a Honda rider,
Joey was a Suzuki man before
he switched in 1981.

Joey savours a hard-earned pint after
another gruelling TT victory. It is
a TT tradition for the winning rider
to be bought a beer before facing
the world's press. Joey enjoyed 26 of
these during his glittering career.

Sibling rivalry. Joey, with trademark No. 3 and yellow helmet, leads his brother Robert at the North West 200.

The grid can be a tense time for any rider, but here Joey's 125cc sponsor Andy McMenemy lightens the atmosphere.

Sign on the dotted line. Joey puts pen to paper flanked by his longtime sponsor, John Rea (left) and Honda team manager, Barry Symmons (right). Some of Joey's antics had Symmons tearing his hair out at times but he knew what a great rider he had.

A focused Joey strides
to the grid at the 1986
Ulster Grand Prix
shadowed closely
by his manager
Davy Wood.

Roger Marshall,
perhaps Joey's
greatest rival over
the years, in action
at Suzuka.

Throughout his career Joey hated having a team of mechanics forced upon him,
preferring to work on the bikes in his own quiet way.

transport and, although the paramedics did the best they could, it wasn't enough to save him.

The crowds went home mostly unaware of the Herron tragedy. The news that he had died in hospital was announced later that evening to a shocked public. Suddenly Dunlop's double success seemed unimportant; Joey himself was even unaware that his closest friend had crashed. It wasn't until much later that the full story was to be told.

Tony Rutter told me years later: 'I only knew about it when I was listening to the car radio on the way home. I don't recall much about the accident but I remember being one of the riders whom Tom tried to catch on that last bend.'

Brian Reid, who was watching the race at Juniper Hill, told me: 'There were three riders in front of Tom when he tried to pass them. He hadn't a chance and his bike went into a slide. After that he hit a concrete post. I will never forget it.'

As for Neill, he is convinced to this day that Herron thought that the three riders in front of him – Rutter, Sayle and Parrish – were disputing the lead and that he had a chance of catching them before the finish. 'Joey Dunlop was so far in front, Tom wouldn't have known this,' said Hector. 'He was obviously trying to win the race. He must have felt he was so close.'

It was a desperately sad Hector who picked up Herron's Suzukis and took them to the Isle of Man for the TT races. 'Tom had sent his van on to the island by freight and I was taking the two bikes in my van,' he said. 'When Tom was killed I was left with the bikes and accessories. I gathered up the machines, put them in my van and when I arrived in the Isle of Man I was told that someone would be coming to collect them. About mid week, two Suzuki officials arrived at the private house where I was staying. They were racing manager Rex Whyte and another top man Martyn Ogbourne.'

Whyte was another personality who was to fit into the Dunlop story. But at that time he had barely heard of Joey and was surprised when over a drink Neill mentioned to him that Joey would very shortly win the Classic 1000cc TT which was at that time the biggest race of the week. 'Are you serious?' Whyte said to Hector. 'Of course I am,' replied Neill, 'And I'll have a bet with you to prove it.'

There is a discrepancy as to what happened next. Hector is convinced he was talking about the 1979 TT, but of course Dunlop did not win the Classic until the following year. Whyte also remembers the bet, but he too is not clear as to when it was made. What is not in dispute is that both men had a wager and Hector won. Joey did win the big race the following year and Rex paid for dinner for Hector and his friends in a top hotel. What is more important, however, as far as Dunlop's career is concerned, was that Whyte agreed to have a look at Joey with a view to him riding for Suzuki.

Rex Whyte was a quiet, unassuming man who was a regular visitor to the Ulster Grand Prix in the days of the Formula One World Championship. He was always courteous with time for everyone and when I asked him about his memories of the early Dunlop he replied: 'I first saw him when he won the Jubilee TT in 1977. He made it look so easy and afterwards he didn't say a lot. Hector did emphasise to me that Joey would win the Classic TT but I'm not sure when he said this. Hector did however introduce me to Joey and I must say I couldn't understand him very well. But then I also had difficulty understanding Hector!'

Whyte also contributed to the general picture of the off-course Joey when he told me: 'Joey generally kept to himself and as far as I was aware most of the time he slept in his van. I never really got to know him well but I feel I was privileged to watch him race in his prime. It was his natural ability on the big bikes which prompted me to sign him up for the Suzuki Formula One team in 1980.'

Well, 1980 was still to come but 1979 still had some way to go and Joey's proudest moments were just around the corner. The Ulster Grand Prix is a race which every rider in Ireland wants to win and Joey was no exception. Once again the famous Suzuki comes back into a story which is in itself a fascinating tale of a rider's simple faith in the people he grew up with.

Neill had persuaded Joey to ride the big RG again; Dunlop was also riding the 750 Yamaha for John Rea. The stage was set, but two days before the race things started to go wrong. Practice for the Ulster took place on Wednesday and Thursday evenings. And on the Thursday it was virtually a wash out. While this was bad enough, worse was to come for Neill and Dunlop. After a few laps news came over the tannoy that Joey had crashed at Ireland's Corner.

Hector and the Mouse jumped into the van and headed out over the back road to see if they could find Joey. While obviously concerned for Joey's safety, Hector was also aware that if the bike was wrecked, it would be the end of the meeting for him.

Hector explains: 'So we got up to where Joey had fallen off and we were walking up the road to Ireland's Corner when we saw the bike sitting there with not a scratch on it. I said to the Mouse, "He must have broken down." We headed further up the road and I met a first aid man coming in the opposite direction. I said "Is Joey up there?"

'"Yes," he said. "He is sitting up on the bank smoking a cigarette. He said his wee finger is off. He has his hand tucked into the leathers and he won't let anybody near it. I hope you have better luck."

'I said to the Mouse: "Take the bike up to the paddock and I will go and see Joey." So I went to where Joey was sitting and he was having a quiet smoke. I asked him what had happened. "I hit the back of John Newbold's bike," he explained. "My hand went up the exhaust pipe and I think I have taken my wee finger off."'

'"Let me have a look," I said; he took a lot of persuading before he agreed. I took his hand out of the leathers very gently. The glove was still on and the wee finger was still there so I said to Joey: "It's not off – your finger is still there."'

It had only been knocked out of joint but Joey was certainly not keen for Hector to tug it back in, so Hector coaxed him to the first aid room for some professional attention. Dislocated finger or not there was serious doubt, in Joey's mind at least, that he would be racing come Saturday.

Hector continues: 'On Saturday morning, Mouse arrived with

the bike. It was a nice sunny day and we wondered would Joey turn up. Mouse had the bike sitting ready but of course Joey was late. Eventually he arrived and I said to him: "Are you all right?" He replied "Och perfect. The wee finger is fixed." I said to him: "How did you get it fixed?" He replied: "I got it charmed."'

It turned out that Joey had been to see his old friend Matt Gibson in whom he had tremendous faith. Matt had taken a look at the finger, worked his magic and convinced Joey that he would now be able to race.

What happened afterwards is still recalled breathtakingly by all concerned. Joey was at the back of the grid in this 500cc race because he had not put in enough practice laps. All the odds appeared to be stacked against him and with a field of top class riders starting in front of him, Joey appeared to be well out of the picture at the end of the first lap when he was in 11th place; it looked as though Joey had no chance and that victory would go to either Dennis Ireland, John Woodley, Rutter or John Newbold.

Ireland was the leader on the first two laps but there was really nothing in it with Woodley and Rutter close behind. Rutter then took up the running when he scorched inside the two leaders at the end of the second lap. At this stage Joey had made up a reasonable amount of ground and was now seventh. Woodley went into the lead at the end of lap three with Rutter a close second, hotly pursued by Newbold and Ireland. But the big news was Dunlop appearing in fifth place with a lap of 113.25mph.

Could Joey make up all that ground with six laps to go? This was the question on everybody's lips and excitement mounted to fever pitch when Joey moved into fourth place, then third behind Newbold and Woodley. Finally, came the announcement everybody was waiting for – 'Dunlop is ahead at Cochranestown'.

After that Joey got the bit between his teeth and gradually increased the daylight between himself and the second-placed man Newbold to win comfortably by almost eight seconds at an average speed of 112.76mph. Joey's victory was all the more remarkable in view of the fact that he was riding a two-year-old machine against the up-to-date Suzuki models. A delighted Neill quipped: 'After this they will want me to work for Suzuki full time!'

Joey said: 'I thought I had no chance when I was sitting on the fifth row of the grid. It was only when I began to catch Ireland that I realised that I could win and once I had got in front I thought about nothing more except staying there. My hand gave me some trouble early on, but it was more discomfort than pain and I feel fine.'

The pace of Joey's effort was such that on lap six he came within 0.20mph of beating the lap record set the previous year by Herron. As if that victory weren't enough Joey went on to greater things that memorable day at Dundrod.

The 1000cc event was the main race of the afternoon with Dunlop, Haslam and Marshall, the big three. They left the rest of the field for dead in a superb three-way scrap before disaster struck for Haslam when his Yamaha began misfiring. But Haslam was not the only man with problems. On the warm-up lap, Marshall discovered an air lock in his fuel system. Hastily swapping tanks with the one from his spare 750 Yamaha, he hoped the problem would be cured.

Marshall stayed with Joey for the opening five laps and each time as he flashed along the 'flying kilometre' in front of the grandstand in Joey's slipstream he had to flick open his fuel tank cap to cure the air lock. Then he lost his tow after a momentary mistake and Joey appeared to have the result well within his grasp. As they raced through the start and finish area to begin their final lap there were only 400 yards in it. Inch by inch Marshall fought his way back and Dunlop knew he had a race on his hands.

Dundrod is an extremely fast circuit with smooth bends and in later years nobody knew them better than Dunlop. But in those days he and Marshall would have had an equal chance and as they scorched round the final right-hander and into sight of the chequered flag, they were locked together. Marshall had the inside line and the fans held their breath as Joey swooped just before the flag for a famous victory.

'My visor steamed up on the final lap and this caused me to

make several mistakes,' Joey explained later. 'I never thought I would win one race today, never mind two.' This Dundrod double was a watershed in Joey's career. After that everything was on and ever upwards. The World Formula One Championship, which was clinched that day by Ron Haslam, would three years later have a new king – Joey Dunlop – who would rule for five years.

CHAPTER 6

PULLING A STROKE

If anyone were to ask me to pick one race out of Joey Dunlop's many illustrious triumphs then I would unhesitatingly go for his memorable victory in the 1000cc Classic at the 1980 TT.

This was the stuff of dreams. A fairytale story. Joey took on the works boys headed by Mick Grant and left them all with egg on their faces. And to add lustre to the legend, Joey won with the aid of what could be regarded as a typical Irish 'stroke'. Not that there was anything illegal about it but Joey went into action with an oversized petrol tank; which meant that he only had to pit once instead of twice as was normal. This ploy paid major dividends and was still talked about 20 years after it happened.

Yet while that unique petrol tank almost certainly contributed to Joey's victory, it also nearly brought about his downfall. On the very first lap, the strap holding the tank to the bike snapped and Joey had to ride through the rest of the race with the tank wedged between his knees and his chest. It was an impossible situation but this never-say-die rider managed it and his efforts that day have gone down in motorcycling folklore.

Just imagine it. Joey rode literally throughout the race with a tank which threatened to fall off at any time and he still managed to win and beat the lap record. That was the measure of the man. He always did something which the others never expected. He let nothing get him down . . . his only goal was victory and that day in the Isle of Man he certainly came good with a vengeance.

However Joey might not have been in the Isle of Man at all that year; in fact he came close to quitting road racing altogether. It all happened after yet another disaster in the North West 200 a fortnight earlier when Joey's brother-in-law and closest friend Mervyn Robinson was killed in the 500cc race. Joey stood back and took a long and hard look at his future after that tragedy. Immediately after Robinson had been killed both Joey and his brother Jim, who had also been racing that day, pulled out of the rest of the meeting. But it seemed as though Joey might have more permanent plans for he gave the impression he would race no more.

I remember speaking to him a few days after the North West and he told me he thought he would just pack it in. 'I don't see any point in it,' he said. 'Mervyn and I were a team and now I am devastated.'

But Joey had road racing in his blood. I think it would be fair to say this. He was never really going to find another vocation. He was always going to race on the roads and he was always going to go to the Isle of Man. After what seemed an eternity during which his career teetered on the brink of extinction, Joey eventually made up his mind to continue . . . and the rest, as they say, is history.

On the fateful day at the North West, Robinson was reluctant to wear the number 31 which is, of course, a mirror image of 13. Aside from the obvious superstition he was afraid of history repeating itself. The previous year, Frank Kennedy had been killed wearing the same number. Mervyn mentioned this to his friends and said that he wasn't too happy about riding with what he regarded as a jinxed number plate but eventually he decided to go ahead. Mervyn Robinson was to suffer the same fate as Frank Kennedy. At a fast section of the course known as Mathers Cross, Robinson lost control and crashed. He died two days later in hospital from head and neck injuries.

At the inquest, which was held in August of that year, 32-year-old Robinson was described as 'Just unlucky.' A 'misadventure' verdict was returned by the coroner who later, while expressing sympathy with the relatives, praised the daredevil spirit of Robinson and others in the sport like him. The coroner said some people had suggested that the sport was getting too dangerous but he did not accept this and added that these young men were of the same calibre as those who had landed on the Normandy beaches or helped to win the Battle of Britain, sentiments which seemed old fashioned 20 years later. 'If they were not taking part in motorcycle racing they would be doing something else,' he said.

Eye witnesses told of seeing the machine, a Yamaha, 'sliding away' and the rider being thrown into the air when the bike hit a grass verge. One experienced motorcyclist, who had formerly competed in the race, witnessed the crash. He said he did not think speed had been a factor and that Robinson was 'just very unlucky.' A race scrutineer, who examined the machine afterwards, said there was some evidence of pressure seizure in the left-hand cylinder but this fault could have developed afterwards. It was not sufficient to have caused the accident.

So what did go wrong with Robinson? My view at the time – written a week after the accident – was that the North West promoters, in trying to compensate for the previous year's first lap pile up involving Kennedy, Willing and Stowe, had unwittingly contributed to the accident.

I wrote: 'Last year there was a pile up on the first lap of the opening race and this resulted in the eventual death of Frank Kennedy. The Promoters wanted to avoid a similar situation this time so they decided to start the riders in two groups with a minute between each group.

'Their reasoning was that there would be plenty of room on the road during that vital opening lap and hectic dash to York Corner in Portstewart, followed by the roundabout in Coleraine. The opening race, the 350cc, was accident free, and the second race, the ill-fated 500cc, looked like heading the same way but there was one important weakness in the new starting system which Robinson's crash, to my mind, exposed.

'The organisers had intended that all the fastest riders would be in the opening group and thus be clear of trouble. This group was made up of the quickest riders in practice which seemed a fair enough basis on which to operate. The only trouble was that a normally quick rider would appear in the slower group if his practice times were bad. And this is what happened in the case of Robinson.

'Mervyn, starting in group two, might have made up his mind that he was not going to waste much time getting among the quicker men up front. He really had no need to do this as he had started a minute behind the first batch of riders and therefore should have been working on corrected time as it were for his placing, much like the TT.

'However, a top rider likes to race with the fast men and for much of the trip, Robinson was way ahead of the group B men with little hope of catching – on the road – those in group A. It may have been his determination to get among the action up front which caused his death and perhaps he took one chance too many.'

I still have that opinion over 20 years after Robinson's death.

Joey's first reaction to the death of his friend was, as you might expect, to withdraw from the Spanish Grand Prix which was taking place the following weekend. Joey was being backed by Cullybackey businessman Davy Hoy on a Yamaha in the 500cc World Championship, and it took a lot of courage to pull out. However, he and Robinson were such close friends that Joey's decision was understood by everyone.

Eventually Dunlop decided it was time to make a career decision and he returned to action in the Cookstown 100, coming third in the 500cc race. This gave him back his confidence, something which he felt he might have lost if he had stood back from the road racing scene any longer.

Next it was off to the Isle of Man in a fishing boat. An unusual form of transport. But Joey was always his own man and he had his special reasons for travelling in this manner. Explaining his boat trip, Joey said that he had wanted to race at Cookstown the weekend before TT practice started and the problem was there were no suitable ferries which would allow him to do that and still get him enough practice; so he decided to obtain the use of a fishing boat owned by his friend, Newtownards businessman Archie Lappin.

This fishing boat, called the Tornamorna, was later to dominate the headlines when it sank while taking Joey and his brother Robert to the 1985 TT. Those on board narrowly escaped drowning.

However that disaster was still to come when the 28-year-old Dunlop set sail from Strangford Lough on a late May evening in 1980. Joey was set to ride the 750cc Yamaha owned by John Rea, on which he had finished sixth the previous year, and he had reasonable hopes of success. However with Honda riders of the calibre of Mick Grant and Ron Haslam up against him, it was obvious it was going to be a tough task.

The inimitable Hector Neill then came up with a possible winning solution. Hector was helping Joey to prepare for the Isle of Man and midway during practice week he said to him that during the previous year's Manx Grand Prix, Hector had run a Suzuki with Ronnie Wilson on board which was able to do three laps without stopping. Hector mentioned this to Joey and said that with Honda using their quick fillers, Joey should try to get himself an edge.

'Why don't you try a big tank on it, and say, do one pit stop?' Hector said to Joey.

'Och, I dinny know,' said Joey. 'Would it work?'

Hector was certain that it would and told Joey that if he could get the fuel measured he would definitely get three laps out of the tank. So the next item on the agenda was to get a tank which Hector could alter. Joey borrowed one from fellow Ulster rider Sam McClements and Hector took it down to a body shop in Douglas and asked the man in charge if he could cut the tank and make it an inch larger. The man had done work for Hector before so he knew what was required. Hector, of course, didn't tell him who the tank was for as he didn't want to give the game away.

So the tank was widened and tested and it wasn't leaking. It held the right amount of fuel and on race day, Friday, Joey Dunlop pushed his bike to the starting line and prepared to face the might of Honda and Suzuki. But there was a problem.

'We should have put extra straps on the tank,' explained Hector. 'But we just left it at one and it was stretched to the limit.'

'The race started and by lap two Joey was in the lead. At this stage the Honda crew were standing by waiting for Joey to come flying in. But what did he do? He just scorched straight down the road. I can still see the look on Honda manager Barry Symmons's face. He knew when he looked down at Joey's team what they were planning. The Hondas came in as planned but even with their quick filler there was no catching Joey. Even when the tank strap broke and he had to hold the tank on with his knees, Joey kept going and when he came in that one time to do a pit stop, he didn't say anything in case the scrutineer might come round to the bike and notice what was going on!'

The man who held the lap record, Honda rider Mick Grant, said to me years later: 'We were humiliated. We thought we had the best bikes on the Isle of Man. Ron Haslam and myself were the two works riders and then this scruffy little Irishman comes in and wallops us. We had noticed he had been working really hard all week in practice trying to get the bike set up. But we had no idea what was happening until race day when he came in for that one fuel stop. He really put one over on us – but good luck to him. That was the start of the Joey Dunlop legend.'

The story of the race itself was really a battle between Grant and Dunlop. With the previous year's winner, Alex George, in hospital in Douglas recovering from severe chest injuries received in a crash during practice, it was thought that the main rivals for first prize of £10,000 would be Grant on his factory Honda and the Senior TT winner Graeme Crosby on a Suzuki.

But right from the start there were shocks. First Grant lost ten seconds when he stalled the Honda at the clutch start and then Crosby made a spectacular getaway, wheelieing and losing ground down the Glencrutchery Road.

At Ballaugh, halfway round the first lap, Dunlop led by four seconds from Australian Graeme McGregor on a Honda with Jeff Sayle, who had switched from a similar Honda to a Yamaha, third ahead of Grant and Chas Mortimore (Suzuki), and Crosby down in sixth place. By the time it came to the Bungalow at the side of the Mountain, Dunlop had increased his lead to seven seconds from Sayle who had got ahead of McGregor. Down the drop to the start, Sayle had closed the gap fractionally to begin the second lap just 6.4 seconds behind the flying Dunlop.

McGregor had lost ground and was being challenged by Grant with Manx Grand Prix winner George Linder an impressive fifth on a Yamaha ahead of Mortimore. Crosby was in seventh place as they pulled into the pits at the end of the first lap. He reported the big Suzuki would rev only to 9000. After changing plugs he got away but having lost over five minutes at his pit, the Australian obviously had no chance, and, still plagued by the same trouble, he eventually retired at the end of the second lap.

He was not the only one in bother. As is so often the case in the Isle of Man, the first lap took a terrible toll. Prospective place man, Billy Guthrie, got only to Quarter Bridge before pulling out, while Stan Woods was next to go with a front wheel puncture. Then Charlie Williams, out on his 350cc Yamaha after his double win of the previous day, stopped at Ballaugh Bridge with his engine over-heating so badly that he dared not go on. He was soon joined by another TT winner, Alan Jackson.

While all this news was coming through Joey was pressing on, relentlessly increasing his lead over Sayle while Grant jumped to third place when McGregor's Honda stopped at Bishopscourt on the second lap.

Although Grant was catching Sayle, Dunlop was pulling away from the works Honda, increasing his lead over Grant from 18.4 seconds at the end of the opening lap to 26 seconds after two laps. And then to everyone's amazement, Dunlop did not pull in to refuel at the end of the second lap, but sailed straight through to start the third. It was on this manoeuvre that the race eventually turned. With Sayle stopping to refuel, Grant took over second place.

Meanwhile Joey was setting a tremendous pace. The second lap was just five seconds outside the record and by Ballaugh on the third lap he had increased his lead over Grant to 31 seconds, with Sayle, who refuelled in just 13 seconds, hanging on in third place. The leaders were now well clear of the pursuing pack. Sayle's luck ran out on the Mountain however. His steering damper had broken and he was forced to retire.

With the Australian out of the race it was a straight fight between Dunlop, the privateer on the Yamaha, and Grant on the factory Honda. Leading on the road, Dunlop made his lone pit stop at the end of the third lap, the halfway stage. Using a regulation issue filler it took his pit crew an agonising 53 seconds to replenish the massive tank and as he accelerated away, Grant roared into the lead.

The Honda pit crew used their sophisticated fillers to good effect getting their man back into the race in just 12 seconds. Grant had gained no less than 41 seconds on that single stop, turning a 22.2 second deficit at the lap into a 10 second lead by the next time check at Ballacraine, six miles into the fourth lap.

Grant held his advantage to the end of the fourth lap, but Dunlop had clipped a couple of seconds off the Honda's lead by the time they completed the lap – just 7.6 seconds separated the leaders as they roared away down Bray Hill for the fifth time. Could Dunlop catch Grant – or would Grant with Honda's massive backing triumph again? Ears were strained for news from all around the course. At Ballacraine, Grant's lead was down to 5 seconds; by Ballaugh it was just 2.4 seconds and at Ramsey Dunlop had his nose ahead by half a second!

Up the long Mountain climb, where the circuit rises from near sea level to over 1,000 feet, the big Honda clawed back a second so that Grant led by half a second at the Bungalow. As they flashed through to start the last lap, Grant led by a fifth of a second – and Dunlop had broken the lap record! His fifth lap was completed in 19 minutes 47.2 seconds (114.41mph). The Ballymoney rider was really flying and it was only a matter of him keeping going to win the race.

By Ballaugh, Joey had edged four seconds ahead and by Ramsey his lead was seven seconds. If the Yamaha kept going, Dunlop would be home and dry. And that's just what happened – to such good effect that on the final lap Dunlop broke his own record with a lap of 19 minutes 38.8 seconds (115.22mph). Realising that the race was lost, Grant eased his pace fractionally to finish second well ahead of fellow Honda rider Haslam.

Surrounded by autograph hunters, Dunlop described the race as one of the hardest of his career so far. 'I had trouble throughout practice,' he said. 'The wheelspacers had been in back to front and the bike wouldn't handle. I worked until 2am this morning trying to get things sorted out. My father and my mechanic worked all night.

'To enable me to have that one refuelling stop, I had to fit a special eight-gallon tank. I had to take it very easy on the opening stages of the first lap because of the extra weight and because I was scrubbing in a new tyre. I thought I was going to have to retire on the first lap going towards Ramsey. The tank strap broke and I had to be extra careful on the bumps. I was scared it would come out of the frame and pull off the petrol pipes.

'Because of this trouble I had one big moment – at Ballaugh Bridge. I took a long time at my petrol stop because last year in the 250cc race I ran out of petrol when I was too fast – once bitten twice shy. As the petrol tank was getting lighter, and I was in good form I felt the lap record would go. I expected Mick Grant to be much closer. I thought he must have retired but I realised he hadn't when I heard he was arriving for his fuel stop just as I was leaving.

'On the last lap, my only trouble was when the rip-off on my helmet visor would not come off. With so many flies stuck on it, it was difficult to see clearly.

'After Mervyn Robinson's death at the North West 200 I had cancelled all my entries apart from the TT. But now I'm back and I intend to continue the season.'

Exhausted at this point, Grant said that he had ridden as hard as he could. 'The trouble was the gearing was all wrong. It was far too high,' he said. 'I could use only top gear a couple of times a lap –

this in turn messed up my cornering. Half the time I just didn't have the right gear for the corner. Someone got their sums badly wrong. It was certainly the hardest TT I've ever ridden in.'

The deciding moment in the race, according to Grant, came at Quarry Bends on the last lap. Grant said: 'I was trying just a shade too hard and drifted three feet off line. It was a nasty moment and I realised then that I had better cool it just a little.'

Watching the Classic TT with more than a passing interest was the Suzuki manager, the 'grey fox' Rex Whyte. After seeing Dunlop's record-shattering win he knew for sure that he had at last found his 'third man', the rider who would ensure that Suzuki would win the Formula One World Championship. But more of that later.

At the beginning of TT week the Formula One race had developed into such a bad-tempered affair that it overshadowed the entire meeting. The crux of the matter was this: Honda objected to Suzuki's alleged manipulation of the rules which moved Crosby, who was Grant's main rival in the battle for the Formula One Championship, from No. 3 to No. 11 to share the same start time as Grant. Twenty minutes before the start, with ACU approval granted for the switch, Honda put in their blocker. Three minutes before the off Crosby was told he would have to revert to his early number, but he refused.

It was an unsettling move which had race favourite Grant off on his allotted number, on his works Honda at the same time as Crosby. It was a case of Honda versus Suzuki. The lap record holder versus a relative TT newcomer.

But the accusations didn't end at the start. The finish was even more bad-tempered. Following rumours over the previous year's petrol tank capacity which was officially limited to 24 litres, much talk centred on the works Hondas' capacity and their ability to go through the six laps with only one stop, while other slower men needed two fuel stops.

When Grant came in to finish first and beat Crosby and Sam McClements, it was noticed that there was a dent in his tank and this did nothing to quash the rumours. A Sunday morning jury meeting was called to adjudicate on protests by Gordon Pantall, who was the entrant of fourth place finisher Alan Jackson. Pantall claimed that Grant's tank was illegal. The jury decided to defer ratification of the results until they met at a later date, probably Tuesday, by which time they would have been able to hear Honda's side of the story.

As for the actual race itself, Grant's Honda coughed its way from the start to Ballacraine on lap one. Fuel starvation was suspected as he was led by McGregor and stayed only marginally ahead of Crosby with Haslam and Jackson close behind.

Grant didn't actually get ahead until towards the end of the second lap. At the Bungalow on lap one McGregor had a 14 second lead over Grant and Crosby. As Grant got into his stride, and he and Crosby diced it out on the roads, McGregor's lead was gradually whittled away. At Ballacraine on lap three, Grant, Crosby and McGregor were together separated by a fraction of a second which meant that on corrected time Grant and Crosby were 10 seconds ahead of McGregor. But after another few miles, McGregor was out. His clutch cable had broken.

McGregor's retirement left the big two with a comfortable lead over Jackson with McClements coming through from behind. Haslam was also out, a victim of mechanical trouble. Suddenly Grant turned on the pressure. His TT experience told and he was able to pull out a 10 second advantage over Crosby on the Ballacraine–Ballaugh section.

The battle appeared to be over.

By the end of lap five Grant led Crosby by half a minute and then on the last lap, Grant eased and Crosby had to speed up when he realised that McClements had pulled up to within four seconds of him. So Grant won by 10.8 seconds with Crosby only two seconds ahead of McClements at the finish.

For former Manx Grand Prix winner McClements, it was the ride of his life on his private Honda. In his bid to catch Crosby, he had set the day's fastest lap on his final circuit. A 33-year-old self-employed motorcycle mechanic from Bangor, Co Down,

McClements had a day to remember. Sweat was pouring down his forehead into his eyes as he spoke afterwards. 'It was like having a bag of salt thrown into my eyes. I wouldn't have liked to have gone any quicker on that last lap.' Sam's £1,800 third place prize money was his biggest in 10 years of racing. His previous biggest prize was £340 in the North West 200. Tragically once again, Ulster was to lose a great rider for in 1989 McClements was killed at the Carrowdore 100.

But, from the race focus shifted to race politics and the not inconsiderable action off the track. With Pantall protesting about the size of Grant's tank it took 42 hours to settle the race. Two jury meetings took place before Grant was eventually cleared of riding with an outsized tank. In a Douglas hotel on Monday, at the time the 500cc race should have been running but for rain and mist, the international jury threw out the protest and declared Grant winner of the £4,500 first prize.

After a weekend of bitterness, Grant and runner up Crosby shook hands before Belfast's Billy McMaster who announced the verdict. McMaster, who was the doyen of motorcycling officials, said: 'Both sides expressed interest in preserving the sporting nature of the TT. It could mean that the rules would have to be tightened up for future Formula and endurance racing.'

Both Pantall and Honda racing co-ordinator Barry Symmons agreed with the jury's sentiments over improved liaison between the scrutineers' tent and the racing officials. They also agreed that for Formula One and endurance racing the fuel tank capacity of the first three finishers should be checked.

After the hearing, Grant admitted he had ridden with a 28-litre tank although the regulations stipulated a 24-litre maximum. Grant said: 'The tank was big but there were only 24 litres of space because it was full of bottles and ping-pong balls. I banged the tank on the first lap to try to cure fuel starvation. Then, at the finish, I banged it again to make sure it wasn't oversized had one of the bottles accidentally burst.' It was that punch to the tank at the finish and the dents which set the protests alight. Crosby was talked out of an initial protest but Pantall then stepped in to make it official.

By the time that was done, the race winning Honda had been released from the scrutineers' tent and had been ridden back to the Honda garage by the mechanic, Nigel Everett, so any evidence had officially gone. Honda did have a dented tank measured on Monday. It had a capacity of 23.7 litres.

When Crosby heard the jury's outcome he walked up to Grant, patted him on the head and smiled. He was far from happy, but at least they were speaking again! But what of the race result and its implications for the championship? The fact that Crosby had finished 10 seconds behind Grant, meant that with one more round of the World Championship to come it was a mere formality – or so it seemed – that Honda would win the title.

That final round was the Ulster Grand Prix over the Dundrod circuit and Grant only had to remain a close second to Crosby to win the title as Crosby was highly unlikely to beat Grant by more than 10 seconds at Dundrod. However, this figured without the 'Joey factor' and the promise he had shown in winning the Classic. Rex Whyte realised that if he could sign Dunlop to ride for Suzuki then this could potentially push Grant into third place and, with Crosby winning the race, the title would go to Suzuki for the first time. It seemed like a good plan and Whyte set out to put it into action.

He made his move after having talks with Hector Neill and he set up a deal with Dunlop for the Ulster. There was also another factor in the story. Ron Haslam was riding for Honda and so was Sam McClements, whom Honda had signed up for a works bike at the Ulster. McClements could, in fact, be the fly in the ointment but they weren't to know that at the time of the 1980 TT.

So Whyte went to Neill, who approached Dunlop, and eventually Joey agreed to ride for Suzuki at the Ulster, with a view, I'm sure, to riding with the works team long term, although as it turned out this didn't materialise. Whyte initially signed Joey up to ride for Suzuki in the Formula One race at the British Grand Prix in Silverstone and to Whyte's amazement, Dunlop finished second to

Crosby. 'I didn't know he was such a good rider on short circuits,' he told me years later. 'He could have had a future there, had he not decided to stay on the roads. At the time I signed him for Suzuki and that vital Ulster Grand Prix, there were simply no other racers around who had experience like Joey had on roads. Many of the top men just didn't want to know about the Isle of Man, the Ulster or the North West 200. They were only interested in the Grand Prix racing on tracks. Joey was the ideal man and I wasn't going to let him slip through my fingers.

'When I spoke to him and told him of what I had in mind he wasn't at first very interested at being made to finish second because he felt he could win. After a great deal of debate he then agreed to do as we asked, provided that we allowed him to do his own thing in the other races. I said that was perfectly alright with me, and that's the way it was.

'So Joey joined our team at the Ulster Grand Prix with a view to giving Crosby the championship. That was the plan. You might say the race was fixed from that point of view, but that was the way of it in those days. Race orders were paramount to everything else.'

Of course, it could have gone wrong. Someone could have fallen off – in fact Haslam did fall off when trying to slow down on the last lap – but as it turned out everything went as Whyte had planned. It was a great day for Suzuki.

This was team tactics at their most blatant and many of the fans went home disappointed when they saw Joey Dunlop, who was obviously the fastest rider on the course, slowing down and virtu-ally escorting Crosby over the line at the finish. It was farcical. That's the way the game had to be played but I know that Joey in his heart of hearts wasn't enthusiastic about it at all. He was always a winner and he didn't like playing second fiddle to any-body. It was probably the only occasion in his life when he wasn't his own man.

As expected, Joey went straight into the lead at Dundrod fol-lowed by reigning champion Haslam who was instructed to forget about the fact that he was about to be dethroned and to set his mind firmly on the task in hand – that he was there to help keep the F1 world title with Honda in the name of Mick Grant. Part of the Honda strategy was lost on the first lap when McClements fell by the wayside with clutch failure and Roger Marshall took a slip road at high speed when the rear brake rod broke.

On the next lap, with Dunlop disappearing into the distance, Crosby settled to the task and moved ahead of Haslam to take second place. But at this stage, things seemed to be going the way of Grant, holding fourth place, and knowing that Haslam would allow him through when the time was right.

On and on, faster and faster raced Joey. Had he decided to suffer the wrath of Suzuki for the glory of a record-breaking victory?

Whyte, as calm as ever, controlled the Suzuki pit crew who seemed far more at ease than the Honda team as this cat and mouse situation developed. No pit signals went out to slow Dunlop who was now getting the encouragement of his local fans to keep going and show the visitors what real road racing was all about. Then on the sixth lap, things took an even worse turn for Suzuki as Haslam retook second place from Crosby with Grant still in fourth.

On the penultimate lap, Dunlop decided to do as he was told and Suzuki could breathe a sigh of relief. After building up a lead of 20 seconds, Joey eased the pace, but it was not Crosby who went to the front as planned, but Haslam. Crosby was allowed up to second to fight it out with Haslam as Dunlop assumed the task of keeping Grant out of third place. The pendulum had swung in favour of Suzuki, however, because second place would have given Crosby a total of 24 points, one more than Grant had he been held in fourth place. Haslam had to act and Grant had to force his way past Dunlop.

On into the nail-biting last lap roared the four leaders. And it was on this lap that it all happened. Haslam was planning to slow or even stop at the Hairpin to allow Grant to get ahead of him, but this plan was given an unrehearsed twist when Haslam slipped gracefully off his machine as he braked for the right-hander. The Nottinghamshire rider quickly grabbed the undamaged Honda and, after making sure Grant had gone by, rejoined the race to take fourth place.

But Grant had failed in his bid to displace Dunlop and the game of tactics ended in Suzuki's favour. Crosby was the delighted winner and the second placed Dunlop was content to have been of service to the first factory to acknowledge his world class potential.

Whyte and Symmons shook hands and tried to persuade the world that tactics had not really played a big part in the final out-come of the championship, while Joey naturally confirmed that there was nothing wrong with his machine. 'I was just told to keep an eye on how the situation was behind me and to make the necessary moves at the right time,' he explained. 'I am disappointed at not winning but there will be another time.'

Crosby, meanwhile, gave the impression that he had won everything on his own merit. 'Just as we had planned,' he boasted. 'I was told to keep an eye on how Joey and Mick were going and Joey was asked to do the same, and the plan worked without a hitch.' Then he added, tongue in cheek: 'Maybe Joey ran into trouble when he had that 20 second lead!'

But Joey had the last laugh of the afternoon, for he went on to win the main 1000cc race. This was virtually a repeat of the previous year with Roger Marshall once again providing the major challenge. For Dunlop it was some compensation for the earlier frustration of the Formula One race. Marshall and John Newbold, on their 750cc Yamahas, made up the best of the opposition while Dunlop again opted for the four-stroke works Suzuki, and quite incredibly shattered the outright lap record!

Newbold led from the flag and he, Marshall and Haslam pulled away from the field as Dunlop began compensating for a lowly grid position. Plagued by bad luck, Haslam went out with a seizure at Leathemstown but by now Dunlop had leader Roger Marshall and Newbold in his sights. It was only a matter of time before he got past. Dunlop had clocked 117.55mph and was well on his way to setting an incredible new lap record of 118.95mph.

On lap five, Dunlop stepped up the pace by four seconds and

stretched Marshall and Newbold to their limits. The race for first place was over but there was plenty of excitement left in the dice for second spot. Newbold passed Marshall on lap six but then decided he would settle for third ahead of Chris Guy, Tony Rutter and local ace George Farlow. For Dunlop it was a double on the day, for he had earlier won the 250cc race. But everyone knew that it should have been a treble.

Treble or not, Joey's victories had put him in line for a works contract and Suzuki were without doubt favourites to sign him for the 1981 season. He travelled to Croydon to talk over terms with Suzuki for whom he had been riding in a private capacity since the British Grand Prix. Whyte made it clear to me at the time that Joey appeared keen to join their camp and they were equally enthusiastic about having him. Joey's adviser, John Boyd, a Suzuki dealer for Northern Ireland, was also in on the talks and it was left to him to make the final financial arrangements between the factory and the rider.

However, on the sidelines, Honda were also making enquiries and it was no sure thing that Joey would sign for Suzuki. The Whyte team were obviously favourites since Joey had ridden for them but there was a feeling among those on the inside that Honda might pounce at the last minute.

'We would want Joey at the TT and Ulster as they formed the two legs of the world championship,' Whyte told me. 'And although Crosby won the championship for us this year, you can take it from me that Joey is the man we will be promoting next time. He is a natural on these roads and there is no point in beating about the bush. Joey is our man and will receive the full backing of the Suzuki organisation.'

That seemed fair enough. In addition, Joey would be offered a 500cc RG Suzuki which would be ready in time for Brands Hatch at the end of October. Whyte added: 'We have been constantly amazed by the ability of Joey Dunlop on short circuits. He deserves the chance to prove himself at international meetings.'

Whyte was also enthusiastic about the chances of Dunlop riding in the World Grand Prix series, although unlike Tom Herron he wasn't asked to ride for the full term. 'Crosby and Randy Mamola are our two world title riders in the 500cc class,' Whyte said. 'But Dunlop will be drafted in during any emergency. In addition, Joey will also ride our Suzuki in the British Grand Prix as well as the 500cc Shellsport series.'

So the stage was set it seemed for Joey to sign for Suzuki. You couldn't have wished for a better deal. It certainly looked good from the point of view of flexibility. Everybody knew that Joey liked to be his own man and he liked a free hand as much as possible, and according to Whyte, that was what he was going to get.

But at Croydon, negotiations broke down and no one to this day knows why. Whyte told me Joey arrived at the Croydon works in an articulated truck. 'He was collecting or delivering something, I don't know what,' said Rex. 'He spoke to Maurice Knight the sales director of Heron Suzuki and then he went away. We heard nothing more until he had signed for Honda. Perhaps Maurice's offer wasn't enough or perhaps Joey was to come back to renegotiate. I really don't know what happened. Joey was a strange person to deal with. We were very disappointed that we didn't sign him.'

So what prompted Joey to so dramatically change his mind? One possible explanation has emerged via Patsy O'Kane, who sponsored Dunlop's brother Robert for a long time. Patsy told me that when Joey signed for Honda Patsy sold him a Mercedes 'to go with his image.' Patsy added: 'After I had sold him the car one night Joey drove me home and I asked him why he didn't sign for Suzuki and had preferred Honda. He told me that he had earlier asked Suzuki for a jacket for his son, Gary, and that the company had sent him the jacket *and* a bill. Joey wasn't impressed. That could have been one of the reasons why the scales tipped Honda's way.'

CHAPTER 7

FROM SUZUKI TO HONDA

Joey Dunlop reached agreement to sign for Honda in the kitchen of John Rea's home in Ballyclare, Co Antrim. It was to be a famously successful and emotional partnership which breathed fresh life into the TT and pure road racing in the 1980s just when both were badly in need of resuscitation.

It seemed at the time as though the floodgates of success would open. The Dunlop deluge was about to begin – the dash to the podium which his fans hoped he would pepper at every available opportunity. Joey may have signed quickly on the dotted line but he knew what he was doing, he was well advised and he knew he was in for a big financial deal. This was in November 1980 and at the time Suzuki felt that the big fish had slipped from their grasp.

Hector Neill told me: 'Suzuki were mad keen to get hold of Joey but the offer they made just wasn't enough. Joey after all was a working man and he was looking for the cash. I really couldn't have blamed him.'

So at the end of 1980 celebrations were held in the Dunlop camp. The breakthrough had been achieved, Joey was to join Honda's Formula One team and the rest would be plain sailing. Or so it seemed. On 27 October I broke the story in the *Belfast Telegraph* exclusively that Joey Dunlop would sign for Honda in two weeks' time. Honda made an offer of a £20,000 retainer for Joey's services and in the words of his financial adviser John Boyd, 'He just couldn't refuse it.'

Thus the saga was about to come to an end and the deal he agreed with Honda had a gilt edge about it. In addition to the retainer, which was a massive one in those days, he would receive a five-figure bonus at the end of the year depending on how he made out in the 1981 World Formula One Championship, for which at that time he was named as Honda's number one rider.

The Honda agreement meant that Dunlop would ride in all three World Formula One Championship rounds – the TT, the Ulster Grand Prix and the Belgian Grand Prix. In addition he would ride the Formula One Honda in the 1981 British Championship. Honda were obviously hoping to regain the glory which had been given to them by Phil Read and Mike Hailwood. Ron Haslam had also won the F1 title for Honda in 1979 but his name didn't seem to have the charisma of Read and Hailwood, so Honda must have reckoned that Dunlop had star quality and that was why they were so keen to sign him. In addition to Dunlop, Haslam and Roger Marshall were also signed for 1981 so the scene was set for what should have been a memorable year as far as Joey was concerned.

However things didn't go quite the way they planned. I was always of the opinion that Honda had signed Joey as a blocker, just to make sure that Suzuki didn't get hold of him, but that they didn't really know how good a rider they had on their hands. In other words they weren't sure what to do with him. It was a bit like a football team buying a big name player and then not knowing whether to put him in goal or in attack. But one thing was for sure, Joey liked to be his own man. That was being emphasised over and over again.

Although he was willing, obviously because of the money and the chance he was getting, to take his place on the Honda team, at the same time you could see that Joey still wanted to look after his own machines, to make sure that everything was as it should be; in other words to be mechanic as well as rider. This was the way Joey looked at it and in view of his results up until then you couldn't have blamed him. Perhaps Suzuki would have been less rigid in the initial stages. Who knows?

However, in the years of fame which followed no one could point a finger at Honda for the way they treated Joey. He became a VIP and years later he said to me: 'I owe everything I have in this business to Honda. They promoted me, they gave me the best machinery and I had a backup team which was out of this world. There were many times when I didn't feel like racing at the TT. You know the way it is – you get a bug or you just don't feel up to it – but because of the Honda backing and because of the commitment they had made to me over the years I always felt that I should never be in the position of ever letting them down, and I don't think I ever have.'

That first year could not be said to be a memorable one from Joey's point of view. The trouble was that Honda had nominated short circuit events for Joey as well as the big road races and to be perfectly honest this wasn't Joey's scene. I know Rex Whyte had said earlier that he had been surprised by Joey's performance in the British Grand Prix at Silverstone in 1980 but at the same time Joey was purely a road racer. That's where he excelled and that's where he was going to give Honda the best return for their money.

By April of 1981 Dunlop must have been wondering if he had made the right choice. Quite literally nothing was happening. He made his debut for the Honda works team at Donington Park on a 1980 Honda Formula One bike but had trouble in the warm up lap for the John Player Classic, and although he took part in the race itself he was never going well and had to retire.

The following week the new Formula One Honda arrived and Joey had his first outing in the British Championship round in Cadwell Park. But again there were problems and he finished seventh. He must have been apprehensive about his future, especially in view of the fact that his team-mate Haslam, who was supposed to be behind him in the pecking order at Honda, had finished third at Cadwell.

My view at the time was that Joey was kicking his heels. He had not been to any warm up road races as was his usual form in previous seasons. In the past he had begun his year at Daytona in March, a sort of 'cobweb shedding' exercise which put him in the right frame of mind for the rest of the season. Honda however had made it clear that they weren't doing Daytona and this meant that Joey had to stay at home.

At the Ulster short circuits of Kirkistown or Aghadowey, Joey also had to take a back seat and wasn't able to race. He also had to miss the Tandragee 100. All this was because Honda had decided that Joey should only ride their machines – quite rightly of course in view of the fact that they had him on a contract. Still, with only factory Hondas to ride he was unable to get in that extra racing which he needed and which always helped to build up his confidence. The one bright light on the horizon was the North West 200; this race had always been one of Joey's favourites, at least at that time in his career.

The North West promoters had slotted in a provisional entry for a Honda works rider but it wasn't until the beginning of May that Joey finally decided he would be doing his career no harm by taking part. He decided to put to the back of his mind the fact that Mervyn Robinson had been killed in the race the previous year; similarly his pledge to never again race at the meeting. The fact that Dunlop had been forced into a diet of short circuit races for most of the early part of 1981 was obviously giving him itchy feet and he was really keen to take part in the North West.

The North West 200 was Joey's first appearance in front of his home fans since the Honda signing. The bike he was to ride was an 1100cc Honda. This was the machine on which Joey had finished sixth at Donington Park in his previous outing and it was expected to be capable of greater speeds than the Formula One Honda which Joey was originally signed to ride with a view to winning the world championship. But whether or not it would be as competitive as the Suzuki and Yamaha machinery being brought over to the North West by Mick Grant and John Newbold and others remained to be seen.

I felt at the time that the Honda would not be as quick as the two-stroke bikes and I expected Dunlop to be more concerned with getting himself into shape for the TT rather than trying to win the North West. I couldn't have been more wrong. That North West 200 was a watershed in Joey's career and was to provide him with his first win as a works rider in front of his own fans.

'Joey Dunlop is Back.' These were the words I used as my introduction to my report on that year's North West which took place on 16 May. It was a jubilant Joey who rode his works Honda into first place and gave a superb display of high speed riding by demolishing the field to win the only superbike class on the programme. He simply breezed round the Portstewart–Coleraine–Portrush circuit and was never tested. With the crowd cheering him all the way over the 11 mile course he won as he pleased by over 30 seconds from Steve Parrish with Dennis Ireland third.

For Joey it couldn't have been easy in the run up to the race. He was the subject of every headline, the centre of attention in the paddock; he was a rider unused to signing autographs yet having to do a PR job all the same. He knew he had to win but there is no guarantee that you can score in these circumstances. What he needed was a fairytale homecoming. And to his great delight this is what he got.

Fair enough, he had scored a double at the North West 200 in 1979, but this was much different. He was on trial in 1981 as a factory rider. Had he flopped many would have started whispering that perhaps Joey just wasn't good enough.

So with all eyes on him and the tension electric in the starting area, the superbikes went off to a clutch start and then, on the run from Coleraine to Portrush on lap one, came the news that everyone had been waiting for – Dunlop was in the lead! The crowd at the grandstand in Portstewart erupted and every eye was trained on the final bend before the straight past the stands. Sure enough it was Dunlop who came through ahead of John Newbold, who was only about three yards behind him with Donny Robinson, one of Joey's neighbours, third.

Newbold was obviously in some sort of trouble despite his second place for he waved his hand at the pits as he passed, trying to signal that he may have clutch trouble. But Dunlop pressed on and at the end of lap two he was four seconds ahead of Newbold with McClements third, followed by Robinson, Roger Marshall and Charlie Williams.

Dunlop powered his way relentlessly towards what looked like an inevitable victory as the race reached the halfway stage. By this point Newbold had dropped out and Marshall was the second-placed man ahead of Robinson. It now looked, barring some unforeseen circumstance, as though Dunlop, still going sweetly on his fifth lap, would give the crowds what they had come to see.

The fastest lap up to this stage was 122.06mph by Dunlop on lap two. This figure was still three miles an hour down on the absolute record for the course set the previous year by Keith Huewen, who was later to become Sky Sports' voice of motorcycle racing. However Joey's speed was five miles an hour down on the record for the longer course set up by Tom Herron at 127.63mph in 1978.

With Dunlop so far in front the big interest now was in the battle for second place – here Donny Robinson was making his presence felt as he held on grimly from Marshall and McClements, both of whom were never far behind. Completing the leaderboard at that stage was Dennis Ireland in fifth place and George Fogarty in sixth. At the end of lap six, with two laps remaining, Dunlop was still out on his own, followed by Robinson who was now winning his spectacular high speed battle with Ireland for second place. Fourth place was now filled by Steve Parrish with Barry Woodland fifth. But really, apart from the scrap for second spot, all eyes were on Joey and the crowd were holding their breath in case anything should happen during those vital last two laps.

Robinson retired at Metropole Corner Portrush on the seventh lap and this brought Ireland into second place followed by Parrish. Dunlop began his last lap with a lead of 30 seconds and after that it was a run to the finish with Joey out in front and never looking like being caught. It was one of his finest moments and a victory he recalled some years later:

'That was a marvellous day for me at the North West,' he said. 'I felt I had a lot to prove as I had just signed for Honda a few months earlier. The North West in those days always brought the best out of me and once I got into the lead I never thought I would be caught. It restored my confidence in Honda and after that I went to the TT with a feeling that I could win.'

A fortnight later Joey left for the Isle of Man in preparation for the Formula One TT, the first round of the World Championship, and immediately he was made aware of his new obligation to promote both himself and Honda. Joey always wanted to concentrate on motorcycling and to do away with all the fuss which came along with the public image. Immediately after the first practice session, when Joey was second fastest on the Honda, he was whisked away for a clean up and brush up operation in order to be present for a publicity photograph. Joey's only comment was that he could have better spent the time putting in another practice lap!

Honda were making no bones about the fact that they were expecting Joey to win this Formula One race but hitherto his fastest lap, in the Classic practice where he lapped at 111.22 mph, had been on the bike on which he had won the North West 200. As for the Formula One Honda – a new machine – Joey wasn't happy about the handling but hoped to have the problem straightened out as practice week progressed. As it transpired the handling problems persisted but still Dunlop was reasonably confident that he would be the man to beat when it came to race day.

On the Saturday the line up against him included Grant, Haslam and of course Graeme Crosby, the man whom Dunlop had helped to the world title the previous year at Dundrod.

Joey wasn't to know that this TT would become one of the most controversial in history. None of it surrounded Joey but at the same time he had major problems in that while in the lead and holding a safe 76 second advantage he had victory snatched away from him when his back tyre began to wear away. However even if he had won it was doubtful whether he would have been allowed to keep the race, such were the moves and counter moves which were going on around this race from start to finish - all of them off track.

The Formula One TT seemed to have a jinx over it. There had been controversy in 1979, there was worse in 1980 and in 1981 it reached its peak. Incredibly Graeme Crosby was given the race by the international jury two hours after Ron Haslam and Honda had been heralded as the winners!

The confusion began before the start. The top works runners had tyre choice problems with a track drying out fast in the strong wind. Immediately prior to the start Crosby switched tyres. But there were problems, and he couldn't take his No. 16 place on the grid. So the start line officials put him at the back of the field.

At first the officials announced that Crosby would not be credited with the delay. It was to be Crosby's hard luck that he had failed to make it to the start. This news was broadcast and Suzuki team manager Martyn Ogbourne immediately slapped in a protest. The merry-go-round had begun. Meanwhile the riders raced on regard-less of the hassle that was building up in the corridors of power. From his back of the grid position Crosby was having a tremendous race through the heavy first lap traffic. Without his time handicap he was into third place in lap one and second on lap three. He took the lead on lap four.

But if you forgot about Crosby, who was officially said to be out of it because of the five-minute time differential which he had 'wasted', the early part of the six lapper built itself into a classic Honda vs Suzuki battle with Joey Dunlop right up there. Joey stormed into an early lead on the new Honda, but after taking things steadily on the opening windswept lap watching for wet patches on the Mountain, Grant had whittled Dunlop's early nine second lead down to three seconds as they pitted for fuel at the end of lap two.

With a quicker pit stop, Grant was ahead by a squeak as pushers shoved both riders back into the action. Dunlop sped away. But Grant's Suzuki wouldn't pick up. It was down Bray Hill before it fired properly. Then approaching Ballacraine the motor began to rattle and Grant called it a day. He said: 'I missed a gear going towards Ramsey. From then the bottom end power went off. I think I bent a valve. Until then everything had been perfect – a really superb TT bike.'

With Grant out of the race it looked like a set piece for lap record holder Dunlop. He was a mile ahead when second-placed Graeme McGregor retired at Ramsey leaving Haslam in the clear runner up slot. But nothing is simple in the TT! Suddenly Joey was in trouble. But his problems, activated by a last gasp tyre change before the start and by a bird committing suicide by flying into the fairing duct and knocking loose two plug leads, didn't worry Honda too much. They had a safe one-two with Dunlop 76 seconds ahead of Haslam at Ballaugh.

Gradually, however, the lead was reduced and by lap four it was dramatic. By Ballacraine, Joey's official lead was down by half to 32 seconds. At Ballaugh it was 21 seconds and at Ramsey it was 12. At the end of the lap during the scheduled refuelling stop, Honda's mechanics noticed much of Dunlop's back tyre had worn away. So they had to change back wheels. More than a minute was lost in the pits and Joey surrendered the lead to his team-mate.

By Ballacraine, Manx Radio's first commentary point, Haslam was 76 seconds ahead of Dunlop. It was all over bar the shouting. Though Joey whittled Ron's advantage down to 37 seconds at the finish, there was no way he could have regained his lost time. Said a disappointed Joey: 'With either the tyre problem or the misfire I could still have won, but the combination of the two made it impossible. I'm very disappointed for Honda. After all they employed me to win the TT and I didn't deliver.'

So around 5.05pm Haslam was heralded as the winner of the Formula One TT, his first Isle of Man victory. The popular Nottingham rider disclosed that his journey in the race had been trouble free. 'The bike never missed a beat,' he quipped.

But what of the Crosby appeal? Two hours later, at precisely 7.57pm, Martyn Ogbourne was called into the stewards' room and told the result had been changed. Immediately Honda men Gerald Davison and Barry Symmons went into consultation with the stewards. It wasn't a good moment for the TT. Crosby was given the race by virtue of the fact that the stewards decided to ignore what had been a near five-minute time penalty, had they taken into consideration Crosby's starting point at the back of the grid. In effect, the FIM had ruled that Crosby had incurred no time penalty and, that being the case, he had been in the lead from lap four until the finish.

In many ways it was a crazy TT and it left a lot of bitterness in the Honda camp. As the season moved on to the second round of the World Championship in Ulster – there was no Belgian round – the rift between Honda and Suzuki had widened. The decision of the stewards in the Isle of Man meant that Dunlop, instead of being placed second in the race behind Haslam, had now been pushed back to third. This was not the confidence-booster he had hoped for as he faced one of the biggest races of the week, the Senior Classic. Sadly for Joey, this race was to end in more disaster with him having to push in to the pits after having run out of fuel at Signpost Corner when in the lead on the third lap.

Trailing Crosby by five seconds at the end of laps one and two, Dunlop had just edged himself into the lead after taking 1.8 seconds off his own lap record set the previous year. Then the tank ran dry. A disappointed Joey said: 'The petrol ran out at Cronk-ny-Mona and I freewheeled to The Nook. Then I began to push. It was a nightmare. The bike was so big I had at times to pull it along with one hand on the bars and one under the seat. I only made it to the pits by aiming for one telegraph pole at a time and then having to sit down for a rest.'

After Joey had restarted and refilled he revved up the motor to try and get a new record. But leaving the Gooseneck a cam chain broke and Joey was out of the race. 'It would be fair to say that it wasn't one of my better days,' he reflected. 'Had I known the margin would be so small in this race I would have had a larger tank with a welded lump inside – just like last year.'

Said Symmons, 'We used a 28-litre tank and reckoned on using 9.2 litres per lap. But we couldn't have known that we would have three 115 mph laps.'

So the 1981 TT ended for Joey with a long push in the sun. The Classic was won by Crosby with second place going to Grant and Alex George finishing third. Apart from Joey's unfortunate finish, the lasting memory of this race was the protest by Honda over the decision earlier in the week in the Formula One race. They decided to field their riders in an all black outfit which included a black bike. This became known as Honda's Black Friday. As it turned out the results showed that it was a black day for Honda in more ways than one.

The next major date was the Ulster Grand Prix in August and Dunlop knew he had to produce the goods if Honda were to regain the championship. He was heartened by the fact that Symmons flew into Belfast shortly before practice and said: 'We would hope that Dunlop and Haslam will fight out the race and win on their merits without any obstructions in the way of team orders. I don't rule out the possibility of Joey being told to win the race even though Ron finished ahead of him in the TT. However, no decision will be made until the practices begin and we have some idea of Suzuki's potential.'

This, in effect, meant that Joey was being given the green light to win the race at the Ulster before what was expected to be a record crowd. Honda were still in a sour mood over the Crosby incident at the TT and there was more than the usual needle in the race. Their bitterness fuelled their decision to introduce an 'insurance policy' by signing Donny Robinson because of his high success rate over the course.

Symmons told me: 'We have brought Donny into the side hoping he will relegate Crosby to fourth place. This being the case it won't matter to us who wins and Ron and Joey can have a free for all. This is the key to the matter. Donny must push Crosby back and if he can't then tactics will have to be changed.'

At this stage, one could be forgiven for sympathising with

Graeme Crosby – Barry Symmons was on his trail like a giant Rottweiler!

And so to practice. Joey immediately staked his claim by becoming the fastest rider on the final night with a speed of 118.42mph in the Formula One class which unofficially broke the lap record. Crosby was second at 118.21mph with Haslam third at 117.89mph. They were followed by Grant, Newbold and McGregor. This was just the boost Dunlop needed – but would it be enough? Sadly not. The race turned into one of the most disastrous for Joey in his long career.

Dunlop had been expected to win or finish second. Even third. But what happened? Joey was in terrible form, nothing went right and he ended up fifth behind Haslam, Crosby and Grant. It was another bad day for Honda and the result gave Crosby the championship. No one really knew – certainly not Joey – what went wrong that afternoon.

'I don't know what happened to the bike,' he said. 'But the back end kept spinning over the slippery surface and I had no chance of getting into the race. It could have been the choice of tyres. Needless to say I am bitterly disappointed.'

Controversy entered the race at the start when Haslam and Grant got a 'flyer' and many were of the opinion that the race should have been restarted. Dunlop mentioned this to team manager Symmons, but Barry said he didn't wish to pursue it. At the end, Haslam scored one of the easiest victories seen around Dundrod, finishing 24 seconds ahead of Crosby. But it wasn't enough to give Haslam the championship for he needed to finish two minutes ahead of Crosby – and that was impossible around Dundrod in wet conditions.

Honda, of course, had been hoping that Haslam and Dunlop would relegate Crosby to third place but once the first lap had been completed it was obvious that Joey wasn't going to be at the races. He was fifth at the end of the opening lap as Haslam and Grant came round almost together, with Haslam holding a slight advantage. There was even more dismal news for Honda when Donny

Robinson was reported to be touring on the opening lap. He eventually came into the pits saying his bike had gone on to two cylinders and was suffering from electrical trouble because of the damp.

Meanwhile Haslam established a firm grip on the race and never looked like losing. On lap three he was virtually out on his own but it was to no avail from Honda's point of view. Although Grant was still second and Crosby third, it was only a matter of time before team orders would require Grant to ease up and allow Crosby into second spot thus ensuring him of the number of points he needed for the title.

With Dunlop still labouring down the field, Robinson now out of the race, and their fourth rider, Alex George, never in the hunt, Honda had a hopeless task and they knew it.

Afterwards Crosby said: 'Of course I'm pleased I've won the championship but I will never again race under these conditions. Grant had warned me before I went out what to expect but I thought he was kidding. I soon found out he wasn't. When I was close to a rider I couldn't see for spray and I had to back off. It was ridiculous.'

One might say typical Dundrod weather!

Haslam said: 'I am pleased to have won for that makes it two wins out of two. I still think I should have held on to the TT result. I decided to go quickly because I wanted to get away from Crosby and Dunlop whom I thought were fighting it out for second place. I was amazed when I came in and found out that Joey was so far behind.'

It was a hollow victory on a bad day for Honda. A glum-faced Barry Symmons summed it up perfectly: 'We played two, won two and lost one!' he said.

There was no doubt that Joey was having to take a back seat to his Honda team-mate Haslam at this stage and there was further evidence of this when Haslam went on to win the Macau Grand Prix in November. Heat exhaustion prevented Joey from finishing the second leg of the race after he had ended up third in the first.

Haslam's win broke the Japanese dominance of the event but it did nothing for Joey's peace of mind.

He did sign up with Honda again in 1982 and received crumbs of comfort in Barry Symmons' view that although the honeymoon period was over, there was a great deal to be learned from the 1981 season. Still, for Joey there appeared to be a long, hard road ahead. He could never have dreamt that the following year he would be world champion.

CHAPTER 8

WORLD CHAMPION

The year 1982 loomed with Joey very much in Ron Haslam's shadow. Joey still had a lot to prove in the season which lay ahead. And as if Haslam wasn't enough there was another rider on the horizon who was scheduled to give Joey some headaches. This was fellow Ulsterman Norman Brown, who had the public personality which Joey lacked.

From Newry, Co Down, Brown was backed by the ubiquitous Hector Neill who had now lost contact with Dunlop's career. Hector had produced a machine for Brown, and Norman, a winner at the Manx Grand Prix in 1981, was making steady progress. By the time 1982 came along Brown's name was on everyone's lips as Joey was still trying to rekindle the flame. In many ways it was something of a watershed in the careers of both riders. Brown was looking for a TT breakthrough, which he got in that year's Senior, while Joey was hoping to improve on what he had already achieved. Brown rode Suzukis and his victory in the Senior TT of 1982 was a performance which almost rivalled that of Dunlop in 1980.

But Joey had other things on his mind. He was about to begin a season which, in the view of some observers, could make or break his career. The first big race for him was the North West 200 in which one of the superbike races had been designated a round of the British Championship. Joey knew he had to prove he was still in a winning frame of mind, as the fans felt there was a question mark hanging over him.

An interesting story concerning that year's North West was told to me by Billy Gibson, who worked for Rea Distribution and was a close friend of Ron Haslam. Joey was very superstitious and when he discovered his picture was on the front of the 1982 North West programme he was very unhappy about it – Mervyn Robinson and Frank Kennedy had both featured on the front of the programme and both had been killed in the race.

Joey allegedly threatened to quit the meeting so the race organisers quickly contacted the printers at the last minute and asked them to replace the picture of Joey with one of someone else. Ron Haslam was the rider who got the vote.

Billy told me: 'This was all done behind closed doors and the printers gave me the original programme with Joey on it, but the caption inside reads 'Ron Haslam'.' Billy reckons this is the only programme of its kind in existence.

The year 1982 was to see the first of Joey's five consecutive world championships but that prospect seemed a million miles away to anyone who watched him during North West practice. He looked like a rider short on confidence. Joey was one of three Honda riders on 1123cc machines. The other two in the team were Haslam, of course, and Wayne Gardner, who was later to make his name as World 500cc Grand Prix champion. But in those days he wasn't all that well known and was regarded as the third string in the Honda team. Haslam was the man Dunlop had to beat, for Ron was becoming Joey's *bête noir*. Everywhere Joey went Haslam seemed to come along too and give him a tough time.

The Suzuki team was made up of Grant – who was a regular at the meetings and had been since 1975 when he won on a Kawasaki – Marshall and Newbold. It was a cracking good line up and a major performance was expected, especially from Newbold, who two years earlier had been virtually beaten on the line by Keith Huewen in a dramatic finish to the second superbike race.

Race day dawned and as usual excitement was high. The first

race on the programme was the British Championship superbike event, won by Haslam, but before very long the winner soon became irrelevant as news of a fatal accident emerged. Newbold, who was watched by his wife Alison, his lap scorer, appeared to clip the rear wheel of team-mate Grant when both were disputing second place behind the eventual winner Haslam. The accident happened, on the second lap, at Juniper Hill, only a few yards from where Tom Herron had died in 1979.

Immediately after the race Barry Symmons said: 'Although Newbold was a Suzuki rider, one of the members of my team, Haslam, has decided not to race again today. He is deeply upset by this tragedy as he was a close neighbour of John.' Rex Whyte added that Marshall, who had finished second to Haslam, would also take no further part that day.

Newbold had raced regularly at the North West since the mid Seventies and had been successful in the 500cc race in 1977. At the time of his death he was a leading contender in the British Super-bike Championships of which the North West was the third round.

With this nightmare scenario as the background, Haslam won his first North West 200 title. Meanwhile Joey was soon out of the race. His bike went on to one cylinder at the end of the first lap and he toured into the pits, where Honda mechanics worked feverishly to make necessary adjustments. Joey went out again but he was only feeling his way and was never going to get back into the race.

Haslam, who had never finished a race at the North West before now, was always in a high speed shuffle which involved four riders for most of the race. The others were Grant, Marshall and new-comer Graeme Wood. Wood was the surprise package of the race, leading for two laps near the finish before ending up in third place as Haslam pipped Marshall in a dramatic run for the line.

Joey's second race that day was in the back-up superbike race but again he was out of luck. He was forced to take second place to Grant after tyre and handling problems. So it wasn't a very happy chappie who went to the Isle of Man TT that year. The only good news was the fact that Honda had given him a new V4 for the

Classic TT. This bike was reckoned to be the fastest machine around at that time.

Keen to erase the memory of Honda's embarrassing Black Friday protest of the previous June, Joey was hoping the immense power of the V4 would be enough for victory despite its thirsty fuel consumption. For the six-lap Classic, Dunlop needed two fuel stops while his Honda team-mate Haslam, who was many people's favourite for the honours, needed only one on his 1123cc machine. Joey said at the time: 'I reckon you lose almost a minute with an extra stop. It's not only the stopping and restarting that matters, it's the time it takes you to get back into your rhythm.'

Dunlop was also keen to have an early TT ride on the V4 to see just how much power it would emit. 'It's possible in the TT to have too much top speed,' he explained. 'There are also a series of bends before Ramsey where too much power can be a bit of a handicap. It's alright having the power but it's necessary at the TT to be able to use it.'

But, sadly for Joey, it was all academic in the end. He never got to race the V4, for during practice it developed a cracked frame and left the Isle of Man for the United States. Joey reverted to the Formula One Honda for the F1 TT but unfortunately for him it was a case of different bike, more problems. Once again, Haslam broke new ground by winning his first TT; Joey was left with a bundle of suspension problems and second place.

It was Grant who set the early pace and a new lap record. The race was dominated for four laps by Grant and Suzuki, but then it became a Honda one-two. Grant had built up a half minute lead when he refuelled at the end of the second lap. On lap three at the Bungalow, Grant had asserted his superiority with a 23 second lead with Haslam in second place and a troubled Dunlop third.

Having put early tyre problems to the back of his mind, Grant faced up to what became a season-long gremlin, a fading front brake. Steadily the Grant–Haslam gap began to be whittled down. Grant was having braking problems and Haslam was getting into the groove. At the end of lap three, Grant's lead was around 30 seconds. With his front brake back to the bar he had only a six second lead at Ballaugh and soon after that the Suzuki gave up. 'The plan was to go fast at the start and get a cushion against the opposition, I didn't particularly want to race very hard on the last lap in that heat,' explained Grant. 'The bike was sliding about from the start when the front brake went. Then, after Ballaugh on the fifth lap, I had a monster oil leak. Drenched in it I was slowed at May Hill and finally stopped at Ramsey.'

Dunlop gradually dropped back as his suspension collapsed and his new motor – replacing the one blown up in the final practice – would only rev to 9,000 instead of the normal 10,000.

Joey then had to endure further disaster in the Classic TT. Without the new American V4 machine Joey rode a slower Honda but he was still in contention when a broken chain put him out of the race with one lap to go. Dunlop was lying second to New Zealander Dennis Ireland after the leaderboard had been wrecked by a series of sudden retirements. First the leader Charlie Williams went out just after Ballaugh on lap five, then the fourth man Steve Tonkin retired at Ballaugh and the third man Rob McElnea – who was to become Dunlop's main opponent the following year – followed soon afterwards. This left Ireland in the lead from Dunlop, but when Joey went, Ireland went on to win from Jon Ekerold.

So it was a rather disgruntled Joey who went off to Portugal for the second round of the Formula One series. Yet his chances of salvaging championship points were improved dramatically when Haslam decided not to take part. The race was won by Wayne Gardner, with Joey again in second place. This meant that Joey had 24 points from the two rounds which was six more than the second place man Dave Hiscock. So, from being dejected after the Isle of Man TT, Joey was now in the happy position of only needing to finish fourth in the final round, the Ulster Grand Prix, to win the championship for the first time.

But lurking in the background was Norman Brown. Here was a competitor with almost as much talent as Joey and certainly the potential to be a future world champion. Brown had stolen Joey's thunder by winning the Senior TT on Hector Neill's Suzuki. Now Brown was heading for the Ulster Grand Prix and a head to head with not only Dunlop but Haslam. He had been signed up by Suzuki for the Formula One race and had made up his mind, he was going to give his all.

The 1982 Ulster turned out to be a thriller. One of the greatest of modern times. It ended up with Dunlop the new world champion although the hearts of the huge crowd who turned up to see the show went out to Brown, who was in the lead for most of the race before crashing on the last lap. But for all Brown's disappointment he did smash the lap record with a speed of 118.10mph and led the race for five of the ten laps.

Nearing the finish it seemed that Brown, in only his first competitive ride for Suzuki, would perform the impossible and win. With two laps to go he was ahead of Haslam with Dunlop in a poor third and obviously in great difficulty keeping going. Then on the last lap Haslam moved fractionally ahead of Brown as the riders flashed through the start and finish area. This was high speed 100mph roulette at its best and it had been like this since the start of the race. A classic in every sense.

With the crowd tensed up waiting for a finish which would see Haslam and Brown scorch over the line together, news came through that Haslam was on his own at the Hairpin and he eventually finished well ahead of Dunlop with third place going to the third member of the Honda trio, Gardner. There was a sense of foreboding about the finish for everyone knew that Brown had been in close contention and must have fallen off. Then Haslam declared that he and Brown had been battling for the lead at Wheeler's Corner when they came up against slower riders. 'I braked but Norman came on past me and I chased him,' Haslam said. 'I caught up but our machines touched and Norman fell off. Luckily he is only badly shaken.'

There were those among the Brown supporters who claimed that Haslam had pushed Brown off his machine. Norman to his credit made no protest. At the finish Dunlop looked in a rather dazed mood as he was crowned World Champion for the first time. The crowd give him a tremendous reception after he had crossed the line 26 seconds behind Haslam. But there were mixed emotions for Joey. He would have liked to have won the title with more style. But to his credit he had fought a problem with faulty brakes for three quarters of the race and he was lucky to finish.

Just what would have happened had he retired from the race I hesitate to forecast. It was one of those days when Joey just *had* to win the championship. It was as simple as that.

After the race he told me: 'It's marvellous to win the title but it just hasn't sunk in. People say I'm now going to retire but I have no intentions at this stage. To be honest I just don't know what's going to happen next. This is a day I will always remember.'

Young Brown, it was later learned, was taken to hospital with a suspected broken wrist. His season was to continue, but the following year, he joined the tragic list of Ulster riders who ended their lives on the track. He was killed when pulling in to retire in the British Grand Prix at Silverstone.

Joey was in a much brighter mood that day at Dundrod than he had been all year. And who could blame him for, despite the fact that he had won the title by virtue of three runner up places, he was still champion and he intended to hold on to that crown.

Later that year, Joey went to Earls Court in London to collect the Shell award for his achievements during the 1982 season. He was accompanied by the ever present Hector Neill, who was collecting an award on behalf of Brown, who was unable to attend. The pair met at Belfast airport and flew to Heathrow before going on to Earls Court to collect their prizes. As the evening wore on, Hector suggested to Joey that they ought to leave for fear of missing their return flight.

'Ach, no rush,' replied Joey. But, by the time they left and reached Heathrow the last flight had gone.

Hector takes up the story from here: '"I told you this would happen," I said, "What are we going to do now?" Joey said: "We might as well stay for the night," but I wasn't going to pay for it so I went to a phone booth and rang a co-sponsor of ours and said "Look, Joey and I are at Heathrow and we have missed our flight back to Belfast. We aren't exactly carrying a pile of money with us so is there anywhere we can stay cheaply for the night?"

'I was told to put the phone down and ring back in ten minutes and something would be arranged. So I lifted the phone ten minutes later and next thing I knew I was told to get Joey and myself into a taxi, go two miles down the road and sign in at the Skyways Hotel. Everything would be arranged they said.

'So Joey and I got into the taxi and arrived at the hotel and looked at the impressive front door. Joey said nervously: "I don't think we'll be staying here." I said "Let's play it by ear." So we walked up to reception and I said: "Is there a room for Mr Neill and Mr Dunlop?" "Yes sir, third floor, room something or other."

'So we marched over to the lift up to the third floor and we entered this smart room with en-suite and two massive twin double beds. Joey took a look around and I said: "It's a bit grand Joey!" I sat down on the bed and looked around the place and someone knocked on the door. I told Joey to answer the door, but he said: "I'm not answering it – they are probably up to put us out." I said: "Go and answer it." As soon as Joey opened the door in walked this guy with a bottle of champagne and a tray with two glasses and set it on the table with a chit at the side. I said: "Joey, sign that chit." Joey said: "I'm not signing it."

'Anyway, he signed it and the guy went out and the two of us drank the champagne and the whole time we kept discussing about who was going to pay for the bill. We had dinner booked which was all part of this package so I went down and there was this Caribbean evening, Joey and I sat down and I said: "What are you going to eat?" Joey said: "I'll follow you."

'So we had all this Caribbean type fish and stuff and Joey and I picked our way through it and behold we were lucky enough to find that the second part of the menu had meat cooked on a grill so it turned out to be a pleasant evening.

'We went back up to the room and I said: "Joey we will just get up early in the morning and sneak out." Joey looked horrified but agreed it was a good idea. It was at this stage I told him my co-sponsor had taken care of us and he would be paying the bill!'

If 1982 had left Joey a little bit unsatisfied as a champion who had never won a race, 1983 was entirely different. This was the year when Joey's career blossomed to such an extent that he soon became a household name. He also established himself among his peers as a rider of the highest quality.

His major opponent during that world championship year was Yorkshireman Rob McElnea, a rider with tremendous talent who later became one of the top operators on British short circuits. McElnea had begun his career on roads and was a great admirer of Joey. But in 1983 McElnea, as the number one rider for the Suzuki team, reckoned he had a marvellous opportunity to lift the World Championship.

There were three rounds that year and by the end of the season Joey had won the TT and the Ulster Grand Prix, while McElnea lifted the Dutch TT, which was the round in between. The Dutch TT gave both riders a tremendous thrill for it was staged at the same time as the Grand Prix world championship meeting.

'That meeting at Assen was one of my all time favourites,' said Rob. 'It was my first time at a major event and I felt I had a real chance of winning the world title for Suzuki. Because the Formula One race was being held on the same card as the Grand Prix events, there were over 200,000 spectators at the meeting. I had never raced in front of anything like that before and I was really revved up for the occasion. Joey and I had a great battle. Joey led for most of the race, but I got him on the last lap. The crowd went ballistic. There was such a buzz. I'll never forget it. Immediately afterwards Joey and I went back up to the top of the stand to watch the 500cc race and Joey brought a large bottle of vodka!'

McElnea emphasised that if Joey had wished to be a top class rider on the tracks he could have done so. 'Riders like myself were keen to do the Grand Prix races while Joey was purely a road man,' McElnea told me. 'Let's put it this way. We were 80 per cent committed to short circuits and 20 per cent to the roads. It was the other way with Joey. What would have happened if Joey had decided to be 80 per cent committed to short circuits and 20 per cent to roads? All of us would have had to look for another job!

'He was as quick as any short circuit rider I had ever met when he put his mind to it. He really loved racing but the pure road courses were his theatre. He felt out of it elsewhere. Yet he had a great talent. What a pity he didn't go on to try to win the Grand Prix world championships. I think he would have gone close in that high grade.'

The good news for Joey in the 1983 season was that Honda at last decided to do what everybody said was the obvious thing – they let him be his own man. No longer was Joey to be tied down to team orders in a sense that only Honda mechanics would look after his bike. Joey was now in a position where he was allowed to oper-ate himself and he was much more relaxed at the beginning of 1983 than he was at any time in 1982. Other good news was that he was told at the beginning of the year that he would have a Grand Prix 500cc machine as well as the new V4 in the three Formula One rounds.

But the North West was the first race to come into the picture. The previous year there had been talk of Joey riding one of the new Hondas at this big meeting but the bike never materialised. In 1983, they were ready and available before racing even began. Joey natu-rally was keener than ever to retain the world championship and what was more important to him was winning at least one of the rounds – something he had failed to do in his two-year career as a works rider. The North West seemed to be a natural place to run in the new V4 in preparation for the first world title round in the Isle of Man.

Davy Wood told me at the time: 'I reckon a race at the North West would be ideal. Joey will be going there anyway on the Formula One bike which he has on loan from Honda as well as the 500, but if he were able to have the new V4 on time well that would really be something.'

There is no course like the North West for testing a high speed machine to the limits and although the alterations to the circuit had made the race slower, this was likely to be up Joey's street for the new artificial bends with the introduction of chicanes would give him a greater idea of the handling of the bike.

In addition to allowing Joey to look after his own bikes, Honda had also agreed he could ride in road races other than those chosen for him by the factory. This meant that he was back on the local roads and in early May he won the unlimited cc class at the Tandragee 100 in Co Armagh. Dunlop was up against the cream of Ulster's road racers and, despite torrential rain, he took them apart with the exception of Brian Reid who finished four seconds behind in the runner up spot. Norman Brown finished the course 57 seconds behind Joey in third place and this sort of result was just what Joey needed to gain confidence for the looming North West 200 and of course the TT.

Shortly before the North West it was announced that Joey would have two special 'hush hush' bikes in his bid for glory. The bikes were 500cc and 850cc Hondas. They arrived on the ferry accompanied by Japanese mechanics. This was the first time this sort of operation had been mounted for an Ulster race since the heyday of Honda in the mid Sixties so Joey was getting the special treatment. The new NS500 machine would be making its first appearance in the United Kingdom. The other bike was a V4 which Dunlop was expected to ride in one of the superbike races in the North West and this would be the machine which would hopefully carry his hopes in the F1 series.

The most interesting point about the news, however, was that the North West would see Dunlop on a 500cc Honda for the first time since he joined the factory team. With fellow Honda rider Wayne Gardner a non-starter Dunlop was likely to be favourite. Joey didn't let anyone down. In a dream debut at a rain-wrecked meeting, he won the 500cc race first time out on the new Honda. Joey averaged 106.05mph to win from Graeme Wood with Gary Lingham in third place. Having had only four laps practice on the bike, his was a surprise win and he became the first Ulsterman to win this class at the North West since Billy Guthrie from Moira, Co Down in 1973.

Before the race Joey reckoned he had little chance of victory as it was difficult to become acquainted with the new machine so quickly. After a pedestrian first lap which ended with Dunlop out of the first six it looked as if he would have to wait until later in the day for his first win. Then it all happened at Portrush on lap two. Dunlop squeezed ahead of Brown and he had increased his lead by the end of the second lap. Brown was suffering. Joey had chosen intermediate tyres for the conditions but Brown had gone for tyres that would suit dry roads and he was now losing ground rapidly. In third place at this stage was Wood, with Lingham fourth, and Brian Reid was also in on the act.

It was Reid in fact who made the only real challenge to Dunlop as the race reached the halfway stage. At this point Dunlop was only a few yards ahead of Reid with a sizeable gap between Reid and Wood. There was no doubt that the race was going to be decided by the Dunlop–Reid battle and when Reid edged ahead at Metropole Corner it looked as though we were going to be in for a split second finish. Brian was still right on Joey's tail at the end of the fourth lap but then next time round his hopes were dashed when he developed a flat tyre and had to pull in at the end of the lap while still in second place.

'The bike was wobbling all over the place,' Reid said afterwards. 'I am bitterly disappointed. I really thought I had a chance of winning when I passed Joey at Portrush but that's the way it goes.'

Meanwhile, with no apparent opposition, Joey was able to ease up and he cruised to a comfortable win from Wood, with Lingham third followed by the relentless Brown. Afterwards Joey said: 'I didn't think I would win that as the Honda is completely new to me. On the first lap I took things easy but then when I pushed ahead on lap two as the rain came pouring down I realised I was in with a great chance for I had chosen the right sort of tyres.'

As for Honda, their faith in Joey had been justified. Barry Symmons said: 'The choice of tyres was made by Joey himself. He knows the course backwards and we left it up to him. Let's say we are just delighted with this dream debut.'

Joey received the man of the meeting award that day at the North West; in addition to winning the 500cc class he also took the main race of the day, the North West 200 Superbike, edging out Brown.

And so to another TT. Machine problems looked like giving Joey another headache when practice began. The gremlins had been dogging him right from the start and on one of the practice sessions he broke down when the fuel breather became blocked. Still, as one well known Ulster sponsor said at the time: 'It's better having your problems in the practice rather than in the race.' Consequently, no one would really rule Joey out of it.

The poor weather kept speeds relatively low and no one had beaten Grant's lap of 113mph in the opening session on the Monday. Although he had no quick laps, Dunlop was pleased with his performance on the 500cc Honda and it looked as though he could be a major factor in the Classic race, which ended the week on the Friday.

But the big race was the Formula One and Dunlop, although he was favourite, still had these nagging doubts regarding the ability of the V4 to last the trip. He needn't have worried. In an amazing performance, Joey set the island alight on the V4 Honda by not only winning the race but breaking the lap record from a standing start and setting a TT race average of 114.03mph – that was almost half a minute quicker than Crosby's best of two years earlier. By leading at the end of each of the six laps he collected £10,250 in prize money – a one-race TT record. Second place went to Grant with McElnea third, but the day belonged to Joey. He was on top form, out of sight on the roads and breaking every record in TT history.

An exhausted Joey said afterwards: 'That was the hardest race of my life. It was much harder than any other TT and it proved my old adage – bad practice good race!'

Grant agreed: 'It was tough, I could hardly hold on after four laps. The temperature was much higher than in practice and the suspension settings were too soft. My tyres went off in the early stages. Then I had a cold and with my wrist not being 100 per cent it made it a hard race.'

Grant had one frightening moment – at May Hill in Ramsey where he went up on to the pavement. Strictly not advisable!

Joey, meanwhile, had a trouble-free race. From the start he stormed into an early lead and by Ballacraine, Manx Radio's first commentary point on lap one, he was already seven seconds up on Grant and leading on the roads. By Ballaugh Joey was 17 seconds ahead. Joey, who had shaved off his beard the day before especially for this race, had increased his lead to 19 seconds at the Bungalow. It was all over bar the shouting . . . or was it?

After both riders had refuelled in less than 10 seconds, Dunlop increased his lead to more than half a minute but, going into his fourth lap, Joey pointed down to his rear tyre and the Honda mechanics got themselves ready for a new back slick. At the end of the lap Dunlop pitted for refuelling and a much needed new rear tyre. The entire stop lasted an agonising 61 seconds. That lengthy stop meant that Grant was now ahead. At Ballacraine, he led Dunlop by 12 seconds with Suzuki team-mate McElnea close up, but by Ballaugh on the fifth lap Dunlop had cut Grant's lead to only two seconds.

Dunlop's incredible performance continued and brought gasps from Honda co-ordinator Symmons when Barry heard at the Bungalow on lap five that Dunlop had a 19 second advantage. With the race in the bag, Joey eased back marginally and his lap – his only flying one – was three-fifths of a second slower than the record-breaking standing start opener. Such was their pace, both Dunlop and Grant broke the two hour barrier for the six laps over the Mountain circuit.

So Joey had at last scored his first Formula One TT victory and, crucially, he had done it in style. A record race average of 114.03mph was coupled with a record lap of 115.73mph. He couldn't have wished for more.

The next round of the championship was the Dutch TT, in which Joey had finished second the previous year. Could he go one better?

Well the man to beat was obviously McElnea, who was fast establishing a name for himself as a Suzuki front runner.

Given the importance of the race in Joey's quest for a second consecutive world championship, one might be forgiven for thinking that an early night and a good sleep was the order of the day – but not our Joey. In fact, his antics on the eve of the race in Holland had team manager Barry Symmons tearing his hair out. It happened like this.

Because the Formula One race was at the same meeting as the World Championship Grand Prix, it meant that Norman Brown, who was competing in the 500cc series, would also be there. Accompanying Brown were the 'team' of Hector Neill and Stanley 'Mouse' Morrow. This pair had been instrumental in Joey's early successes and now, of course, they had a new kid on the block in Brown. Hector had hired a motorhome plus a caravan and was all set for using them before Joey suddenly arrived at Assen in a Ford Capri.

'Where are you to sleep, Joey?' enquired Hector.

'Och, in the car,' came the reply.

Hector told him that he could stay in the caravan with Norman and the Mouse and Dunlop said 'Great job.'

Somewhat inevitably after a few drinks later that night, a party broke out in the caravan. The Mouse was playing the accordion, somebody else was playing saucepans, and all you could hear were the wild shouts of the partygoers. This went on into the early hours of the morning.

The following day at about 9.30am Hector and his team got up and sorted themselves, but there was no Joey. Nobody had seen him and he wasn't in the car. Practice was shortly due to start and down came Barry Symmons.

'Has anybody seen Joey?' said an anxious Barry.

Hector, Brown and Morrow said they hadn't seen him anywhere. Then Mouse remembered that the previous night he had seen Joey sleeping under his car with a blanket over him. He had wakened Joey and said: 'Don't let Ireland down Joey. The rest of the world championship contenders are staying in hotels. You are the World Champion and you're lying out in the open. At least get into the caravan.'

No one could remember if he had or not but they started to search all the same. Eventually Barry went down to the bottom of the caravan, lifted a blanket and there was Joey lying sound asleep.

'Do you think he will be alright?' said Symmons. 'Don't worry,' said Mouse. 'We'll get him there in good time. Joey has never missed a deadline in his life.'

And of course Joey did arrive on time for what turned out to be an epic Formula One race. He was beaten by McElnea but he had a two point lead going into the final round of the world championship, his home race at the Ulster Grand Prix. Things couldn't have been better and he looked on target for retaining that title.

In order to make sure that Joey clinched that crown with the minimum of fuss, Honda sent him a new superbike for the Dundrod race. A 920cc machine was flown especially to Belfast during practice week. This was a larger version of the V4 and it was also bigger than the Honda on which he had finished second in Holland. Symmons said at the time: 'We believe the new bike which has been tested at the Suzuka Marathon race in Japan will provide Joey with the best possible chance of clinching the championship.'

Dunlop was backed up by one other Honda rider, Roger Marshall, winner of the 1000cc race the previous year. Marshall was to ride the smaller 850cc Formula One bike which he had been using all year and his role was to keep McElnea at bay. They needn't have worried for on the big day it just simply wasn't a race. 'Joey Dunlop – by a distance!' This was my description of Joey's 1983 Formula One win in the Ulster, for the rest of the field were simply nowhere. Joey, riding superbly, turned what was supposed to have been a knife-edge struggle into a procession and he won the race just as he pleased to retain the championship on the same track on which he had lifted it the previous year.

This was a Dunlop tour de force – make no mistake about it. Right from the fall of the flag he had the whole affair wrapped up and ready for packaging and at the finish he completed the course 33 seconds ahead of Grant with McElnea third. McElnea told me years later: 'When we went to the Ulster and it started to rain I knew I had no chance for in my view Joey was totally unbeatable in those conditions. Thursday practice was handicapped by the poor weather, yet I still managed to finish in pole position. But it didn't matter a bit.

'It pissed down on race day and although I got 'hole shot' [meaning that McElnea got away first] Joey had different plans. He just flashed past me as though I was stopped and 'flew' down the flying kilometre. I looked over at Grant and I shook my head and said to myself, 'What are we going to do with this guy?' At that level Joey Dunlop was quite simply a class apart.'

Before the race it was thought that Dunlop would have had to bring the normally thirsty Honda into the pits near the end of the race and although he had a huge lead with three laps to go everyone in the starting area was anxiously looking for signs from Honda that Joey would have to pull in. But he just kept going round and round the Dundrod course he knew so well, maintaining a steady pace and always keeping his nearest title challenger, McElnea, well in arrears. In fact McElnea was second for 11 of the 13 laps and never looked like cutting down on Joey's lead. The only doubt throughout the race involved that threatened pit stop and once it was obvious that Dunlop had no intention of pulling in, the race was a foregone conclusion.

Afterwards Joey said: 'Honda left it up to me to pull in if I reckoned I needed to top up and I decided to wait until Suzuki stopped before I did. They didn't, so I kept on going.'

Symmons echoed Joey's sentiments: 'I can tell you now we never intended to stop for fuel. At a recent race in Japan, the consumption of our machine proved superior to Suzuki, but we let it be known that we would have to stop and top up. This was a ploy in order to encourage Suzuki to try to complete the race without stopping and had it been dry, they would have been pushed to do so. As it was, the wet roads kept the speeds down and we never had any sweat.'

Dunlop never came anywhere near the lap record set by Brown for Suzuki the previous year. In fact he really didn't have to. The fastest speed he attained was 110.10mph on the ninth lap. Grant would, I felt at the time, have been much closer to Dunlop had McElnea not been in the running for the championship. He deliberately stayed behind his team-mate giving him every chance but when it was obvious that he couldn't catch Dunlop, Grant swiftly passed McElnea and took a comfortable second place.

But it was Joey's day and despite the fact that the race was forgettable as a contest no one could deny him his moment of triumph.

At the end of the year Joey once again had a crack at Macau. And once again he was beaten by his Honda team-mate Haslam, who won the race for a record third time with Marshall, also on a Honda, in third place. The Macau Grand Prix was never destined to be included among the list of Joey's triumphs. But he wasn't worried. To Joey it was only a holiday affair. He was already concentrating on defending that Formula One title in 1984.

CHAPTER 9

THREE IN A ROW

Throughout the many years that I watched Joey Dunlop race at top level I can only remember him being angry on two occasions. I mean *really* angry.

It took a lot to make Joey lose his cool but when he did become annoyed at something he let it show. Not, as many others did, by losing their tempers and bawling out officials and other riders – that wasn't Joey's style. Instead he normally retreated to the inner confines of his van with his motorcycles and had a quiet smoke before deciding his next move.

The most recent occasion was at the Ulster Grand Prix in 1999. Dundrod is an unforgiving track and nobody knew that better than Joey. However the 'golden boy' David Jefferies was appearing there for the first time and in the opening superbike race he attacked it with gusto. He was all over the track and eventually won with what was quite frankly a hair-raising display of high class riding. But Joey wasn't impressed by his cavalier attitude. He approached Dave afterwards and advised him that Dundrod could be a dangerous place. It's unclear what happened next but Joey was obviously not at all pleased by Jefferies' response!

For the final Superbike race it was a determined Joey Dunlop, with a steely look in his eyes, who pushed the Honda up another couple of notches. He gave a performance which was better than anything I had seen from him during the latter part of his career. He was simply superb but so was Jefferies. They battled round Dundrod as if no one else were there and at the finish they had shattered the lap record before Joey just got up by a few feet. It was totally breathtaking. Sadly, it was to be Joey's last performance on his favourite track.

Fifteen years earlier, in 1984 – a much more important season for Dunlop for he was the reigning Formula One champion – there was a similar rift between Joey and his team-mate Roger Marshall. It wasn't a disagreement about how to ride Dundrod as was the case with Jefferies many years later. It was a case of Joey getting the feeling that Honda wanted Marshall to win the title that year and not him. At least that's what the fans thought and an incident at the Dutch TT – the second round of the F1 TT championships, which had been extended in 1984 to five rounds – did nothing to allay their fears.

With Joey in the lead, Marshall had come in for one of the fastest pit stops of all time – so fast in fact that there were many accusations that Marshall hadn't cut his engine in the pits at all, as is customary. Marshall won the race and Joey had been robbed of a potential victory. Roger refuted any suggestions that he had executed a dodgy pit stop. 'We did a quick refuel,' he told me. 'That was where I won that race but I know Joey's fans weren't a bit pleased and thought that I had done something that wasn't quite legal. That was just nonsense.'

Whatever the truth of it both riders came to the Ulster Grand Prix neck and neck. Each knew that they had to win there to get an edge for the final round, which was taking place in Belgium. Marshall was in many ways the favourite if you judged by the number of rounds he had won up until then. But Dundrod was Joey's favourite track and that counted for everything.

There was supposed to be a raging feud between the pair at this time, but years later Marshall denied this. 'Joey and I had a knife-edge battle for the Formula One title that year,' he said. 'And when we came to Dundrod it was anybody's race. I became very angry after the finish because I thought that Joey had undercut me on the last lap at Irwin's Bend. As we were negotiating it, Joey's bike came under me and I nearly went on to the grass. I was furious.'

You can say that again. After Joey had come in as the winner and was wheeling his bike into the paddock, an indignant Marshall charged down the pit area, shaking his fist and demanding that there be a protest. He told team manager Barry Symmons that he had been nearly knocked off his Honda on the last lap and he wasn't the least bit happy about it. He was out to make waves in a big way. The suave Symmons quietly calmed him down, however, and nothing more was said about it.

In later years Marshall told me: 'Well I do believe that Joey went under me at Irwin's Bend. After the race I was incensed and I insisted that a protest be lodged. But I calmed down and I think you remember before the final round at Zolder in Belgium I made a point of shaking Joey's hand before the race started. We were always good friends.'

And Joey's view? I will always recall that immediately after the Dundrod race I went to speak to him in his van. He sat back, pulled a large drag on his cigarette, looked me straight in the face and said: 'Roger doesn't like to be beaten does he!' That sentence spoke volumes for Dunlop's sentiments. On those occasions Joey Dunlop was a man you just didn't argue with.

Marshall and Dunlop had totally different personalities and this was what made that 1984 championship so fascinating. While Dunlop liked nothing better than to 'disappear' after a race in one of the far corners of the paddock where he could spend the time working on his machines with no interference and certainly no spectators to ask questions, Marshall was like a buccaneer as he strode through the paddock signing autographs and chatting up the many attractive camp followers who attended these races.

Cosmetically, he was made to last forever and as he said himself: 'I certainly liked to party. Everything as far as I was concerned was a great laugh. You had to enjoy yourself or there was no point in being there.' He didn't always get on well with Symmons. 'We had a mutual respect,' Marshall said. 'But I was a rebel, I didn't like to conform. In those days I liked to do my own thing. But Barry had the best team and they were very well organised. He was very serious about his job while I was a bit of a 'jack the lad'. But it all worked out well.'

Despite what appeared to be a frivolous nature of Marshall's character, there was no doubt that he was a big rider for Honda at that time. And, in spite of their rivalry, he had tremendous respect for Joey. 'I knew I could race up with Joey in any road race with a mass start but at the TT he was a total master. He was so confident at the beginning of a TT and that's what gave him an edge. He would be a few seconds up on you before you realised it and you never cut those seconds back. He was an undoubted 'King of the Island'. That was his throne and I wouldn't dispute that.

'In 1984 Joey's fans were under the impression that Symmons had signed me up to take the title and that Joey would take a back seat. After all he had won the championship the previous year. But nothing could be further from the truth. We were both racing on our own merits and it was a case of 'may the better man win.''

I asked Roger the question which everyone wanted to know, especially since Joey's death. What made him so popular among so many thousands of fans? Roger, who is now team manager with the Reve Ducati road racing team, thought long and hard about it before he said: 'He was the people's champion. He never changed despite his many successes. He was always the same Joey Dunlop who started out all those years ago. He was very hard to get to know although I roomed with him during that 1984 season and found him a pleasant personality. But Joey was a very deep type of person. You could never probe his thoughts. That didn't annoy me. We got on well on and off the track and that's what it was all about.'

Although, by Roger's own admission, Joey wasn't as much of a party animal as other riders, he fondly recalls the events of one night during that 1984 championship, after the Portuguese round at Vila Real. 'We all went out for a hectic evening to celebrate Mick Grant's birthday,' Roger told me. 'At midnight we decided to do a lap round the course in Joey's car and Joey was the driver. He went so quickly that two of the mechanics were immediately sick. Barry Symmons came in the next day and wondered why Joey was staying in bed. I had to say that he had a touch of the flu!'

The 1984 season began in earnest for both men at the North West 200. Roger felt he had his best chance ever of winning the race (he had not triumphed there before) for he was leading by 45 seconds but once again his challenge came to nothing. He clipped the tyres of one of the riders in front of him because his visor was fogged up. The race eventually went to Dunlop but Joey wasn't pleased afterwards because he felt he hadn't beaten Marshall fairly and squarely.

Joey was almost a non starter in that year's race. A crash at Mondello Park near Dublin the previous weekend had raised doubts about his fitness to ride. He was practising for the unlimited cc class at the Carroll's Race Of The Year when he fell off his 500cc Honda and injured his wrist.

After an overnight rest Joey found he was unable to race the following day as the wrist had become swollen, so once again a visit to his old friend, the 'charmer', was called for. This was Matt Gibson, the man who had helped him at the Ulster Grand Prix in 1979. Joey went to see him in order to be fit for the North West 200 and to make sure in his own mind that he could race at the top of his form. His injuries weren't serious – sprained wrist and bruised shoulder ligaments – but they were painful. He had to face a medical before taking part but everything was okay; he was ready for what was now a round of the Motor Cycle News Masters championship.

Joey's chances were strengthened by the absence of Rob McElnea, his old adversary from the previous year, who had decided to compete instead in the Austrian Grand Prix. But Mick Grant was there again and Rex Whyte turned up to have a look at the race with a view to what his plans might be for the TT, which was just around the corner.

The MCN Masters Superbike race turned out to be something of an anticlimax. Although Joey won, and won easily, the fact that

Marshall had fallen off took a lot of the satisfaction out of Joey's success; Mick Grant was another who fell by the wayside. Dunlop finished winner by nine seconds over Steve Parrish but he wasn't over-enthusiastic about the performance. His machine had misfired throughout the race and his visor – as was the case with Marshall – had steamed up giving him plenty of trouble.

Later in the day Joey took out the new 250cc bike which Honda had given him but this let him down and he had to stop at Coleraine on the first lap. Altogether not a very exciting day for Dunlop fans – just that one hollow victory in the superbike event. Joey's build up for the TT was not what he would have liked it to be.

Joey's fans always expected the best from him and I suppose you could say they felt a bit let down after that North West performance. I said at the time the fault was not Joey's even though he must have been still suffering a hangover from that Mondello Park crash. The core of the problem was that Honda had failed to supply him with a machine which suited the occasion and as a result it was Honda, not Joey, who had disappointed the faithful.

So it was on to the TT. Could Joey add another win to that of the previous year, even though the Honda appeared to be vulnerable? We hadn't long to wait. Mick Grant came up with the fastest lap in Formula One practice with a speed of 112.55mph but Joey sneaked into the picture in the final practice session with a speed of 107.93 mph; Grant was eventually fifth on 102.80mph. This was an important morale booster for Joey. As he said shortly before the race on Saturday 2 June: 'Practice is one thing. Racing is another. The Honda is going well after the misfiring at the North West for we have had a new exhaust system fitted and I am hopeful I can win for the second year in a row. Last night, although I was fastest in the official practice, I was having a quiet evening and just 'bedding in' the bike.'

The 'bedding in' certainly paid off – in fact it took everyone else in the race the following day by surprise – for Joey slammed his way to yet another epic victory despite the fact that he had to stop an incredible four times before he took the chequered flag. The Honda once again was misbehaving but Dunlop was always a man known for his determination and an unerring ability to get the most from his machine. He kept going despite all the problems to win by 20 seconds from Marshall with Tony Rutter in third place. In the process Joey still managed to set a lap record of 115.89mph. What a man!

Two of Dunlop's four stops were for fuel which was par for the course but he also halted twice 'out in the country'. On one occasion at Union Mills he actually kicked the bike in frustration. He had noticed that an exhaust was broken. He said afterwards: 'I had a job getting the bike away again. In fact two young lads offered to come and assist me but I waved them away and started it on my own. I could have gone harder but for all this trouble.' This exhaust problem meant that when Joey came in for his second pit stop he had to change the back wheel and this cost him further ground.

There was no hint of these troubles at the start of the race. Joey stormed into an immediate lead and by Ballacraine, seven miles out on the first lap, he was five seconds ahead of Marshall who was tied with Suzuki's McElnea. Ten miles further, at Ballaugh, Dunlop had increased his advantage to eleven seconds. Approaching Ballaugh, McElnea, who earlier in the week had set an unofficial new outright TT lap record of 116.45mph, had caught right up on the road with Grant, whose 750cc Suzuki had been rebuilt only just in time for the 2pm start.

Leading on the roads, a determined Dunlop was on his best form and, as he hammered into lap two and headed for Quarter Bridge, he was only just seconds outside his own lap record set the previous year on the bigger 850cc Honda. Relentlessly Joey pressed on. His 25 second first lap lead was extended to 32 seconds at Ballacraine on lap two. As Dunlop, who was clocked at 152mph in the speed-trap, passed the Highlander pub he was relieved to hear that his arch rival Grant was out. The Suzuki gearbox had expired on the Mountain Mile. Joey was a huge 1½ minutes clear on corrected time when he stopped to refuel. Marshall lost time in a bungled

37 second pit stop during which petrol spewed all over the Honda and a loose exhaust was tightened up.

Then, on lap three, the problems started for Joey. It was that dreaded misfire. So bad in fact that his massive lead disappeared and Marshall claimed a five second advantage over Joey with McElnea also in the picture. But Joey Dunlop was never a rider to let the mere detail of a misfiring engine slow him down. He soon cut back Marshall's five second lead and regained a two second advantage at the Bungalow on lap three.

Joey had pulled up to a 25.8 second advantage at the end of lap four but then, incredibly, more problems. He was forced to make a 57 second pit stop to refuel and change the rear wheel. With Marshall refuelling immediately after him in only six seconds, Roger was expected to be in the lead when they reached the Manx Radio commentary point at Ballacraine. While Joey remained ahead on the road, Marshall was 24 seconds ahead on corrected time. So Joey had it all to do all over again. In the high speed Ballacraine–Ballaugh trip, Dunlop gained eight seconds. It was building up into a tremendous last lap battle between the two Honda stars. By Ramsey, Marshall's lead was down to 11 seconds and at the Bungalow it was only five.

Could Joey do it? Well his fans had no doubts and as Joey stormed into that final vital lap with all guns blazing he was cheered on by his supporters waving a white battery of programmes which rivalled any ticker-tape reception on Broadway. It was Joey all the way and although he was signalled to slow down at the Gooseneck he still managed to have enough in hand to set a new lap record.

That was win number one in TT week and now he was ready for the Senior on the Monday. This was a strange sort of race, ending in controversy when Joey stopped on the last lap while leading by 45 seconds from McElnea. The official reason for Dunlop's stoppage was that the Honda had broken a crankshaft. But afterwards there were rumours that Joey had run out of petrol after gambling on that dramatic last lap. This view was reinforced by the fact that the Honda team were on the line at the end of the fifth lap – one from the finish – waiting to 'top Joey up' only to see Joey fly on through.

There was still confusion the following day about what had actually happened. Davy Wood told me: 'There definitely was petrol left in the tank when Joey's bike was wheeled in by the ACU organisers. The figure given to me was 5.2 litres and this would have been sufficient to see him home.

'He certainly didn't run out of fuel but it was a strange race to say the least. Joey came in at the end of the second lap to refuel as scheduled but we were surprised when he came in again after the next lap. It appears he became disoriented because of the sun in his visor making it impossible for him to see any type of signal.

'The real problem for Dunlop, unknown to us, was a broken oil seal along the gearbox,' continued Davy. 'This caused the engine to cease breaking the crankshaft. It was unfortunate to say the least for he had the race won.'

Joey went out again for the 250cc race and, believe it or not, he did run out of petrol this time – again on the last lap. Nine seconds behind Graeme McGregor Joey retired at the Verandah with 10 of the 226 miles to go.

On then to the Classic, the big race of the week after the Formula One. This took place on the Friday and Joey had high hopes that he would end TT week with a spectacular victory. Alas, for his supporters, it was not to be. He was beaten by 14.2 seconds by the previous year's winner McElnea, who averaged a record-breaking 116.12mph over the six laps. Grant, on a Suzuki, finished third more than a minute behind Dunlop.

It would have been nice for Joey to have won another TT that week but really his thoughts were firmly fixed on the next round of the World Formula One championship in Holland. Of course, this was the race which saw the so-called feud between Joey and Marshall boil up over Roger's refuelling stop. Whatever the truth, Joey felt that it cost him the race. Up until then Joey and Marshall had been neck and neck leading the field and it looked as though they would take the race down to the wire. Then came that controversial refuel.

Years later, as we know, Marshall denied not cutting his engine but it is interesting to reflect on what Barry Symmons said at the time: 'The Dutch TT affair appears to be a running sore,' he said. 'But I can tell you there was nothing in the regulations that tell you a rider had to stop his engine when refuelling. Despite this I pointed out that Honda riders should stop their engines and Dunlop did this. I wasn't in the pits at the time but unfortunately Marshall didn't cut his engine. In my view he only gained 1.5 seconds on Dunlop. At the finish Joey was 17 seconds behind Roger so it is nonsense to say the pit stop cost Joey the race.

'In addition it should be pointed out that there was a protest lodged by a Dutch rider objecting to Roger's pit stop. Had this protest come four minutes earlier, the probability is that Roger would have been ruled out under FIM regulations. I can just imagine the reaction there would have been in Ulster had this happened to Dunlop. You know it is completely wrong to suggest, as some people have, that we would like Marshall to win the title this year. You can take it from me that Dunlop's machine is every bit as competitive as Marshall's. In fact I would say it is a better bike but try convincing others of that.'

So that was Barry's view, but the whole scenario was a strange one to say the least.

The next round was in July at Vila Real in Portugal, a place renowned for its heat. Joey struck the first blow when, after a sedate opening to practice, he smashed Wayne Gardner's two-year-old lap record. He finished in front of Marshall, who was also on form, and the stage seemed to be set once again for a marvellous head to head between the Honda pair. While Joey looked good on the bike it was obvious to most onlookers that he was going to have some very serious problems with the heat during the 100 mile race. He did only 10 consecutive laps in practice and confessed afterwards to being exhausted. 'I don't know what it's going to be like tomorrow. But I will give it everything I have got,' he said.

As it turned out the heat did get to Joey. After finishing second to Marshall, he collapsed as soon as he got off his bike. His legs buckled underneath him when he tried to dismount and he was taken to a medical unit where he was detained for half an hour. Speaking after his recovery he said: 'Towards the end of the race I had it in my mind that I might not actually finish but I was determined to collect those championship points. It was like an oven out there.'

The 25-lap race, which was started late in the evening to avoid as much sunshine as possible, looked like being a classic. Both Dunlop and Marshall, who were tied on 27 points for the championship prior to this third round, were desperately anxious to win. On the seventh lap Dunlop set a new lap record with an astonishing time of 2 minutes 43.58 seconds which was almost five seconds faster than the existing record of Gardner. Marshall came in for fuel at the end of lap 13 and, two laps later, Dunlop was also into the pits. Even at that early stage it was becoming obvious that something was wrong with Joey.

As the race entered its final stages Joey continued to fall adrift of Marshall, who was looking more and more like the winner. The time separation at the end of the hundred-miler was 1 minute 7 seconds, which bore no relationship to the excitement that had been provided by the two men at the earlier stages of the race. It was heat that beat Joey and nothing else.

The next round of the championship was once again over Joey's favourite circuit, Dundrod. But with the handling of his Honda still leaving a lot to be desired and no one quite sure whether or not he would need to refuel, Dunlop must have had a head full of doubts on the eve of the race. Yet such was his sheer class that everyone had faith in him to overcome these problems and to set the world championship alight by scoring a vital win. Throughout practice there had been an atmosphere between Joey and the rest of the Honda camp over the handling of the bike. (At one point he told me that he wouldn't be *riding* the bike, but simply *hanging on*.) You could almost cut it with a knife, but through it all Joey consistently managed to lap at high speeds and the same could be said for Marshall. At the end of the day it was Joey who managed to get pole position as he topped the leaderboard at 117.17mph.

In addition no one appeared to be quite sure about the refuelling plans for the race. The previous year there had been similar doubt – as it turned out Joey rode straight through, but it was wet then and as the roads were now dry it was thought he and Marshall might have to pull in. But that was fraught with problems. It was feared that the prospect of both men in their pits at the same time in the latter stages of the race would set fire to an already highly volatile situation.

Fortunately for the Honda camp, one moment of humour relieved the tension. During one of the practice evenings, Roger pulled into tell Barry Symmons that a goat was running down the track.

'A goat?' said the usually stoic Symmons.

'Yes,' repeated an agitated Marshall. 'A goat, I saw it myself.'

Symmons obviously felt that Marshall was imagining things but Roger eventually convinced both Barry and the rest of us who were listening at the time that in fact someone's goat had escaped from a nearby farm and had been running down the track. 'I tried to pass it at least a dozen times but it kept running across the course,' Roger said. 'I was lucky I didn't hit it. I don't know what would have happened.' No one would confess to owning or knowing anything about the goat. The unfortunate animal disappeared and nothing was heard of it again. A figment of Roger's imagination? I don't think so. Years later he was still adamant that there had been a goat on the Ulster Grand Prix course – for the only time anyone of us can remember.

The race itself was heart-stopping stuff all the way. By the end of it all Joey came out in front – but not without a great deal of controversy and the drama of Marshall ordering Symmons to protest after that last lap incident. As Dunlop crossed the finishing line about three seconds ahead of Marshall he raised his fist in a victory salute but shortly afterwards the pit area erupted when Marshall threw down his Honda and dashed to Symmons to tell him he wanted a protest lodged – and quickly. Marshall wouldn't say at the time what the protest was about and neither would Symmons.

Joey later told me his story of what happened on that dramatic last lap. 'Marshall took the lead at the end of the Flying Kilometre,' he said. 'I was just behind him and getting my chance to get past. It came at Irwin's Bend where I squeezed past Roger but I didn't touch him. After that I went clear and was never headed again.'

Marshall wouldn't say anything about the incident but Symmons commented: 'You can't protest about alleged dangerous riding. I have told Roger this but he is not very happy about it. Still, there is nothing in the rules to cover this situation and needless to say I am embarrassed by the whole affair.'

The race was a memorable one throughout with Marshall making the early pace. Surprisingly, Grant split the Honda riders on the Suzuki which meant that Dunlop was third. For the first four laps it was Marshall, Grant and Dunlop with literally nothing between them. Then Joey made his move on lap five and closed up on Grant to take second place. It looked as if he would move into the lead but Marshall held on as Grant counterattacked and pressed Joey for second spot. Dunlop and Marshall were now disputing the lead, leaving Grant further and further behind and it was later learned that Grant had lost his exhaust pipe.

The battle between Marshall and Dunlop raged on with speeds gradually climbing before Dunlop set the fastest lap of the day at 117.74mph on lap ten. Marshall also had a high speed of 117.53mph and it was anybody's guess who would take the flag. Then came that dramatic last lap. All heads in the grandstand turned towards Quarry Bends, anxiously waiting for the riders to come into view. The programmes went up. It was Joey nearly three seconds ahead of Marshall.

There had been no refuelling required, contrary to expectations, and Dunlop said afterwards: 'I was conserving the fuel in my tank and that's why I didn't make my move until late in the race. I didn't want to take the chance of losing it in the pits.'

The Ulster Grand Prix of 1984 made history in that Joey became the fastest rider in the race since it was launched in 1922. He became the first rider to lap the course at over 120mph and finished it with a lap record of 120.62mph. Marshall also lapped at over 120mph in an epic 500cc race which saw Dunlop win from Grant and Marshall.

Joey had a treble at the meeting, equalling the record of Tom Herron who achieved a similar feat in 1978 and John Williams in 1973. The treble also gave Dunlop eight wins at the Ulster Grand Prix, another record. This put him one ahead of Dubliner Stanley Woods, who scored all his successes over the Clady course. Mike Hailwood, Giacomo Agostini and Ray McCullough were the other joint winners with Joey.

In addition to his eight Ulster Grand Prix successes, Dunlop also won the Killinchy 150 15 times since his first victory in 1976. This was a truly remarkable record which in due course made him king of the Dundrod circuit. Joey's 1984 performance was, to my mind, the best I ever saw from him over the Dundrod circuit and I have been watching the Ulster Grand Prix for 30 years.

Back to the championship and the Ulster result meant that Joey and Marshall were level at the top with one round to go – at Zolder in Belgium. Joey, with a wry grin, told me: 'That round is going to be really worth seeing, isn't it?' This race would decide whether or not Joey would hold on to the title which he had gained at the Ulster Grand Prix two years earlier.

The effect this race had on the Ulster folk was electric. Everywhere I went people were asking me 'Will Joey do it?' and I replied 'Of course he will.' It was like the old days of a world title fight in the King's Hall in Belfast when people discussed in bars and elsewhere who they thought was going to win. Joey had grabbed the public's imagination and all the talk of a dispute with Marshall was fuel to the fire.

The race, when it did come, was something of an anticlimax but at the end of the day it was Joey who won the title. Before the race started Marshall shook hands with Dunlop, an obvious gesture following the row which had erupted at the Ulster. Then, after the race, in which Marshall was forced to retire, he came in to see Joey in his caravan and warmly congratulated him on winning the title for the third time.

After having been eighth fastest in practice, Joey looked to have a poor chance of winning but the wet weather which had plagued the practice session dried up on race day and Dunlop was able to get to grips with the tight Belgian track. He and Marshall dominated the race from the start and Joey was ahead when Marshall retired on the 14th of the 36 laps with a broken head gasket.

After 26 laps there was slight controversy when Dunlop pulled into the pits for refuelling and found he was blocked by another rider. Grant was also in the pit at the same time and he had similar problems. In fact it looked as though he was getting in the way of Dunlop at one stage. As a result, Joey lost a lot of ground which he made up rapidly, but at the finish the best he could do was second place to Dutch rider Mila Pagic, who was riding a Kawasaki. Third place went to Roger Burnett on a Ducati.

And suddenly the 1984 season was all over. Joey was champion again. He had achieved a third consecutive championship. But for Joey, like so many successful sportsmen, it was the actual titles that mattered. He had scant regard for trophies won as Mervyn White, secretary of the North West 200, discovered when seeking the return of a North West silver cup at the end of that year.

'Joey was building a new bungalow and when I arrived he was up to his eyes in sand and cement,' said Mervyn. 'I mentioned the trophy to him and he nodded towards his children who were play-ing in the sand alongside him. To my horror they were using the cup to make sand castles! That was Joey.'

CHAPTER 10

SINKING AT STRANGFORD LOUGH

The night of 25 May 1985 came close to rivalling the Titanic disaster in the minds of Joey Dunlop fans, for it was on that date that Joey was nearly lost to the watery bowels of Strangford Lough in Co Down.

Ever since 1980, when he won that memorable Classic race in the Isle of Man, Joey had regarded travelling to the Isle of Man in the fishing boat Tornamona as a superstitious act. If the boat had been lucky for him in 1980 then it would be lucky to him forever more. That's the way he looked at it.

As we have discovered, Joey was not a conventional world champion. The public at large believed that riders of Dunlop's calibre travelled to race meetings in style – certainly not in the cramped conditions of a hired fishing boat. But that's the way it was in those days for Joey and nobody thought any the less of him for using this mode of transport.

So on a fateful Saturday night, a week before the TT, Joey and his brother Robert, along with 10 others, set sail as normal from Portaferry harbour on the 'lucky' Tornamona. They weren't to know what lay ahead of them . . .

Also on board were a number of bikes which were going to the TT, not all of them accompanied by their respective riders. One of the bikes which should have been on board was that belonging to

Brian Reid and it was this omission which caused all the problems and which nearly led to Dunlop and his co-passengers drowning in the murky depths of the lough.

All went well at first as the riders set sail and Joey recalled that he was making sausages, bacon and egg as a fry up for the rest of the lads. They were in good spirits and why not, for Dunlop certainly fancied his chances for the treble at that year's TT races. He was world champion and he was going for broke.

Then, as the boat neared the open sea the Tornamona received a call from the quayside at Portaferry. A lorry had driven up and on it was Brian Reid's bike. The call was to bring the boat back again to pick up Reid's machine. The skipper answered the call and they all agreed that they should return to the quayside.

It was to be the worst move they made . . .

The Tornamona turned round, reached harbour and eventually loaded Reid's bike on board – Reid himself was flying to the Isle of Man – and set sail again. This time, however, the tide had turned against them and by the time they got to the exit to the lough, about three miles away, the seas were swelling. The boat was tossed and turned on the high swell and eventually crashed against the rocks before being torn apart.

Dunlop and the others, who had gone to bed in the hope of grabbing some sleep, thought they were dreaming. Joey gave his version of what happened next in his own matter-of-fact way. 'I had just dozed off and I was wakened by a loud crash then the lights went out,' he said. 'We got up and looked over the side and saw the boat had struck the rocks. We managed to free the dinghies and were just clear of the boat when she sank. One of my friends had to be coaxed into the life rafts as he was convinced this was the end of him and he was going to stay on the boat.'

When Joey and the others were eventually rescued and stood shivering on the quayside, Joey explained to gathering reporters that he had been travelling to the Isle of Man since 1980 on the Tornamona because he thought it was lucky for him. A coastguard spokesman confirmed later that he had received a distress call from the boat at 17 minutes past midnight saying it was taking in water fast and was sinking.

Portaferry lifeboat was launched immediately but because of the rough seas a stronger offshore vessel from Donagadee, Co Down – a similar type to that which saved passengers from the ill-fated Princess Victoria in the North Channel in 1953 – was called out as back-up. Coastguard rescue parties from nearby Ardglass and Portaferry were mobilised and an RAF helicopter equipped with high density 'night sun' lighting was called in from Aldergrove, near Belfast airport.

Twenty one minutes after the original 'mayday' call the skipper of the Tornamona radioed the coastguard again to tell rescuers that water had reached their batteries and, as they were losing communication, they would be abandoning ship. The 12 men took to the life rafts and fired flares to draw attention to themselves. Thirty seven minutes after the drama began Portaferry lifeboat pinpointed the rafts and took them in towards shore. The men were then transferred to a larger boat helping in the rescue operation and all were landed safely in Portaferry at 1.23am on the Sunday morning.

By this time the Tornamona, with its precious cargo of finely-tuned powerful motorcycles and expensive parts, had disappeared, leaving Joey and his pals gazing forlornly at the murky depths. How were these bikes to be recovered? Brian Reid recalled the tale to me.

He said: 'My memory was that the Cookstown 100 road race took place on the Saturday but the normal ferry for the Isle of Man left on the Friday, so if you wanted to go to the Cookstown you couldn't get the ferry from Belfast. We had organised to do the Cookstown with one bike and then send it along with Joey in the fishing boat to the Isle of Man. Joey's own bikes had already gone to the island.

'So we went to the Cookstown and it poured. I felt as if I was getting the 'flu or something and, as the bike was brand new, I thought I would rather not go out on it on a dirty day not feeling well. I decided to pack up and go home early and get ready to go to the Isle of Man, so I didn't race that day at all.

'Billy McKinstry, an auto electrician who was sponsoring Sam McClements at that time, said he would take my bike down to the fishing boat along with Sam's and would collect it later that evening.

'All the rest of my bikes were away at the Isle of Man. They had gone on the ferry on the Friday. Because I wasn't feeling well Billy said that he would take my bike down with the bike belonging to Sam McClements.

'Dunlop and the boys had told me that the bike had to be at Portaferry by 11pm that night as that was the time at which they were leaving. So McKinstry arrived at my home in Dromore, Co Down to pick up my bike and he wasn't in any particular hurry because it was a long way off until 11pm. We loaded the bike up had a bit of a chat and as far as I was concerned that was the end of it.

'Then at about three or four o'clock in the morning I was woken out of my sleep by another rider, Noel Hudson, who had rung to say that the boat had sunk. I thought 'boat . . .? what boat . . .? what are you talking about?' So he gave me the number of the local police station at Portaferry. I rang them and they said that the boat had sunk and all the bikes were down but that everybody had been rescued from the boat.

'What had actually happened was that Billy had driven down to Portaferry with the two bikes but when he got there the boat had gone so he was about to turn and come back home again when somebody in a boat shouted up: "Are you looking for the fishing boat?" Billy said he was, so they said: "Well they have just left only about 10 minutes ago, do you want me to radio them and ask them to come back?"

'Billy said that would be a great help. So they radioed the fishing boat. The Tornamona turned and came back and they loaded the two bikes on to the boat. And seemingly they wasted so much time doing this that they missed the tide and when they went back out again the tide was against them and they were making no ground. Instead of going forward, they were going sideways and they ran on to the rocks. They shouldn't have turned back, they should have just kept on going.

'Needless to say I never slept the rest of the night after that phone call and as soon as it came to eight o'clock I was on the phone ringing round several people I knew to try and organise divers. The divers were keen to get going, just to see the bikes and get them up. As soon as I arrived at Portaferry all these men were there ready to go down to help me get my bike but the people who owned the boat wouldn't let them dive because of salvage law. Apparently if you dive into a boat and you are the first one there you actually own the salvage so I think they were afraid the divers would claim the boat. But these guys weren't interested in that, they just wanted to dive for my bike.

'They were diving all day and as I stood there watching bikes coming up I became more despondent for none of them was ever mine. It was getting frustrating. Eventually they had to leave it and it was the following day before my bike was raised to the surface.'

Meanwhile, Joey had gone home to Ballymoney but news of the sinking had spread and the media wanted to hear Joey's story. My good friend Harold Crooks, who at that time was representing Downtown Radio, Ulster's best known commercial radio station, was one of those seeking an interview. He went to see Joey in his mobile home in Ballymoney but when he got there Joey had other ideas.

'Sorry Harold,' he said. 'I'm dashing down to Portaferry to see if I can help the boys rescue their bikes.'

'I won't be a minute,' insisted Harold. 'Just a quick interview. Besides the television people are coming as well.'

But Joey would have none of it. He said that in a few minutes he would be finishing his lunch and then getting into his Ford Sierra and heading down to Portaferry. 'I don't care where your television people go,' he added.

At this stage the TV people did arrive and persuaded Joey to let them follow him to Portaferry. So Joey set off and the TV people set out after him. However, instead of heading towards Portaferry, Joey headed into the town of Ballymoney with the TV people hot on his tail. In and out of every street went Joey until eventually the TV people caught up with him and asked him where he was going. To which Joey gave the classic reply: 'Well I'm hoping to find a shop open so I can get a packet of fags!'

Being rescued from a watery grave is, you will agree, not the best preparation for the Isle of Man TT races. But Joey Dunlop had a personality which was unique. Nowadays, you would say he was totally focused. In those days he was just described as one who lived wearing blinkers or was 'single minded'. No matter what way you looked at it Joey was able to block out the trauma of what he had been through. In later years no doubt, those having experienced a similar close call with death would have gone straight to their stress counsellors.

Lifeboat man Gabriel Rogers praised the courage of the 12 men on the Tornamona, saying they had kept their cool throughout the terrifying ordeal and had done everything they had been told by the rescue crew. 'They all remained calm and acted in a responsible manner,' he said. 'The reason for this could be because they are used to facing danger when they ride their bikes.' Chillingly, he continued: 'If the conditions had been just a little worse Northern Ireland could well have lost one of its world champions. There is no doubt they were all very shaken with the experience and Joey said afterwards that he had never been so glad to see anything as he was to see our lifeboat.'

But once on the safety of land the matter was closed for Joey. As far as he was concerned, the only therapy he knew was the scream from a high speed Honda as it belched down the Mountain at the Isle of Man. And that was where he was heading next. After having supervised the salvage operation which had lifted the bikes from the lough, Joey decided on the Monday it was time he was in the island.

Understandably, on this occasion, Joey left by air, saying at the time: 'I'll never travel by sea again. I am trying to get a flight now to see if I can get a bit of TT practice in this evening.' Recalling the drama for the final time he continued: 'I am just about getting over it. It's not something I want to go through ever again. It's not every day you wake up and find water pouring in on top of you at a depth of about two feet. We thought we were near ourselves [the end] but we managed to get the dinghies over the side and get into them. Once we were away from the boat we knew we were safe and that help was on the way.'

Joey put the whole affair behind him when he reached the Isle of Man and having set the fastest lap in practice he was once again hot favourite for the Formula One TT race which he was attempting to win for the third year in a row. In order to give himself as little time on his hands as possible before the start he went to bed early the night before and slept late.

Joey, as everybody knew, was a man who didn't like to have his thoughts interrupted just before a race was due to start. He found this irritating and he liked to arrive at the grid as late as possible. This was a habit he developed early in his career and it never left him. In fact, I remember on many occasions fellow riders and members of the Dunlop camp asking: 'Is Joey going to turn up at all?' But we always knew he would be there. He just didn't like walking about doing nothing.

Joey appeared to be very happy with his Formula One Honda that year and he had every reason to be, considering he had set the fastest laps in practice. Another man happy with his lot was Brian Reid, who was racing his new 500 Formula One Yamaha for the first time since it had been rescued from the deep.

On to race day, and with Dunlop favourite, everyone was expecting one of his vintage performances. And they weren't disappointed. He pulverised the opposition despite a last lap scare when the Honda began to misfire. He saw his chief rivals Marshall and Grant drop out but not before he had smashed the lap record with a speed of 116.43mph on the opening lap. Dunlop won by a staggering 5 minutes and 10 seconds from Tony Rutter and Steve Parrish.

Setting a scorching pace from the drop of the flag, at Ballacraine on the first lap he had taken the V4 Honda to a three second lead over Grant with Marshall, who was still Dunlop's Honda team-mate, a further two seconds down in third place. By the time they got to Ballaugh, Dunlop had extended his lead over Grant to 10 seconds. On the long climb up the Mountain for the first time it was still Dunlop. Astonishingly the 33-year-old reigning world champion had pulled out a further 20 seconds on Grant to lead by 30 seconds. Then the two-pronged Suzuki attack on Joey lost a prong when Graeme McGregor came a cropper at Greeba Castle. However, he was perfectly alright despite the spill.

With such a comfortable lead, Joey settled down to give the crowd a treat and he was in a steady rhythm from lap two. The third lap saw the pace slacken off slightly as a result of earlier fuel stops. Dunlop went round in 112.34mph while Marshall lapped at 111.95mph. Dunlop's lead was 40.4 seconds by that stage.

The fourth lap of the race saw Marshall quit while holding second place. Marshall's 1984 works Honda ground to a halt at the Mountain Box and, with Marshall out, Grant moved up into second place well over a minute behind Dunlop. It was a procession from then on as Joey claimed an easy victory.

That wasn't the end of TT week as far as Joey was concerned. He scored a treble at that 1985 meeting by winning the 250cc race and following up on the final day with victory in the Senior TT. This treble was the first achieved in the Isle of Man since Mike Hailwood had recorded two hat tricks in 1961 and 1967. It strengthened the argument that Joey Dunlop was one of the greats – not that anyone really doubted this at that time.

So it was one down with five more rounds to go for the Formula One TT World Championship, which that year was a six-round series. Joey had always been favourite for the Isle of Man round, but the tougher tests were to come on the Continent with the Dutch TT in June, followed by the 'hot house' Villa Real in Portugal and a new round in Barcelona. This would be followed by the Ulster Grand Prix where Joey was very much at home. If the title was still undecided by that stage, the final round was scheduled for Hockenheim in West Germany.

Joey had never won a Continental round of the world championship so he was more than a little nervous as he set off for the Dutch TT. The race was one of the toughest in Dunlop's chequered career.

Immediately before the start it poured with rain and only stopped just before the flag was lowered. That meant Dunlop's wet tyres would almost certainly wear out long before the end of the 25 lap race. His rear wet tyre wore away in chunks and after his refuelling stop he found a 31 second lead fast disappearing. Faring much better with tyres, Mick Grant was closing fast. With nine laps to go Dunlop was leading by eight seconds, the next lap it was six, the next it was down to a slender one.

From then to the end of the race little separated Dunlop and Grant, who didn't refuel. It was a desperate last lap with Grant levelling with Dunlop but never actually getting into the lead. Both survived wild last lap slides with Grant going onto the grass as Dunlop pressed home to win by three tenths of a second. What a finish! 'It was all very easy at the start,' reflected Joey. 'I was determined to pace myself better than last year. After the fuel stop though, it was tough. Even going for the finish, it was difficult. In fact I was lucky getting any power on at all.'

The next stage was Vila Real, where the oven-like heat had wrecked Dunlop's chances the previous year in that famous race with Marshall. But if Dunlop thought it was hot in 1984, then he had to think again in 1985 for the heat on that July afternoon was furnace-like. And at the end of the race once again Joey required resuscitation, his body lying prostrate on a stretcher. This was the picture which was indelibly left in everybody's mind, although there was a happier caption for this time Dunlop was the winner and not the runner up.

Brian Reid, who was leading the World Formula Two championship at that time, also rode at Vila Real that day and he could describe the conditions probably better than anyone. 'It was unbelievably hot,' he told me. 'This was a mountainous area so the extreme heat appeared to be trapped with nowhere to go. As a result it was stifling. I remember asking someone at the time and they told me that the temperature was round about 130 degrees. I didn't think you could live in those temperatures!

'I hadn't qualified all that well in practice for the Formula Two race and I remember my leathers were opened up a bit as I went to mount my bike on the starting line. The leathers weren't zipped right up to the top and it wasn't long before I found myself glad that this was the case. When I went to the line and was about to put the bike out of gear the flag dropped so I just had to go there and then. When I started racing I couldn't get the leathers zipped up because of the wind which was blowing in and I rode the whole race with my leathers half unzipped.

'At the end of the day it was probably a good thing for it kept the air circulating and enabled me to stay cool. The road temperature that day was 140 degrees and I recall Rex Whyte cracking open an egg and frying it on the pit wall which I found hard to believe at the time but it did happen.

'When I finished the race all the guys just gathered round and poured water over us. It was just so hot. Tony Rutter collapsed once the race was over. He stopped the bike and just fell down unconscious. Then I stripped off and dispensed with my leathers. So many people were lying round me I thought I was in a field hospital but I felt fine after I got that water thrown over me.

'Gary Padgett said he also felt good and we just jogged down the pit lane to prove a point. As for Joey, well his race was later on and he won, but after his race Joey also collapsed. I can still recall him lying unconscious with people pouring ice over him just to get him cooled off. These are scenes which you never really forget.

'There were so many people dehydrating and passing out. Some riders lasted only three or four laps and had to stop. Your head goes light in those conditions and I just drank gallons and gallons of water before the race started so that I could think straight.'

Not everybody could stay cool in the heat, however, and the big event ended in scenes more like a battlefield than a Formula One race. The race had seen a titanic fight between Dunlop and Graeme

McGregor but, as Dunlop crossed the line, a local Honda production champion, Manuel Joao, jumped the red lights out of the pit area and was knocked over by a bottle of water thrown by Barry Symmons. In the heat of the moment, Joao's mechanics were so angry that they attacked Symmons and tried to kick the daylights out of him!

In a hotel later that evening, Symmons asked Mick Grant's mechanic, Nigel Everett, why he hadn't got involved in the brawl. At which Everett quipped: 'I thought seven of them were enough for you Barry!'

Back to the race and with the Portuguese Honda still lying on the track where it had crashed after the bottle-throwing incident, third place man Grant crossed the line 49 seconds behind McGregor.

Because of the oppressive heat the start had been delayed until 6.30pm, but the race really came to the boil as Dunlop and McGregor continually swapped places. The outcome was in doubt until both the leaders stopped for petrol on lap 18. Topping up with three litres in five seconds Joey was soon out again and before long he had the race wrapped up. Honda had scored their third successive victory in Formula One. The positions in the championship after three rounds saw Joey leading on 45 points followed by Grant with 22 and Tony Rutter on 18.

Meanwhile, Reid was also throwing down a challenge for the Formula Two series so it looked as if there would be two Ulster riders on the World Championship rostrum at the end of 1985.

At Barcelona, Joey clinched the World Championship for the fourth year in a row only he didn't know this was the case at the time. He survived a sweltering struggle to score on his Honda and cruised home virtually unchallenged in a race which was overshadowed by a multiple crash.

An oil slick from Andy McGladdery's exploded Suzuki engine was the cause of an accident in which Tony Rutter and Graeme McGregor were the most seriously hurt. It happened on a 140mph right-hand bend between the start and the chicane on this torturous 2.3 mile circuit. Ray Swann, who ran over Rutter after Spaniard

Domingo Pares went down, escaped with extensive arm and leg bruising and Nat Wood, who was surprised to find himself in the front row at the start, was discharged with a broken collar bone and ankle. But Rutter was in a coma with serious head injuries and McGregor badly concussed as ambulances and police cars mingled with riders on the circuit. Local ace Juan Garraga was also injured in the crash.

Joey, who had taken over the lead from McGregor and Garraga on the 12th of the 42 laps said: 'I saw oil and straw all over the road as I came up the hill. I ran straight through it. My bike didn't seem to slide at all but it was obvious that other people had problems. If Garraga and McGladdery hadn't crashed they would have given me a lot of trouble.'

The accident on lap 14 put paid to what had promised to be an exciting scrap with Garraga and fellow Spaniard Paul Ramon giving McGregor and Dunlop a hard time at the front. At the finish Joey won by 42.57 seconds from unknown German Dieter Rechtenbach, with Dutchman Kees Van Der Endt third.

Reid also won his Formula Two contest so it looked as though the two Ulster riders were poised to clinch the championships at the Ulster Grand Prix. This was certainly the case with Reid, but shortly after the Barcelona meeting Dunlop received word that the always doubtful final round in the World Formula One Series, in Belgium, had been cancelled due to lack of interest from the promoters. (Many Europeans had never regarded the F1 title as anything more than a second division series.) This meant that Joey was already champion after Barcelona and didn't need to ride in the remaining two rounds at the Ulster and in Germany.

It took a lot of the excitement out of the championship but at the same time it ensured that Joey was the title holder for the fourth year in a row. So there was no pressure on Joey as he moved on to the Ulster and he won this race looking round as they say. Joey even had time to stop and refuel before beating the Suzuki pair of McGregor and Grant. He quipped after his win: 'I had to refuel in every one of the rounds. At least I was consistent.'

Unbelievably, in view of the atrocious practice weather, the Ulster was run in hot temperatures and Dunlop looked as though he had just come in from the desert when he finished. 'I really enjoyed this race,' he said. 'I knew the Suzukis weren't going to stop to refuel so that's why I tried for a big lead early on. It paid off and I was able to come in and refuel any time I pleased. I am now looking forward to winning the final race in West Germany.'

The day didn't end so successfully for Brian Reid. Although Brian clinched the World Formula Two Championship for the first time, within half an hour he was being helicoptered to hospital with a broken thigh after crashing in the 250cc race which followed. His sponsor Mick Mooney commented: 'My heart sank when I saw that he hadn't come round for the fifth lap. It just shows you what can happen in sport at this level. We had planned all sorts of celebrations. Now they must wait!'

Although Reid and Dunlop had been racing together for a number of years it wasn't until they travelled to Portugal to receive their 1985 gold medals that they really got to know each other. But their meeting got off to a curious start.

Reid said: 'We went to the FIM Congress and we were staying in the same hotel. I had flown there independently so I was waiting for the coach to take me to the Congress that night to receive my gold medal. As I was standing outside the coach waiting to board, I looked up and saw Joey Dunlop. He walked my way and then he just walked on past as though he hadn't seen me! I thought to myself, 'My god, I came the whole way to Portugal where there are only two Irish riders and he doesn't even speak to me.' It was then that I realised that Joey was deep in thought and miles away when the incident happened. When we got on the coach he was the total opposite. He sat down and we chatted away.

'After receiving our medals at the Congress we went back to the hotel and chatted again and then we decided to sit in the bar. That was the first time I really got to know Joey and I spent the night talking to him until four o'clock in the morning. It showed me that once he had loosened up he was a great man to be with.'

Being world road racing champion might have been enough for some people but Joey still had another goal during that golden summer of 1985. Joey had always wanted to dispute the contention, in some people's minds at least, that he wasn't a top class short circuit rider. One of the riders he had set his sights on beating was England's Alan Carter, who had been showing such tremendous form in the World 250cc Championship.

At the Killinchy Club meeting in September 1985 in Kirkistown, Joey eventually achieved his ambition. A huge crowd had come out to see Carter and Joey in action. Carter was the undisputed king of his class in England and had finished seventh in the World Championship Grand Prix series that year. However, Joey was no respecter of reputations and although he felt he had a tougher job than usual before his home crowd, he soon got to grips with a race that had everything.

Carter led for the first two laps with Dunlop poised in second place then Joey moved ahead on lap three. Joey clung on but, with two laps to go, he ran into trouble at the chicane. As the riders screeched through the starting area for the last lap Dunlop was about five yards behind the flying Englishman and it looked at this stage as if he had lost out. But we reckoned without his fighting spirit and at the bend at Colonial One, Joey outbraked Carter to slip into the lead again and hold on to the finishing line, where he only had the width of the bike to spare at the chequered flag. 'That's a race I always wanted to win,' said Joey with a wink. 'I reckon it proved a point.'

In October Joey went on to make it a clean sweep of six out of six in the world championship by winning the final Formula One round in Hockenheim. Joey was unbeatable on the 750 Honda, but the most amazing gamble of the race was pulled off by Swede Anders Andersson on his GSR Suzuki. Anderson hung on for second place without a pit stop during the 100 mile race, a feat which perplexed the British Suzuki riders, all of whom had to make pit calls.

Not so lucky was German Ernst Gschwender, who pressed Joey

hard over the first 14 laps and took a 12 second lead after Dunlop's fuel stop on lap 15. He was losing two seconds a lap to the recovering Dunlop when he, too, pulled in to re-fuel on lap 18. Still, he had the chance of third place thanks to a quick pit stop, until the last lap when his petrol tank split.

Also in action that day – but in a different race – was a rider who was to cause a dramatic shift in Joey's fortunes. Belgian Stephan Mertens won the 250 Euro race on the same card. Four years later at Brands Hatch he crashed into Dunlop and almost ended Joey's career . . . but that was still a long way off.

The year 1985 had gone wonderfully well for Joey and fittingly there was icing on the cake for the popular Ulsterman. He was already the Motor Cycle News 'Man Of The Year' but it soon became clear that Ulster's greatest motorcycle road racer would receive a higher accolade.

At the end of December in the New Year's Honours List the 33-year-old 'People's Champion' was awarded an MBE for his services to motorcycling. For Dunlop the award ended a triumphant year in which he had escaped tragedy in a boating accident in May and gone on weeks later to become only the second rider in history to win three TT races in one week; not to mention a fourth consecutive world championship.

The celebrations had started and looked like continuing well into 1986.

CHAPTER 11

TROUBLE AT HONDA

B y the time 1986 came along, Joey Dunlop's position at the pinnacle of motorcycle road racing looked impregnable. He had won the world championship for the fourth year in a row, he was riding on the best possible machinery, and he also knew that he had the opposition licked. Unless there were some surprise packages in the 1986 season, Joey looked certain to retain his title not only that year but in the foreseeable future.

But the 'foreseeable future' can be totally unpredictable as we all know. Who would have thought in early 1986 that by the end of the year Honda Britain, the Rothmans supported team, would be no more; Barry Symmons, the long time team manager would be looking for another job and Joey Dunlop's career itself would be balanced precariously on a knife-edge?

Looking further ahead, who could have predicted that in 1987 Joey would lose his title and would never regain it? And who would have dared say that by the time 1989 came around Joey's very future would be threatened by injuries received in a horrific crash at Brands Hatch in the spring of that year?

All of that, however, was ahead of Dunlop as he prepared for 1986 and another tour de force. He had been set up with the best possible bike. A new Formula One Honda had been flown in from Japan and Joey was the team leader along with Roger Marshall and

Roger Burnett. The difference was that Joey would ride the Formula One bike in all the world championship rounds while Marshall and Burnett would compete on their machines in the British championship. This seemed a neat picture with Honda obviously giving priority to their number one man Dunlop.

The 1986 world championship series started unusually early. Joey had to begin the defence of his title at Misano in Italy in April. It was an unfortunate start to stay the least. In fact it was downright frustrating. The Rothmans 740cc Honda ran out of fuel on the very last lap when Joey was challenging for the lead. The four times world champion had been battling at the front when he had to make a lengthy refuelling stop which cost him 27 seconds on the leading bunch. During the ensuing 25 laps he fought magnificently to reel in his main rivals and was just about to overtake the eventual winner, Italian Marco Lucchinelli, when his Honda spluttered to a halt.

Lucchinelli went on to grab the 15 points for first place ahead of Sweden's Anders Andersson with Australian rider Rob Phillis finishing in third place.

So as far as Joey was concerned this was a non-event but it was soon to get better – much better.

Dunlop's son Richard was due to be born the weekend before the North West 200 in early May; at the same time Joey was expected to ride in the second round of the World Formula One championship in Hockenheim, West Germany. It turned out to be a happy occasion on both counts for Joey's wife Linda gave birth to the newest Dunlop on the Saturday, and the following day Joey celebrated by romping to an eight second victory over Suzuki rider Paul Iddon at Hockenheim.

Joey's preparation for the North West 200 couldn't have started on a better note. Apart from the opening two laps he commanded the German race and had built up a 20 second lead by the time he pitted for fuel on lap 16.

Iddon's ability on his works Suzuki to go the full distance without a stop meant that he actually took the lead on lap 16 and held it until lap 19 when Joey resumed control and pulled out his winning margin. In the early stages of the race Joey had battled with the German Suzuki star Ernst Gschwender but on the third lap the German's machine blew up in a big way leaving Dunlop unchallenged until the fuel stop.

So Joey took the 15 points, Iddon had 12 and that man Andersson, with the benefit of a second place at Misano, scored 10 valuable points to maintain his interest in the series.

Next up was the North West 200 which was Joey's favourite dish at this stage in his career. However, in 1986 he had to make an unusual preparation for this international meeting. The reason was that, as a new father, he had to look after the household chores or at least make an attempt to do so! 'I'm in a bit of a mix up at the minute, taking the children to school and visiting Linda in hospital and I haven't had time to even look at the course,' he told me as he jetted between hospital and North West 200. It was certainly an unusual preparation for Dunlop whom you just couldn't imagine involving himself in domesticity.

However, despite the changes at home Joey was still the coolest customer on the block when it came to practising for the North West. He had three machines for the meeting – the world championship F1 Honda, the 500cc and the 250cc. He told me at the time he was more than pleased with the way the new F1 had been performing but he added: 'We will not really know its potential until the North West. This will provide its sternest test.'

The main opposition was again Roger Marshall who was riding the F1 Honda on which Joey had won the championship in previous years, so it looked again as though it would be Marshall versus Dunlop in the Superbike races. Unfortunately from the spectators' point of view, or perhaps fortunately from Joey's angle, Rob McElnea, who had been involved in a real cracking finish with Dunlop the previous year and who had forced Joey to set up a new course record at 120.55mph, was missing.

I asked Joey at the time if the absence of McElnea made any difference to him. 'Not really,' he told me. 'But obviously a rider of his

class makes you go all out. This time I feel the big danger man will
be Roger and we will know more about that on the day.'

As it turned out the race was a total anticlimax. Marshall did win
the opening Superbike race, but Joey was an absentee for he had
ridden in the earlier 250cc class and banged his knee – an injury
which required stitching.

To please his fans, Joey came out for the final Superbike race
of the day and managed to beat Marshall. Still, as Joey told me
afterwards: 'My knee was stiff for most of the day and racing out
there at the finish seemed to ease it. I suppose you could say I'm
glad I came back and that I won. If I hadn't won I might have felt a
bit differently.'

For Marshall there was an unfortunate ending to the North West
week. His car had failed to start after the meeting and he was forced
to send a message to England for a special part. This meant that the
rest of the Honda riders left without him. Still, knowing Roger, I'm
sure he found plenty to do with his time during his short stay on the
North West coast . . .!

Joey's next major outing was at the Isle of Man TT and the pace
had hotted up. He had failed to score in the opening Formula One
round in Italy but he had won in Germany and now was ready for
what he always regarded as the supreme test.

Before the Isle of Man races however, tragedy struck the Dunlop
camp when Mel Murphy, who was Joey's mechanic throughout all
his world travels, collapsed and died while timekeeping and lap
scoring during a sponsored motorcycle run to raise funds for the Sir
Bob Geldof charity Sport Aid. Joey was taking part in the run, which
was a 24-hour motorcycle marathon through his home town of
Ballymoney, when the news came through that Murphy had died.
He was greatly saddened as we all were, for Mel – who was only 35
- was one of the characters of the sport.

The TT was delayed two days due to atrocious weather. But Joey
didn't mind. When they finally set off, half an hour late on the
Monday, he took the race by the scruff of the neck. He waltzed
away with the four-lap, 115 mile TT opener, coming home ahead of

Honda team-mate Geoff Johnston with a winning margin of almost a minute. Andy McGladdery finished third.

'I had to wait a day or two to take it but it was worth the wait,' said a jubilant Joey after his fourth TT Formula One victory in a row. 'It all went pretty smoothly. I had to change a tyre after the second lap and it didn't cause me any problems.'

Dunlop, who was riding the RGV Honda 750, went off like a rocket from the drop of the flag. Just eight miles into the race at Ballacraine he had opened up a three second lead over West German Klaus Klein, who was to die in tragic circumstances the following year at the Ulster Grand Prix.

Out in front, Dunlop continued to pile on the agony as far as opponents were concerned and stretch his lead even further over the new second place man McGladdery. Further back came Marshall, two seconds behind McGladdery, with Johnston riding the ex-Wayne Gardner Formula One machine a further five seconds down on Marshall.

Up over the Bungalow for the first time, Dunlop had moved even further ahead of McGladdery and Johnston, who were 14 seconds off the pace. By the end of that opening lap, Dunlop had clocked a speed of 112.88mph which was some 15 seconds ahead of the rest of the field.

With Dunlop in scintillating form the lead increased lap by lap and even when he came into the pits for a tyre change there was never any doubt that he would win the race. This was undoubtedly Joey at his best and he must have been thinking at the time that there must have been no one among his likely opponents for the rest of the season who could peg him back.

Well, he was in for a shock.

Four years earlier Norman Brown had, for a short space of time, threatened the Dunlop supremacy. As we have seen he later died in an accident at Silverstone. But in 1986 another Ulster racer rose up to challenge the great man and he too looked as if he might throw Joey off course.

This was Neil Robinson, no relation to Joey's brother-in-law

Mervyn but a brother to Donny Robinson who lived near Joey and who had competed regularly in the World 350cc Grand Prix series. It was Donny, you will recall, whom Honda brought in at the last minute at Dundrod in 1980 to try and ensure a World title win for Grant when Dunlop handed it on a plate to Crosby.

So Neil Robinson was in the line up in 1986 and he certainly looked to be a lad with a future. Promoted by fellow Ballymena men John Smith – a former road racer – and Trevor Armstrong, Robinson had the right PR. He looked good, he spoke well and he had the ability on the track to bring thousands of fans through the gate to watch him. In many ways he looked as though he might upstage Joey and that, in the late 1980s, was to think the unthinkable.

Robinson had competed in a few short circuits at that time and was keen on taking in the Grand Prix series. However Suzuki felt that he had as good a chance as any of stopping the Dunlop tidal wave in Formula One and they signed him up to ride in the next round of the world championship – the Dutch TT.

Robinson gave everyone a taste of what was to come by leading the race – until he had to drop out when the chain came off his Suzuki, leaving Joey victory on a plate. Dunlop was naturally pleased to win and he was also delighted for Robinson, a rider he had known all his life.

So the celebrations began after the prizegiving ceremony and perhaps they went on too long for shortly afterwards, a car in which Dunlop and Robinson were travelling went off the road on the Assen circuit and ended up in a ditch. Joey had a twisted ankle and Robinson had minor bruises, but it meant that both of them had to miss the next day's racing. They were taken to hospital but were released shortly afterwards. Ballymoney amateur photographer Derek McIntyre was also injured in the crash and needed seven stitches in hospital. It was an unfortunate ending to what had been a memorable day as far as Dunlop was concerned.

Robinson had set the fastest lap in the Dutch TT at 98.14mph so he obviously fancied his chances when the circus moved to the fifth

round at Jerez in Spain. Here Paul Iddon scored something of a surprise win from Graeme McGregor with Robinson in third place and
Andersson fourth. Joey could only manage fifth spot and so he
really had to pull out all the stops when it came to the sixth round at
sweltering Vila Real.

Needless to say Joey did the trick again. Just when it appeared as
though the cards were stacked against him he scored a dramatic
victory and also broke the lap record into the bargain. This was one
of Dunlop's best ever days for he held the lead for all but one of the
25 laps around the streets of the Portuguese town and ended up
with a fantastic average speed of 96.69mph.

Until the closing stages, when Dunlop had to call in for fuel, he
had the race all his own way, but then Paul Iddon closed the lap
dramatically after Dunlop's fuel stop to produce an exciting climax
to this sixth round of the series.

Earlier in the race Robinson had ridden superbly to keep Dunlop
in sight but when his fairing worked loose he had to pull into the
pits, losing almost two minutes When he came back on to the track
the best he could do was fight his way back to fifth.

So with two rounds remaining Joey's task of keeping the World
Formula One championship in Northern Ireland looked a comfortable one. He had now scored 66 points with second place
challenger Iddon on 49 and Andersson on 46.

The next round was at Imatra, Finland and Robinson, who was
still seeking his first win, must have thought he had the race
wrapped up for he was leading by a comfortable margin after Joey
had gone in to refuel and he increased his lead after Joey's pit stop.

But then disaster struck with a vengeance. Robinson developed
a slow puncture in the rear tyre and dropped back to third. Misery
for the young Co Antrim rider yet again. But his finest hour was still
to come . . .

Dunlop won in Finland by eight seconds from his nearest
championship challenger Iddon with Robinson 17 seconds further
adrift. This meant that Joey had clinched the championship for the
fifth year in a row, for his victory gave him 81 points from the six

rounds – 20 points ahead of Iddon with Andersson, who was fourth in Finland, third overall, followed by the remarkable Robinson in fourth place.

As Robinson had only taken over the works Suzuki in the Dutch round in June his performances had been of the highest class. He would most certainly have had a win if the gods had been kind to him but he still had the Ulster Grand Prix to come and Dunlop knew that Neil wasn't going to go down without a fight.

Everyone predicted that Robinson would give Joey a close call at the Ulster for, with Joey having already won the title, there was no pressure on him to take any chances. At the same time Joey always liked to win at Dundrod as this was a course he liked better than most – but no one expected Robinson to beat the old maestro by over a minute.

Yet that was the shock result in the Formula One class after an absorbing race which saw Robinson, the young pretender, come home almost alone with the experienced and all-conquering Dunlop in second place. Andy McGladdery was third. It was almost unbelievable. While the experts had tipped Robinson to come close, no one had expected a result like this and it was only afterwards that the full facts of the case emerged.

Although full credit was given to 23-year-old Robinson, who had only ridden over the Dundrod course for the first time the previous year, Dunlop had a genuine excuse. He was almost involved in a first lap accident which most certainly wrecked his chances. Iddon fell off in front of him at the Hairpin and Dunlop's Honda had to grind to a stop. 'It took me some time to get going again,' a disgruntled Joey said afterwards, 'and I thought that Paul was badly hurt. By this time Neil had gone well clear of the field and I saw no point in trying to catch him on wet and slippery roads. I have already won the championship and I can only say good luck to Neil, for he must have ridden a fine race although I didn't see much of him!'

Iddon, who had been one of the favourites, eventually returned to the paddock to receive medical attention and it turned out he had only minor cuts and bruises to his foot.

However the day belonged to Robinson and rightly so. This was his first success over the course and it was a truly memorable one for he cut the pace right from the start and it would have taken a top form Dunlop to have caught him. Robinson was well clear at the end of the first lap. On lap two he increased his lead and from then on it became obvious that he just wouldn't be caught. What was even more remarkable was the fact that Joey appeared to be having trouble in catching McGladdery and it wasn't until the seventh lap that he eventually squeezed past. At this stage he was 45 seconds behind Robinson and had no chance of winning the race unless Robinson retired.

As the race went on, Robinson built up his lead and eventually passed the magic minute barrier with two laps to go. McGladdery was now a respectable third behind Dunlop and further down the field the action was intense involving Phil Mellor, Sam McClements, Klaus Klein and Andersson. This quartet swapped places throughout and at one time McClements, having his best ever ride, threatened to take over fourth. However he ended up fifth behind Mellor with Luxembourg rider Patrick Bettendorf making up ground to finish sixth.

Afterwards a delighted and rather bemused Robinson received the plaudits of his legion of fans and once he had survived this he was able to talk about the race. 'Marvellous,' he said. 'I made the right choice of tyres and everything went perfectly, but don't be calling me the new king of the road. That title still belongs to Joey Dunlop. I was surprised I didn't see Joey at any stage of the race but my pit kept me well informed that I had a huge lead and that was that.

'The only problem I had if you could call it one was that my visor steamed up. This was only a minor occurrence. I certainly hope to ride for Suzuki next year. I have received an offer from them and at this point in time I am inclined to accept it.'

Tragically Robinson didn't get the opportunity to follow up for only the following month he was killed in a road race at Scarborough in Yorkshire. This was a hammer blow not only for John

Smith and Trevor Armstrong who had been behind all of Robinson's early activities. It was also something which the Ulster public just couldn't quite grasp. A new hero had been snatched from their grasp virtually before he had started to show his true potential. It was Norman Brown all over again.

Then, with the fans still reeling at the loss of Neil Robinson, came a thunderbolt from Honda. They were pulling out their British team for 1987. It was right out of the blue, no one expected it and with Joey Dunlop world champion for five years it was something which set the Ulster public reeling. Now it wasn't a case of 'Would Joey be champion again in 1987?' It was more a matter of 'Would Joey have any bike at all in 1987?'

In a statement from London, Honda announced that they were pulling the plug on their racing and motocross teams in order to concentrate as they said on 'dealer support'. They announced that new packages had been sent to their three road racers – Dunlop, Marshall and Burnett – for their consideration. Joey didn't hear immediately of the packages as he had been working in Tipperary on family business and wasn't due to return until later in the week.

The background to the Honda decision appeared to be clouded to say the least. Honda in their statement placed great emphasis on the fact that they considered dealer teams to be essential to their grand plan. And they emphasised that their move wasn't prompted by the fact that Rothmans had decided not to put any more money into the British road racing team.

'I can deny that categorically,' spokesman Graeme Sanderson told me at the time.

Why then this sudden about face?

'Roger Etcell, the new divisional manager of Honda Motor Cycles, decided that Honda's interests would be best served by switching to dealer emphasis and further details of this plan will be announced at a later date,' Sanderson continued. 'What this means in practical terms I'm not at liberty to say nor can I divulge what the packages to Dunlop, Marshall and Burnett will consist of. But I assume that we will encourage dealers to go road racing including

Left With scant regard for the speed limit(!) Joey races to victory in the 125cc class at the 2000 TT, the final leg of his famous Treble.

Below A graphic illustration of the danger of high-speed road racing. Joey skims the graveyard walls at Billown in the 1999 Southern 100 in the Isle of Man. He won the race with a shredded rear tyre.

Bottom Waiting for the off. The Honda pit crew with Barry Symmons (far right) prepare to launch Joey back into action at the 1982 TT.

During an illustrious career, Joey never tasted success in Japan. Here he makes up for it by posing with paddock girls at the 1984 Suzuka 8 Hours.

Riding European circuits was part and parcel of life for Joey during his world championship winning seasons. Here he powers through the field at Vila Real, Portugal in 1986.

Captured on camera. Joey was one of the first motorcycle riders to test the new technology of the on-board camera.

An exhausted Joey is
rehydrated at track side
after riding in the
tortuous heat of the
Vila Real circuit,
Portugal, in 1985.
Joey regularly suffered
in hot conditions but it
was a necessary evil en
route to five world
championship wins.

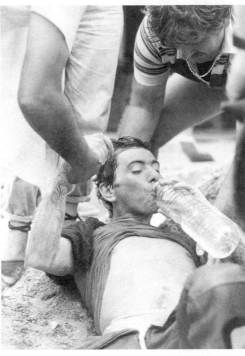

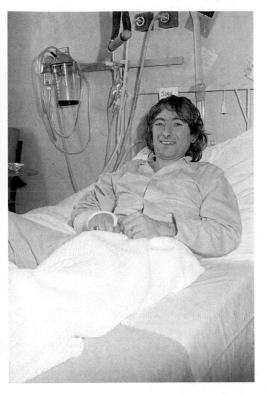

Putting on a brave face
in hospital following
the crash at Brands Hatch
in 1989 which almost
ended his career.

Joey leads brother
Robert at Deer's Leap
in the 1990 Ulster
Grand Prix. This was
his first Superbike
race win following
his comeback from
serious injury.

The second of Joey's visits to Buckingham Palace in 1996 to collect an OBE for services to motorcycling and humanitarian deeds. Wife Linda and family lend support.

Posing with the Douglas, Isle of Man, cub scouts in 1991. Joey rode with a woggle and scarf under his leathers in the following day's 125cc TT won by his brother Robert.

Author Jimmy Walker puts his interview technique to the test before Joey goes to the line for the 1989 Carrowdore 100.

Taking a fag break while working on a steel erection job in Belfast. Joey often worked with his brothers, Jim and Robert, on such jobs when he wasn't racing.

Ouch. That hurt! Joey volunteers to be cut in half during an evening in his honour at Ballymoney Town Hall, organised to commemorate his fourth world title win in 1985.

Left The Millennium Treble. Joey at the 2000 TT with the 125cc trophy.

Below The local press fail to keep pace with Joey's achievements!

Bottom And to the victor, the spoils. Joey gets the full treatment on the podium after winning the 2000 Formula One TT.

Right Joey receives a special award from Winston Buchanan, Chairman of the Temple Club, for breaking Mike Hailwood's record of 14 TT wins.

Below The End. The final race, Tallinn, Estonia.

Bottom An estimated 60,000 people attended Joey's funeral on 7 July 2000.

Joey in full flow on the Island.
This is how his millions of fans around the world will always remember him.

the World Formula One championship and supply them with machinery that they can afford. Of course, this won't have the same impact as a full-blown works team but that appears to be Honda policy at the moment.'

So there it was. No Honda team. Or so we thought. It was then that Davy Wood went into action . . .

Wood, who managed Joey in his heyday, was a former road racer and later became what might be called an entrepreneur in the sport. He was a pugnacious and highly intelligent type who knew all about PR and moved in all the right circles. Davy was a man who had an answer for everything and always seemed able to pour oil on the most troubled of waters.

Davy decided that he would not give up and that Joey would have a bike for the following year. And it was mainly through Wood's efforts that Joey returned to Formula One racing in 1987.

Wood first contacted Suzuki and sounded them out as to whether they were interested but really Davy's heart lay with Honda which was obviously his first love. Eventually in November 1986, thanks to Wood's intense lobbying, the Honda Racing Corporation based in Tokyo announced that they would take in all 10 of the world championship rounds in 1987 and that Joey Dunlop would be their rider.

The spokesman for Honda stated that Joey's new commitment had nothing to do with Honda Britain, who had pulled out of road racing the previous month. 'This is entirely a tie up between Honda Japan and Dunlop,' he said. 'Joey has signed a letter stating that he will race for the company in the Formula One series and naturally we are delighted at the way things have turned out.'

Joey thus joined a select team of stars. Heading it was former world 500cc champion American Freddie Spencer along with Wayne Gardner and world motocross king Dave Thorpe.

The new deal gave Joey the chance to go for his sixth world title and it had nothing to do with any team proposed by Barry Symmons, who had been in Tokyo the previous week hoping to snatch something from the fire. What it also quite clearly showed was the depth of feeling which existed for Joey in the Honda corridors of power. From 1987 onwards there was never any question of Joey being dropped. He had Honda behind him four square until his untimely death 13 years later.

Ironically, in 1987 Joey would be racing against former teammate Roger Marshall who had given him such a close call for the title in 1984. Since then Marshall had had little to do with Formula One and during the 1986 season Dunlop had carried the flag single-handedly.

But Marshall signed for Suzuki at the end of 1986 and looked set to be the number one threat to Joey the following year. I thought at the time that this would provide zest for the racing which looked like losing a great deal of interest following Joey's runaway victory in the summer of 1986. I didn't anticipate that anyone else would come along to upset the flow. I couldn't have been more wrong.

It was a swarthy volatile Italian named Virginio Ferrari who put the kibosh on Joey Dunlop's championship hopes in 1987 – and the little Italian also won everlasting notoriety as the man who walked out on the Ulster Grand Prix.

A bizarre state of affairs existed during the practice sessions for that year's Ulster. Ferrari, who had been in the lead in the championship by two points thanks to wins in Hungary and Holland, took one look at Dundrod and gave the impression that he just couldn't believe what he was seeing.

'It's a dangerous looking course and I'm not at all keen about it,' he told me as I ventured into his caravan to avoid the torrential rain. 'I have to race here and hopefully I can pick up much needed points.' But it was obvious to all concerned that the thought of racing at the Ulster did not fill him with wild enthusiasm. I got the distinct impression that he would much rather have been elsewhere and I must say, looking round at the desolation which was Dundrod on a wet night, I couldn't blame him.

'This is a course which suits Joey Dunlop,' he told me. 'You could say it is Joey's type of track.'

However Joey wasn't saying that at all, for in appalling conditions he skidded during the first practice session and it was this spill which clearly influenced the promoters in having the whole session called off as parts of the track became flooded.

Ferrari meanwhile was 35th fastest with a respectable speed of over 90mph and most of us thought that on dry roads it would be a much different story. What we didn't know was what was going on in Ferrari's head at that point and we were in for a major shock when we turned up for the following night's practice.

'I quit. This course is too dangerous . . . I quit,' he ranted. This was the Italian's reaction as he looked at the high speed fliers during the second night of practice and decided that this most certainly wasn't going to be his scene. The 31-year-old star screwed his index finger to his temple: 'It's crazy. A crazy track. A crazy place. A crazy race. I like to win the championship but I like my life to go on as well. I go home.'

With that, he peeled off his leathers and left road racing campaigners Joey Dunlop and his pals to get on with it.

Ferrari agreed that during the first night's aborted practice session he was prepared to give it another go. But when he saw how fast other riders were going on a dry circuit he had second thoughts. He told me: 'I had a slow look round on Wednesday in the rain, but I saw today how dangerous a place like Dundrod could be when you have to race fast. So I say no thank you.'

The organisers were reeling for this had never happened in the long history of the race, at least not to anyone's knowledge. Race secretary Andy Campbell said: 'I haven't been officially informed that he is pulling out but if it's true it is a big blow to us because we went to a lot of trouble to get him here. Still, if that's what he wants to do, it's his choice.'

And so Joey Dunlop was left without a leader in the Formula One championship to contend with and although he looked his usual noncommittal self at the time he must have felt he had one less hurdle to climb.

This had not been an easy season for Joey, for despite the fact that he had won the Formula One TT yet again and had also followed up by lifting the Senior Classic race – in addition to which he had scored a treble at the North West 200 – his Formula One hopes hadn't prospered and by the time the Ulster came along Joey knew he had a battle on his hands if he was to keep his crown.

It all went back to an incident which took place in Holland earlier in the year which put Joey under more than the usual pressure. In June at the Dutch round of the Formula One series Joey and American Freddie Merkel were involved in a controversial collision which saw Joey knocked out of the race and watching the closing stages from the pits. Dunlop understandably didn't forget that day for the crash meant him losing his place at the top of the championship. This meant that he eventually went into the Ulster round just behind Ferrari while Merkel, perhaps understandably, decided not to turn up. Some of Joey's fans said rather unkindly that he wouldn't dare make the trip, but that's by the way.

Ferrari and his Yamaha team-mate Davide Tardozzi, along with West German Peter Rubatto, were all expected to be in the line up along with the regulars like Dunlop's old Honda team-mate Marshall. However with Ferrari quitting, by the time race day came along the whole meeting was in total confusion and the weather wasn't helping for it was pouring like a bad night in Rangoon.

We weren't to know it at the time but 1987 was to see the Ulster Grand Prix reach its lowest ebb.

The first race – and what turned out to be the only race – was the 350cc which was won by Brian Reid, who the previous year had clinched the World Formula Two championship for the second time. So Reid was on a high, but you couldn't say that for anyone else and especially the Formula One riders who were pushing their bikes out to the track with the rain still coming down incessantly.

The race turned out to be a disaster from start to finish. First of all it was delayed for one hour following the warm up lap when riders complained that there was too much water on the course. At this stage Dunlop dismounted from his Honda and returned to the paddock saying he didn't see any point in racing in the current conditions.

However, after an inspection by the clerk of the course it was decided to go ahead and with the rain pelting down, the riders were sent on their way.

Spray was flying about everywhere making it virtually impossible for spectators to see what was going on. During the first lap Dunlop was tucked in behind Marshall in seventh place after having made a slow start. In addition many riders 'jumped the gun' because they couldn't see the green light starting signal.

At the end of what turned out to be the only lap Marshall was in the lead and West German Klaus Klein was lying in fifth place just ahead of Dunlop.

It was at this stage that tragedy occurred.

With the rain now making it impossible to see across the road from pits to grandstand, Klein appeared to aquaplane and Dunlop, who was close behind him, was almost involved in the accident. Pit attendants and marshals dashed on to the course to try and stop the remainder of the riders going through and although some had started on their second laps, including Dunlop, the message went out officially to stop the race.

When Dunlop eventually returned to the pits he was in a highly agitated state. 'I was right behind that rider who fell in front of me,' he said. 'I didn't know it was Klein but I just closed my eyes and braked hoping for the best. I went on through and afterwards was told the race was stopped. We should never have been out there for the conditions were worse than they were during Wednesday night when practice was abandoned. Water was pouring down the road like a river and I can't understand why we were brought out to the line.

'These were the worst conditions I have ever been asked to ride in. I rode in a cloud burst in the TT but that was nothing in comparison. Bikes were skidding and slithering about everywhere. As far as I'm concerned I won't be racing again today.'

It was later confirmed that 32-year-old Klein, who came from Stuttgart, had been killed instantly when hitting a grass bank 200 yards past the grandstand area. He had multiple injuries.

A decision was made by the clerk of the course, Bertie Hunt, that not only should the race be stopped but the rest of the meeting be abandoned. As Ted Macauley of the *Daily Mirror* said to me, squinting through the rain: 'What a disaster. I can't remember anything like it in all my long experience.'

The Ulster Grand Prix took a long time to recover from 1987 and in later years there were still those who recalled the fact that the Formula One race should not have been attempted.

Dunlop meanwhile had now only a slim chance of winning the championship. His best chances had gone with the wiping out of the rounds of Vila Real, Imatra and Dundrod and worse was to follow for Joey. He travelled to Japan and collided with Ferrari before finishing 12th. Then at Hockenheim, Ferrari won with Joey finishing fourth.

The Hockenhein visit turned out to be yet another disaster, this time of an unusual kind. A bad attack by mosquitoes didn't help Dunlop's chances. Because of the noise in his hotel, Joey had decided to sleep under canvas at the course but he was attacked by mosquitoes on the Friday night and as a result his left eye was partially closed when he went to the race.

Joey however was not making that the excuse for his fourth place and certainly his performance would bear this out. He had set the fastest lap of the race up until the last lap and it was then that he slowed dramatically having decided not to refuel.

Dunlop was third before the last lap and Honda decided that their bike could just about complete another lap without refuelling. As a result Joey lost a vital place. He said: 'We took a chance on that last lap and hoped that I would catch Ferrari and Tardozzi who were first and second. We knew we had a safe fourth place if we refuelled but were hoping for something better.'

The race was not without further incident in that Ferrari and Tardozzi, Yamaha team-mates, almost crashed out of the race on the last lap when their bikes touched. Fate however was kind to them although Joey's thoughts at the time would have been interesting!

And so to the final meeting at Donington. Joey's position with regard to the championship was bleak but also clear. He had to win with Ferrari down in sixth place if he was to retain the title.

In a last ditch bid Honda even gave Dunlop the Bol D'Or winning machine but it was too late. Suzuki's Iddon won the 100 mile race; Marshall, who had been dictating the pace, was forced to pull in for a late fuel stop and this forced him into second place; Merkel came with a late charge but like Marshall was forced in for fuel and eventually finished fourth.

Dunlop, with a brilliant display of world class short circuit riding, was in position to challenge the Suzukis early on but a slipping clutch in the Honda motor that had already clocked 2,300 miles in the Bol D'Or confined his efforts to third place.

It was a disappointing end to the season for Joey as Ferrari finished a cool seventh quite happy to cruise round ensuring him of his first world title. In the final reckoning he had finished with three points in hand of Dunlop, while Iddon's win elevated him into third overall.

The year 1987 – despite those TT and North West wins – was one which Dunlop would recall as the summer when he lost his crown. It was a time when things started to go wrong and Joey had to be hopeful that they could only get better in 1988.

CHAPTER 12

CRASHING OUT

I had the feeling that it was the end of an era when 1988 dawned. And yet I had no real reason for thinking so. After all, Joey had continued his usual rampage through the previous year's TT and the North West 200. But the fact that he had failed to clinch the World Formula One championship struck a warning note as far as I was concerned. Nothing lasts forever and the queue of new guys willing to take on the old gunslinger was growing ever longer.

In Joey's case he could look forward to – if that was the right phrase – competition from riders like Steve Hislop and Carl Fogarty, both of whom were later to dominate the TT in the early Nineties. In addition, he had another Ulsterman on his tail. This was Bangor, Co Down rider Stephen Cull. Cull had been around for a few years and in fact had given the British Cotton team a rare win the 1980 North West 200.

In more recent times Cull had confined his activities to Irish national events but he always rode at the TT and he was always a rider for whom the island brought out his best performances. In 1988 Cull had some top class bikes for the North West and the TT and he looked like being a real threat to Joey.

Joey's cause wasn't helped either by the fact that Honda seemed to have put him on the long finger. They promised him a new Formula One bike for 1988 but it never arrived and he was forced to ride an RC30 under the banner of the Shell Gemini team. To be more explicit about it, Joey *was* the team. There was nobody else. So in effect Honda had said to him 'Go with it Joey. It's all yours.'

Coming up to the North West 200 that year Joey knew he had a lot to prove because he wasn't happy that the RC30 would be quick enough. He was also aware of the fact that Cull was giving the impression that he would be the man to beat – that's the way it turned out.

Cull was always a cocky, confident character and I give him credit for inventing a quip which occurred during that year's TT races. While suffering the frustration of a slow refuel during one of the races, Cull said to his mechanic: 'Do you give out Green Shield stamps as well?' I know this one-liner has been used since but that was the first time I ever heard it and I am reasonably sure that Cull was the man who invented it.

Back to the North West however. Cull had good bikes and he didn't mess about. In fact he took Joey Dunlop apart, winning two Superbike races and the 250cc class. It was complete domination.

I wouldn't have believed it if anyone had told me before the meeting that Stephen Cull would have been able to fall off his bike, remount and still beat Joey Dunlop. But that's what happened in the final race of the day. The two riders were disputing the lead coming into York Corner in Portstewart. Cull was in the lead. But on the climb up the hill he lost control and slipped off. Joey raced past but believe it or not, Cull straightened his bike, climbed on board again and by the time the riders had got to Coleraine and were heading round to Portrush, Cull was back in the lead. He won the race with something in hand and established himself as a major force for the forthcoming TT races.

The omens didn't appear good for Joey approaching the 1988 TT. And he had a number of misgivings: the Honda had not really run up to speed at the North West 200, his early practice times at the Isle of Man weren't the best and he was also concerned by Cull signing up for Suzuki shortly before the race, to replace the injured Andy McGladdery. But all of this reckoned without Joey's perennial powers on the island. Joey rose to the occasion and became the fastest rider ever over the Mountain course on his way to winning the Formula One race for an unbelievable sixth successive year.

Problems in practice? You could forget about them when Dunlop saw the green light. Joey had said beforehand that he would be lucky to get into the first six. He must have been kidding for he was in his old brilliant form as he led the race from start to finish to win at a record race average of 116.25mph, which was 68 seconds up on the second man Nick Jefferies who averaged 115.13mph with Roger Burnett third at 113.09mph.

Dunlop thus became the first rider in the long history of the TT to win the same class six years in a row. In addition he also set a new absolute lap record of 118.54mph on the second lap and this despite slowing down to refuel! Dunlop was in cracking form right from the opening lap and by the time he had reached Ballaugh he was already 17 seconds ahead of Jefferies and Geoff Johnston.

By the end of the first lap Dunlop was leading on corrected time by 14 seconds and at halfway he was 36.8 seconds ahead of the second placed man Hislop, who was one of the unlucky riders at the previous month's North West 200.

But Hislop ran into problems. He toured in at the end of lap four and then his bike failed to restart on time. He eventually got going but had to retire at the end of the fifth lap, but not before giving a warning of what Dunlop could expect in future races. Steve put in a stunning lap just one second slower than Joey's record-breaker and he got to within 22 seconds of the leader with one and a half laps to go.

'I also got a big gouge in my helmet at Doran's Bend,' the young Hislop said. 'I thought I had scraped an ivy hedge but it was a wall.'

Hislop's exit left Dunlop an easy 38 seconds ahead of a brilliant on the road dash between Johnston and Jefferies. Johnston eventually went out on the final lap with brake problems and another top rider to run into trouble was Phil Mellor, who had given Dunlop something of a close call the previous year. Mellor was fifth after lap one but then lost fuel rapidly and eventually finished well down the field.

Burnett too had his problems, for he had to change a wheel after a puncture at the end of the second lap, but he was able to restart and took a creditable third place.

But the day belonged to Joey on his RC30 Honda. He was now looking forward with renewed enthusiasm to the Senior race on Friday in which he was due to meet his North West conqueror Cull.

Dunlop said after the finish that he was surprised the RC30 had gone so quickly. 'I never thought it would be quicker than the RVF Honda,' he said. 'But it was really hauling. I had one problem. The breather was blocked after the second fuel stop and I had to open the cap to let some air in. But apart from that I had no trouble and I enjoyed the ride. I also enjoyed the champagne at the finish,' he joked.

The win earned Dunlop 20 points towards regaining the Formula One championship. He now stood in joint first place with Noboru Miura who had won the opening round in Japan.

That win also put Joey in the right frame of mind for the 250cc TT which came on the Wednesday and once again he won with a record-shattering lap. On his Gemini Honda Dunlop led for most of the race and won by 20 seconds from Brian Reid with Dublin's Eddie Laycock third in an Irish one-two-three.

Dunlop had a 20 second advantage as he pitted for petrol at the end of the second lap, but there was a scare in store for Joey. After the petrol had been put into the tank the fuel cap slipped out of the mechanic's hand and fell into the bottom of the fairing. The mechanics had to lift up the front wheel so the cap could roll out onto the ground.

After this mishap, Dunlop remounted and continued marginally behind Reid. But midway through the third lap Joey was back in command. Reid said: 'Joey was quicker than me on the Mountain and I also had trouble remembering to change gear with my left foot after the gear change had been shifted when I broke my right big toe in practice.'

Five Irish riders finished in the first six. Behind fourth place Brian Morrison came Johnnie Rea and Stephen Cull.

So that was two up with the Senior to go and that return battle with Cull. It was all action on the island! Joey completed the treble as you might have expected. In a fantastic record-breaking Senior race Dunlop won at a race average of 117.38mph and he also smashed the lap record early on.

However, the big story of the race was the new lap record of 119.08mph set by Cull. This was on the second lap but shortly afterwards Cull was forced to lose ground with a broken exhaust; eventually he left the race when his machine spectacularly caught fire. Fortunately Stephen was uninjured. Second place eventually went to Hislop followed by Johnston, Marshall, Burnett and Brian Morrison.

Dunlop set the pace from the start, breaking his own four-day-old outright lap record from a standing start. He clocked 118.66mph which was 1.2 seconds quicker than his Monday time. He led by 4.4 seconds from Cull with Jefferies third but Jefferies then had to retire on lap two at Union Mills.

Both Cull and Dunlop broke the record again on lap two when each stopped for fuel. Dunlop took a second off his previous lap time and that included slowing down to stop at his pit. Cull, whose pit was further along the line than Dunlop's, then clocked the fastest TT lap in 81 years of racing with that speed of 119.08mph, only a fraction of a second above the sub nineteen minute lap.

Midway through the third lap Cull briefly snatched the lead but Dunlop bounced back. He had an advantage of two seconds at the Bungalow and four seconds at the end of lap three. By Ballacraine on lap four, Dunlop was 12 seconds ahead and the record books looked like being rewritten once more.

This was a sensational TT. At halfway Dunlop was averaging 117.45mph which was unheard of. Then came the news that Cull was in trouble. An expansion box holed and he dropped to 25 seconds down on Dunlop on lap four. Cull then lost second place to Hislop and it was the Scot who followed Joey home.

It was a tired Joey who toured back into the grandstand area to face the inevitable questioning from ever present Geoff Cannell. This was Joey's 13th victory in the TT and the obvious question was: 'Are you going to come back for more and try to break Mike Hailwood's record?' Joey gave Cannell that well known world-weary look and said: 'I just don't know. That race took a lot out of me. I'm getting too old for this carry on. Steve Hislop was going very fast. I didn't expect him to be so quick.'

This was the first indication that Joey had given that he was aware of Hislop's threat to his supremacy but the young Scot certainly had the bit between his teeth and he told me some years later: 'I was always keen to catch and match if possible Joey Dunlop. At the 1987 North West 200 he and I had a tremendous battle in the 250cc–350cc race. He was on a Honda and I was on a Yamaha. For six laps of the race we were elbowing each other and I said to myself, "I can't believe it, I'm alongside the great Joey Dunlop and there is nothing in it." Eventually we finished fourth and fifth, Joey just pipped me. Afterwards I went into my van and I realised I had never spoken to the man in my life. He kept himself to himself and I must admit I was a bit reticent also.

'A fortnight later I won the Formula Two TT and at one of the presentation evenings I bumped into Davy Wood. Wood told me that Joey had noticed me after the North West 200 and asked, "Who's that young rider?" Davy had said to Joey, "That's a Scot called Steve Hislop." And Joey had replied to Davy, "That boy will win a TT."

'That was an honour as far as I was concerned. I never dreamed that Joey had noticed me but he missed nothing. When it came to 1988 I was determined to give as good as I had got and after my bad luck in the Formula One race I pushed on to try to beat him in the Senior. I had good machines and I reckoned that my RC30 was as fast as Joey's.

'I didn't win but I still felt pleased that I had come so close. As I stood in the rostrum and I shook hands with Joey, he spoke to me for the first time: "Well done." That was all. Perhaps Joey thought that afternoon that this newcomer would one day beat him. Who knows.'

Despite his historic TT treble – he was the first man in history ever to complete two hat tricks at the Isle of Man races – I had the feeling that Joey's star was on the wane. He didn't seem to have the same enthusiasm for the game. He seemed to have lost a lot of his edge. Perhaps it was the fact that he had suddenly realised that he was getting older. Who knows what was going on in his mind as he trooped home from the island to prepare himself for the next round of the Formula One championship in Holland.

Joey slipped up badly on this round, finishing eighth. He had been fastest in the early practice sessions but he never got into the leading group in a race which was won by Roger Burnett. Joey was in fourth place for most of the race but on the penultimate lap he came in for an extended fuel stop and dropped four places. This was enough to shatter his hopes and he dropped to second place in the championship, seven points behind Burnett.

The next round was scheduled for Vila Real where Joey had mixed memories. Still, for once it wasn't the intense heat which caused the problems. This time it was torrential rain. The race had to be restarted because of the rain and unluckily for Dunlop he was leading when the abandonment came.

After a long delay it was eventually decided to race again late in the evening but because of the fading light the race had to be curtailed to 10 laps instead of 25. Dunlop finished well down the field, taking fourth place overall. Despite this he was in the Formula One lead on 41 points going to the fifth round in Finland. Second place man Burnett was on 35 but he had stated that he would not be competing in any further Formula One rounds.

The Finnish round proved to be a happy one for Joey for he finished in third place and retained the lead in the championship. Winner in Finland was Anders Andersson followed by Peter Rubatto with Fogarty nudging ever closer with a fourth place. Robert Dunlop had his best ever placing in fifth.

So with the Ulster Grand Prix to come along as the next round,

Dunlop had 49.5 points and his nearest challenger Burnett had 35. The future however was much brighter for Joey with the news that Burnett had decided not to take part in the Ulster Grand Prix and, while that was a blow to the promoters, it was a good move as far as Joey was concerned.

He appeared to have the championship completely wrapped up for no one considered Carl Fogarty. In those early days Fogarty showed signs of being a future champion but no one could have guessed what heights he would reach. As the whole world now knows, he later entered the Superbike class, won the world title a record four times and became a major star in the process. But back in 1988 Fogarty was virtually unknown.

'I got on well with Joey Dunlop right from the start,' Fogarty told me. 'Perhaps it was because both of us were shy. I certainly didn't feel like talking much and I always kept my thoughts to myself. I first visited Dundrod for the 1987 race the day the meeting was cancelled. I rode in the first race, the 250cc, only to break down after a few laps. When I came back again in 1988 I realised I would have to learn the circuit on a superbike and to be honest I didn't really fancy my chances of winning that Formula One race. Joey would in my mind always be too quick and I was just hopeful for a place in the first four.

'As it turned out the race was run in wet weather and in those days I was better on wet roads than I was on dry. The opposite was the case later in my career. When I saw the wet roads in Dundrod that day in 1988 I thought to myself "I could win this" and my confidence grew stronger and stronger as the day progressed. I really was surprised I suppose to beat Joey by such a huge margin as was the case but of course as we all know Joey had problems in the race.

'I started to get to know Joey well after that for there weren't very many riders in the Formula One championship in those days. Apart from myself, Hislop and Joey there would have been Dave Leach and Andy McGladdery and one or two others. We were very close but as far as my relationship with Joey was concerned, I was like a kid greeting my hero.'

Fogarty has always had fond memories of racing in Ireland and he told me: 'It was the Irish people who first recognised any ability which I had. In 1987 I also started to ride in the North West 200 and I made it my aim to try and win that race one year. I did eventually do so in 1993 when I scored a superbike double. I felt that being in the same type of competition as Joey Dunlop meant that I was accepted by the Irish fans. In other words they thought Joey was the best and if I could stay with Joey they thought I was good too. He sort of towed me along in his wake.'

Fogarty's father George had finished second to Joey in his first ever TT win, that Jubilee race back in 1977, so I suppose you could say it was a twist of fate that it was his son Carl who took over as Formula One champion in 1988.

Admittedly he didn't take over immediately from Joey because Virginio Ferrari had scored in 1987, but Fogarty's win at the Ulster Grand Prix in 1988 was the race on which the whole championship revolved. Joey had to win that day or at least get a high placing to stay in touch. As it was, he finished seventh and that was really the end of his championship hopes.

Carl had picked up 13 points with that fourth place in Finland and had 33 points which put him 16.5 points behind Joey. He was the only serious title contender left and perhaps only Fogarty himself thought he had a chance of winning at Dundrod which everybody knew 'belonged' to Joey. How wrong we all were . . .

The Ulster Grand Prix that year turned out to be a watershed in Joey Dunlop's career. I often wonder what would have happened if he had won and gone on to retain the title. Would he have continued in the sport or would he have retired there and then? Who knows?

It certainly was a disastrous day for Joey. He was expected to claim a dream victory but the race turned into a nightmare; he made the wrong choice of tyres and this decision gave him no chance as he finished seventh behind Fogarty who was winning an Irish road race for the first time.

It was a marvellous race however, and it had everything the fans wanted – except perhaps victory for Joey. But Fogarty must take a lot of credit for leading from start to finish despite making a stop to refuel; his victory made him a red hot favorite to win the championship with two rounds to go.

Dunlop's sorry saga began during the warm up laps, when heavy rain forced riders to change from slick tyres to the wet weather version. Then when the road dried up they changed again, but unknown to many at the start there was still some inclement weather at the back of the course and this was to cause its own problems. Dunlop went to the start line with a slick rear tyre expecting dry roads all the way, but it was soon painfully clear to his fans that he had made the wrong choice.

Fogarty led from Robert Dunlop with Hislop third and Joey fourth early on. Even at this stage Joey looked to be struggling and he dropped back to fifth on the second lap, retaining the spot after three laps had been completed.

It was then that the drama began.

Realising that he had made the wrong choice of tyres, Joey pulled into the pits and re-emerged with not only his rear wheel changed but he had refueled as well in order to give himself every chance. However time was not on his side and the pit stop lost him 22 vital seconds.

Meanwhile Fogarty continued on his own serene way at the head of the field from Robert Dunlop, Hislop and Nick Jefferies as Joey tried frantically to get back into the race. He was 15th at the end of lap four but with nine laps still to go his fans weren't unduly worried. Next time round he moved up a place but after a couple more laps it was obvious he was making very little impression on those ahead of him.

By this time the roads had dried out and it was now clear that Dunlop had made another mistake in changing to wet weather tyres. And even the fact that Fogarty had to pull in to refuel after eight laps gave him no chance. Fogarty's pit stop took 22 seconds and this allowed the new second place man Hislop to take a brief lead with Robert Dunlop third and Jefferies fourth. Joey was now ninth but his hopes were fading fast as time began to run out.

More drama on the next lap, when the leader Hislop had to refuel, along with Robert Dunlop, and this allowed Fogarty back into the lead which he held until the finish.

As the race drew to its final stages it was still Fogarty, riding superbly, who held every challenge and he finished the race over 17 seconds ahead of Hislop with Robert Dunlop third, Jefferies fourth, Williams fifth and Moran sixth. It was a disconsolate Joey Dunlop who finished seventh and who said: 'That was just one disaster after another. The roads were dry when we did the warm up laps but the rain came on at Wheeler's Corner on the first lap and I was unprepared for it for I had a slick rear tyre.

'I knew at that point that I was going to get nowhere so I made the decision to pull in after three laps and change. This could have been the wrong decision for the sun came out and dried out the course so I might have won had I stayed with my original tyre. It's just one race I want to forget about in a hurry.'

Fogarty's win gave him another 20 points and a total of 53, but Dunlop still led the series with 58.5. Fogarty said: 'I was worried about the weather and was concerned about the way it kept changing. I didn't expect to beat Joey Dunlop round here but I knew I had a good chance of a high placing. The valves on my machine which caused trouble in practice acted up again and my bike lost power over the lead three laps. I was really worried in the closing stages and I thought that refuelling stop might have cost me the race.'

So Joey Dunlop was still hanging on to his lead in the Formula One series if somewhat precariously; however the next round in Sicily decided the championship and ended another disappointing year for Joey.

The title was lost in Sicily even before the race started; Joey crashed in Thursday night's practice and was in hospital for two days with cuts and bruises. Then, during the warm up laps on race day, his Honda broke down and he was forced to watch the race from the sidelines. It was a terrible anticlimax.

Worse was to follow for Joey when Fogarty won the race and, consequently, took a 14.5 point lead over Joey with only one round of the series to come – at Donington Park in September.

This turned out to be just as unhappy as Sicily was for Joey. He finished in eleventh place and the championship went to Fogarty. The hoodoo which seemed to have dogged him from the Ulster Grand Prix continued at Donington, where he wrecked both engines in practice and then had to take part in the race itself by salvaging what he could from the two wreckages. The crank went on the first practice then it was valve trouble in the new engine.

Dunlop also experimented in the race with a new back tyre but he was never in with a chance and said afterwards: 'The Honda was too slow and there was no point in taking chances with it in view of the fact that my championship hopes were non-existent.'

Afterwards Joey made it clear that he intended to ride in the World Formula One championship the following year and also to take in the World Superbike series. But he was hoping for much better luck than he'd had in 1988 where he only won one world championship round – the Isle of Man TT.

Still, he had Mike Hailwood's record to chase. That was always something. Thirteen wins in the TT. Could Joey equal Hailwood's figure and make it 14? It seemed only a matter of time before he did. But fate was waiting in the wings.

In 1989 Joey faced yet another major season and the good news right at the start of the year was that Honda were prepared to give him a full-blown works bike. They also stated however that he would have to ride the machine in the first round of the Formula One series which would be in Japan in May. This meant that it clashed with the North West 200 so Joey had a major decision to make.

To put it another way, the decision had been made for him. Honda had made it clear that they expected Joey to ride in Japan and that was that.

Davy Wood, who was still handling Joey's affairs at that time, said in his view there was no question of Joey missing the Japanese round. 'When you consider that the final round of the Formula One series in Austria has already been cancelled then you will realise that Joey cannot afford to miss another one if he is to win the championship and repay Honda for what is in fact a major gesture on their part,' said Davy.

The following month Joey announced officially what we already knew – that he would be racing in Japan and would be missing the North West 200. He told me: 'I am definitely going to Japan. The Honda people want me to go there and although I am unlikely to pick up any championship points, I have to carry out their instructions. It's very much a public relations exercise. In fact, I think I'm being brought over to advertise the Honda Racing Company,' he joked.

In March of that year a major press conference was held in Belfast at which Joey's plans for 1989 were unveiled. Wood was up front as usual, Joey was there and Joey's father Willie also made an appearance. It seemed to me at the time that this would be a make or break season for him. Certainly he was going for the Formula One world championship, but more importantly and higher on the agenda was Hailwood's TT record. Joey and his team were looking for their place in history and he had only one more win to go to equal the legendary 'Mike the Bike'; knowing Joey's record round the Isle of Man, one win would have been the least you could have expected from him. He usually picked up TT successes in handfuls.

At the same time I noticed an air of anxiety about Joey at that press conference. There was a lot of razzmatazz about the place, more than you would normally associate with the launch of a Joey Dunlop year. In fact I couldn't remember at the time if we had ever had a press launch for Joey before!

Joey appeared to be a bit uneasy in that he had to pose for photographers; he had to make bland comments to people who asked him what he would regard as unimportant questions, and he had to do a promotion job for Honda and the new deal they had offered him. This was never something he was particularly at ease with.

I came away that night with the distinct feeling that this would be the last year we would see Joey racing at the top level. However, I didn't have any premonition of disaster, which perhaps was just as well for only a few weeks later Joey's world crumbled round him.

The name Stephan Mertens meant nothing to Joey Dunlop's hordes of supporters at the beginning of 1989 but by the time Good Friday came along the Belgian rider's name was on everybody's lips. Reason – he was the man who was involved in a high speed crash with Joey at Brands Hatch. It was an accident which could have ruined Joey's career.

Joey said later: 'Short circuit racing can be just as dangerous as the roads and that day at Brands Hatch another rider ran into the back of me. I had no idea at the time who it was. It was only later that I learned that it was Mertins. I knew nothing about the accident until I woke up in hospital but I was off the track for almost a year with a broken leg, ribs, wrist, collar bone . . . you name it. I had a lot of trouble getting fit again and I will never forget that day.

'The thing about racing on bikes is that you ride very close. Once you know the riders you are competing with you can stay within inches of them. It's as close as that. If someone beside you is riding at 140mph and you are at the same speed, it seems as if you are standing still. That was the case at Brands Hatch on that Good Friday, but unfortunately neither Mertins or myself knew each other's style and something just went wrong.'

The Ulster sports world held its breath with the news that Joey had been taken to hospital. After all, Joey was one of those riders who didn't crash. He was indestructible.

He was competing in the third race of the Euro-Atlantic match series when the accident happened, and he was later taken to St. Mary's Hospital, Sidcup, in Kent with a suspected broken wrist and a broken thigh. After an operation it was confirmed that Dunlop's wrist was reset and a pin inserted in his thigh.

It wasn't known at that time just how long Joey would be in hospital but obviously the remainder of his 1989 season was very much in jeopardy. What everyone was thinking was whether or not Joey would be able to make it to the TT. Well, Joey certainly had no second thoughts about that and made it clear he would be there come hell or high water.

After his leg healed he made every effort to get himself fit for the island and at the end of May he flew out for practising. But it wasn't his leg which was causing the problems strangely enough, it was the injured wrist. He told me just before he left for the Isle of Man: 'The leg has healed but the wrist is still giving me some problems. I am flying out on Sunday in the hope that I can race in the island but I feel that the Formula One race has come too soon. I may be fit to ride in the later races but at this stage I am making no predictions. I have to wait and see how I get on during the practice sessions but at the moment I reckon I won't be racing in the Formula One which is the one race I really wanted to have a crack at.'

As it turned out Joey didn't ride in any of the Isle of Man races for he was turned down by the doctor.

Peter Kneale, doyen of the Manx Radio commentary team, still recalls that day. 'I will never forget it,' said Peter. 'Here was this man who was clearly a TT legend hobbling to the grandstand on crutches to see if he would be passed fit to race. His determination was obvious but the answer was 'No'. Still it showed the dedication of the man to compete in a sport which he loved above all else.'

It was a bitterly disappointed Joey Dunlop who left the medical office after having been turned down by the chief medical officer David Stevens. It was Joey's injured right wrist which caused the problem. According to officials it had not healed sufficiently for him to ride.

Although Joey looked downcast as he faced a battery of camera men I had the feeling that at the back of his mind he was thankful that the decision had been taken out of his hands. A lot of his closest friends were relieved that he had been given the thumbs down. After all, many of them still recalled that dreadful day when Tom Herron raced at the North West 200.

There was further bad news for Joey when Honda announced

that, in Joey's absence, their 750cc machine would be given to up-and-coming Hislop for the TT. It was, however, made clear that Joey would have the bike back again when he was fit to ride.

The move to put Hislop on the machine meant a turn of good luck for Ulster rider Phillip McCallen who was later to become one of the great rivals in the closing stages of Joey's career during the mid Nineties. McCallen was drafted in to ride Hislop's RC30 Honda on which he had won the North West 200 and this was the biggest break in McCallen's burgeoning career.

For Joey it was a TT week to forget in more ways than one. Hislop, taking advantage of the fact that he was on the better machine, equalled Joey's achievement of the previous year by landing a treble and so now there were three riders who had won a hat trick of races in TT week – Mike Hailwood, Joey Dunlop and Steve Hislop.

Dunlop meanwhile was concentrating on his comeback but he wasn't fooling anyone, not even himself. He said a few days after the TT that he would be hoping to return at the following week's Killinchy 150 over the Dundrod course. But he didn't resume racing until late July and he eventually came back virtually unobtrusively by riding at a meeting in Fore, an obscure course in Co Westmeath in Ireland. It was really only a holiday for Joey and the family and the week afterwards in Cork was also just an outing.

His first real test was still to come when he announced that he was an entry for the Temple 100 – the meeting where he scored his first ever road racing win back in 1975. Shortly before the Temple meeting I had the opportunity to speak to him at length about what had been a frustrating and in many ways disheartening season.

For once Joey was in a talkative mood.

I asked him about the fact that he had taken so long to come back and he said to me: 'I was at my lowest ebb when I missed the TT and then the Killinchy 250. But what was more worrying was the state my wrist was in. When I came back from England in April I noticed that the wrist wasn't straight so it had to be reset. Then at the time of the TT I became aware of the fact that my wrist was 'seizing' in motorcycling terms. In other words it was locking and I began to panic, thinking I would never have full use of it again. I resolved to fight back however and I can tell you it put all earlier thoughts of retirement right out of my head!'

I pushed him on the retirement point for everyone had been asking when he was going to pack it in and Joey disclosed to me that his plan had been to retire at the end of the 1989 season if he had beaten the Hailwood record.

As it turned out of course he wasn't able to ride at the TT, and one has to wonder what would have happened had he in fact managed to get those 15 wins in 1989. Would he have gone on another year or would he have decided enough is enough?

It's funny the way fate takes a hand in these affairs. The fact that there was no season as such for him in 1989 meant that he had to fight his way back again. The fight back probably recharged his batteries so that once he had broken Hailwood's record – it took him until 1993 – he didn't feel that there was any need to retire. He obviously had the bit between his teeth and he just kept on treating every season with the same enthusiasm and drive which he had shown in his vintage years.

But back to that year's Temple 100. 'Dunlopmania' certainly drew the crowds and they thronged around this narrow course between Saintfield in Co Down and Belfast.

Joey was limping about the paddock signing autographs, smoking cigarettes and looking just his old self. However in my view he was extremely haggard looking and I remember Valerie McBride, wife of Sam McBride, who later became Temple clerk of the course saying to me: 'Is that man really going to ride a motorcycle? He doesn't look up to it. He looks terrible.'

Joey certainly didn't look as though he was fit to run a marathon or throw the discus but racing motorcycles was something he did very, very well and he passed a medical although he had already told the doctors that he didn't intend to do anything startling. Dunlop, contrary to predictions, decided to ride in the 1000cc race rather than the 125cc but he made it clear beforehand that he was only going to do a handful of laps before pulling in. This is just what happened. Joey never became involved at the sharp end of the race and virtually toured round quite sensibly at an average speed of 85 mph on his Honda before coming into the pits with two laps to go.

Afterwards he told me: 'I needed that outing, I found it impossible to stand on the foot rests over the jumps as I normally do because of the pain in my leg. I had to sit on the machine instead of riding it like a jockey. Still, my wrist gave me no problem and this was my main worry. I'm hopeful that after today I can only get better.'

As it happened Joey didn't really improve on that performance. He rode at the Ulster Grand Prix and at the final meetings of the Ulster season – the Mid-Antrim 150 and the Carrowdore 100 – but really he was only touring and it came as no surprise when in September of that year he announced that he would quit for the season. He had never really recovered from those injuries at Brands Hatch on Good Friday. And he did the right thing in deciding to have a well-earned rest.

Joey's decision was made after competing in the Loughshinney meeting in Co Dublin. He was due to take part in the big Sunflower Trophy International meeting at Kirkistown on 14 October, but after consulting his doctor he was advised that owing to the fact that his leg was still giving him pain he would be wiser to call it a day.

So, the 1989 season which had promised so much ended with anticlimax. Would Joey Dunlop ever return to the heights he had scaled in the early Eighties? Only time would tell.

CHAPTER 13

RENAISSANCE MAN

By the dawn of the early 1990s it was decision time for Joey Dunlop. Should he continue in the fast lane and blast on towards Mike Hailwood's all-time TT record – or should he take the easy option and slip down a side road which would eventually lead to him fading from the scene?

It was no secret that Joey's major accident the previous year had damaged his prospects as far as world motorcycling was concerned. But then it was no big deal, for the World Formula One series was on its last legs and in 1990 it was renamed the FIM Prize – which was another way of saying 'We don't want you around any more'.

Carl Fogarty was the title holder and looked unlikely to be dislodged in 1990 except perhaps by Steve Hislop who at that time wasn't taking any particular interest in this fading championship and was looking further afield towards World Superbikes. So Fogarty had it on a plate except for Joey and many observers were of the opinion that Joey's days as a Superbike rider were virtually finished. I think Joey held this opinion also and as he reached what could be called the crossroads of his career – a hackneyed phrase, but one which was apt in this instance. He had to make up his mind about his immediate future. Should he stay with the Superbikes or drop down into the Lightweight classes?

Joey didn't actually announce anything at the beginning of 1990 but I got the impression that he felt his best chances of equalling Hailwood's record would be in the 250cc and the 125cc areas. He had already proved himself a top class 250cc rider at the TT and the 125cc looked to be right up his street, for it had only been restored to the island races in 1989 and wasn't exactly brimming with talent.

It was the obvious target. But few of us realised at the time that the biggest stumbling block between Joey and the Hailwood record would be a member of Joey's own family. Robert Dunlop was the holder of the 125cc TT, having won it in 1989, and he wasn't going to give up easily, nor would anyone have expected him too. As far as personalities go, he was totally different to Joey. In fact, I couldn't see them as brothers at all.

While Joey was reticent, inward looking and kept his own counsel, Robert was entirely the opposite. A cheeky chappie with a quick quip for every occasion, he was the master of the television and radio soundbite. It got to the stage that whenever there was a major motorcycle story about to break Robert Dunlop was always 'one of the usual suspects'. He was the man you could bring in at a moment's notice to give an instant opinion on anything pertaining to the sport. He was superb at it and he obviously had done his homework and knew exactly how much PR mattered in a sportsman's career. Conversely, you couldn't have preached the gospel of public relations to Joey. He just wouldn't listen. But Robert had an English wife, Louise, who promoted him and made him realise that he could be as big a name as his brother.

Did Robert suffer from being under the shadow of his more famous brother? Robert would never say so. Any time I asked him he always gave me a quiet grin, rolled one of his own cigarettes and answered in a non-committal way. He would have made a superb politician, you never got anything out of him but at the same time you always got a quote!

There's no doubt he was upset when he didn't get Joey's Honda for the 1989 125cc TT. Apparently he had been promised this but it all fell through. Robert rode a private Honda and won the race. Afterwards the works Honda boys congratulated him and asked him to join their team at the prizegiving but Robert refused. Was he angry with Honda? Probably, but he would never say.

As far as ability was concerned, Robert was top notch. No question about it. In my view he was the best 125cc TT rider Ireland has ever produced bar none and that includes Joey. He won the British championship in 1991 and he had a superbly smooth and confident style which seemed to assure him of victory without him obviously trying too hard. Louise once told me: 'Bob McMillan, the Honda boss, admitted that if Joey hadn't been around, Robert would have been the number one in the eyes of Honda. They regarded him extremely highly.'

However it wasn't Honda who snapped up Robert Dunlop at the beginning of 1990. It was the new JPS Norton team who, in their all-black leathers, introduced a splash of colour and a chauvinistic element into road racing. After all, Norton was a name which was synonymous with the sport since it began in the early 1900s. The Nortons had faded from the scene under the avalanche of the Japanese machines so when this new and exciting team emerged there was a lot of newspaper interest.

And would you believe it. Who was team manager but Barry Symmons – the great survivor. It was Barry who announced in early 1990 at a special press conference in Ballymoney that Robert Dunlop would be Norton's number one rider in the new season. So it looked as though it would be Robert and not Joey who would be providing the major threat to the Superbike stars Fogarty and Hislop – and he certainly gave notice of his intentions by rattling out a Superbike double at that year's North West 200.

And where was Joey while all this was going on? Well, Honda held him in such high regard that they had given him a new bike straight from Japan for the Formula One series. He also had other bikes which he ran independently, managed by the ever present Davy Wood. They were 250cc and 125cc machines and these were the bikes on which he was to enhance his career later that year.

Joey's fans had an early disappointment when the Motor Cycle Union of Ireland rated Robert as the number one rider in the country, followed by Phillip McCallen who had finished second to Robert in the previous year's Macau Grand Prix – the biggest success achieved by Robert in his career. Joey was rated only fourth behind 1988 Ulster Grand Prix winner Eddie Laycock, a Dubliner who had carried the flag for the MCUI in the World 500cc championships.

It looked like Joey was on his way out but the 'old man' with the wry grin and the eternal cigarette had other ideas and in the Cookstown 100 he fired a warning shot across the bows of those who had thought his days were over. It was just like old times as the crowd rose to Joey after he had won the 250cc McBride Fashions Irish Championship event. Joey was back on centre stage with a vengeance although he would have been the first to admit that he had his share of good luck when Brian Reid pulled in with a seized engine after completing only one lap and McCallen was also forced to retire.

McCallen had made a marvellous start to the season and while it would have been a major success for Phillip if he had beaten Dunlop at Cookstown, it wasn't to be and afterwards Joey, who hadn't won a race since the 250cc class at the Ulster Grand Prix in 1988, said: 'It was just like winning my first road race, I was a bit nervous when I took the lead for I thought something would happen to me. But everything went marvellously well. I didn't even feel those injuries from last year.'

So Joey Dunlop was off and running once again and with the TT looming it looked as though the Hailwood record was there for the taking. After all Joey would be riding in four races on the island. However 1990 was not to be his year at the TT. He finished eighth in the Formula One, 16th in the Senior and retired in the 250cc and in the 125cc, which once again was won by brother Robert.

You couldn't blame Joey for feeling that he was beginning to lose his grip on the big occasion, but those of us who wondered if he was sliding out gracefully were given a sharp and timely reminder of his talent when Joey searched deep down into himself to win a race which is rated as one of the greatest of his career. It was the

1990 Ulster Grand Prix. While Robert was grabbing all the head-lines, Joey was in the shadows. It looked as though he hadn't a prayer. But it was too soon to write off the old maestro and Joey showed once again that when the gloves came off at Dundrod, he had few if any peers.

He reserved his moment for the big race of the day, the Formula One. It was still a world championship event but the title was over. Fogarty had won in the Isle of Man from Nick Jefferies with Robert Dunlop third; then he had scored again at Vila Real with Robert second this time and Joey third. In the third round in Finland, Fogarty won again to wrap up the title. So Fogarty didn't need to come to the Ulster and he gave it a miss.

We were left with a battle between the two Dunlops – and it turned out to be one for the history books. The race revolved around whether or not the Norton or the Honda would refuel and there were some who had a notion that Joey might lose when it came to the pit stop. But Joey had a card up his sleeve. While Robert came in to refuel his thirsty Norton on the ninth of the 13 laps Joey just kept on going – shades of the 1980 Classic TT – and with the crowd urging him on he opened up a cushion which turned out to be a winning one. With his many thousands of fans biting their nails that Joey wouldn't run out of petrol, the little rider who had thrilled so many produced yet another big one from the hat and scored his first Ulster GP success for two years.

It has to be said however that he achieved this win without any sort of opposition from Steve Hislop. As early as the first lap Steve was touring and he pulled in to sort out a faulty gear lever which cost him precious time. Hislop did go out again but it was a token gesture and at the sharp end it was the head to head between the Dunlops which captured the imagination.

They were first and second throughout the 13 laps. To start with it was Robert in front on the black Norton looking every inch the winner while Joey was tucked in behind waiting for his moment to pounce – which he did on the fifth lap. He continued in front for another three laps before Robert caught him again but at this stage

Robert had to refuel, and although the highly professional Norton team took only seven seconds, this gave Joey his chance and he decided to go for broke. Right up until the closing stages most of us thought he would have to pull in some time but Joey had other ideas and to a cacophony of sound from the packed stands took the flag to record a tear-jerking success.

Afterwards he appeared to be overcome by the occasion. 'I had decided early on to try to go through without refuelling,' he said. 'For I knew that the Norton would have to come in. I was relieved to see Robert in the pits for this gave me the advantage I needed. I don't know how much fuel I had left in the tank. I was just too scared to look. I knew however that if the engine began to misfire I would have to pull in. Happily this wasn't the case.'

Robert conceded: 'What can you do? I'm naturally pleased for Joey to win and I must say that he told me last week that he wouldn't be refuelling. In my heart of hearts I knew I would have problems beating him if that was the case.'

Barry Symmons, who had guided Joey to his five world championships, had mixed feelings at the end of the race. 'For once in my life I was just hoping there would be a dead heat,' he said.

This was Joey's best performance in 1990 in what otherwise had been a disappointing year. He had to wait for the 1991 TT and another chance to break the elusive record of Mike Hailwood and this time he had another Ulster rider to contend with who was threatening to make a lot of waves.

Phillip McCallen was a wildcat type of rider who came from Portadown and who, as we have seen, was given his first chance in the big time when Joey couldn't make it to the 1989 TT. After that McCallen just kept improving and had a totally different style to Joey's which won him a multitude of fans. It was almost like the old days of the Armoy Armada and the Dromara Destroyers. Dunlop versus McCallen. Who was the better? The fans argued about it endlessly.

There is no doubt that McCallen was exciting to watch. He looked as though he was about to fall off at every stage of the race.

But he hung in there and became one of the best TT riders of all time. His total of 11 wins over this most unforgiving of circuits speaks for itself and he has a record of four wins in one week in 1996 which even Joey Dunlop never equalled.

However in 1991, the days of TT glory were still in front of McCallen and Joey was preparing himself for yet another crack at the record. He had by now decided that the North West 200 was no longer a key race, serving only as a warm up race for the TT. 'It's too much like a short circuit,' he said. 'I'm not keen on all that close racing any more.' There is no doubt in my mind that Joey's Brands Hatch crash had changed his attitude to racing and perhaps to life. Rather than giving 110% in every race, as he had done before, he reserved his best efforts for special occasions. One of those, undoubtedly, was the Isle of Man.

So for 1991 he was back again and once more Robert was in his way. Joey's best chance according to the experts would be in the 125cc TT. But in a pulsating finish Robert squeezed home after Joey had led for almost three quarters of the race. It was heart-breaking for the Joey Dunlop entourage. For most of the race Joey appeared to be heading for a record-equalling 14th win but with one lap to go Robert, who had cut the gap remorselessly through lap two, eventually moved ahead by four seconds and gradually increased his advantage on the final lap.

The story of the race is simply told. Joey was eight seconds ahead of McCallen at Glen Helen on lap one then increased it to 22 seconds ahead of Robert at the end of the first circuit. Joey was still in the lead at the halfway mark. But then it all went wrong. A broken breather pipe robbed him of his chance when he was in the lead by just over 15 seconds. It was at this stage that he came in to refuel at the end of the second lap and the luckless Joey struggled back into the race with his machine covered in petrol. He was relegated to second place by Robert who took the lead between Ramsey and the Grandstand in Douglas on the penultimate lap.

'The pipe was broken at the pits and from then on petrol was being pumped out all the time and I thought the tank might run dry,' said the disappointed Joey, who even freewheeled down the Mountain on the final lap as a precautionary measure. 'I thought I was in with a real chance today,' he said, before announcing to an amazed audience that he had given up smoking as part of his get fit programme!

Meanwhile, although Robert had won he wasn't getting much of the applause and he must have felt like a party pooper. 'I was having a little fuel trouble myself,' he said. But no one was really listening. The tears were all for Joey. When I asked Robert if he felt like the least popular TT winner of all time he replied: 'I have a duty to my sponsor.' Who could argue with that?

Later that year Joey rose to the occasion yet again with two magnificent wins over the by now hot McCallen at the Ulster Grand Prix. In a simply magnificent piece of riding, Joey rewarded his faithful fans by getting the better of McCallen by a bike's length in the first Superbike race – and then repeating the performance in the final one at the end of the day. In many ways Joey proved that although he was now 39 years of age he still had plenty 'in the tank' for a new boy like McCallen.

Interestingly McCallen was one of Joey's fans even in those days when it would have been easy to have been an enemy because of the intense pressure in both camps. 'I will never forget the first time I saw Joey race,' he told me. 'I certainly wasn't impressed. I was only 12 at the time and Joey must have been about 25. It was the Tandragee 100 and I was expecting to see a superstar like Barry Sheene. Instead I saw a rider covered in oil and looking like a nobody. He didn't appear to be the legend everyone was talking about.'

However those first impressions soon changed to admiration as McCallen realised the talent which Joey possessed. 'The beauty about him was his natural, easy style,' McCallen continued. 'He looked so smooth. He appeared to be so safe. In fact he won without seeming to try. I couldn't compare him to any other rider. I think he was unique. Joey would race round a course at the fastest possible speed and you would still think he was only out for a stroll.'

Joey always looked kindly on the fact that Phillip never forgot that Joey had given him his first chance in the big time. It was Dunlop who got him involved with Honda in the beginning when McCallen wanted a break into racing. Joey pointed the way and McCallen, according to Joey, continued to thank him for years afterwards.

Joey's most memorable race against McCallen was, for me, that 1991 epic. It was the one which I will never forget. With one lap to go the excitement was intense as McCallen launched his challenge against Dunlop. However as both riders raced through the final curve to the finish it was Joey on the inside who just held off McCallen's late surge on the wide outside to get up by a quarter of a second. It was a finish reminiscent of the famous victory of Tom Herron over South African Alan North in 1976 but this time there was no dispute about the winner. Dunlop had got there, if only just.

McCallen had the satisfaction of setting the fastest lap with a speed of 120.12mph but for Joey it was an amazing 27th win over the Dundrod course. He seemed to be his usual matter-of-fact self when talking about it afterwards. 'I always thought I had the race well in hand,' he said. 'Phillip did try to pass me a couple of times on the last lap and then I got in behind a slower rider approaching the final bend, but I knew there was only one line through there and that Phillip wouldn't catch me racing on the outside.'

A disappointed McCallen, who had been on top of the world having had a marvellous season up until then said: 'I thought I might have passed Joey on the back end of the course but my bike started to slide about and I nearly lost it. I tried again at the Quarries but went into another slide and then I made that final effort near the finish but I just couldn't get through.'

Third place was taken by Robert Dunlop, whose Norton managed to finish the course contrary to some predictions. Nevertheless, Robert was disappointed not to have finished closer to the leading pair. He had his own struggle beating off the attentions of Dave Leach, who was ahead of him for over half the race, but Robert battled on and despite missing a gear and almost going into a wobble on the last lap he managed to carve his way through to finish third.

Dunlop and McCallen weren't only involved as a high speed duo at Dundrod that year. Both rode for Honda in the Suzuka Eight Hour race near Tokyo. McCallen had many fond memories of how the Japanese people idolised Joey. 'Joey was a huge hero in Japan,' he said. 'He was like a god with fans mobbing him everywhere he went chanting "Joey, Joey!". The Isle of Man TT races are rightly revered in Japan as the ultimate challenge in bike racing and winners are held in very high regard. It was unbelievable how big a star Joey was in Japan. From the different Press reports I had collected I had been aware that my popularity had risen, but during that trip I was a nobody standing for hours in the hot sun while Joey signed thousands of autographs.'

But that was about as successful as it got for the Irish pair. They were dogged by mechanical troubles, especially frustrating because McCallen had offered to bring his engine with him from home but Honda had insisted they had everything they needed. The race itself was won by Wayne Gardner on a Honda along with Michael Doohan, who later became one of the greatest world 500cc champions. Kevin Magee was second along with Doug Chandler and third place went to the British team of Fogarty and Hislop on Hondas. Joey and Philip failed to qualify for the main event.

And so ended 1991. A satisfactory year for Joey in many ways especially after those wins over McCallen but at the same time Joey still yearned for that TT victory which had now become almost an obsession. You somehow got the impression that perhaps Joey would never equal Hailwood's record. After all, he had been stuck on the 13 wins mark since 1988 and by 1992 he must have been thinking that time was not on his side. However, he needn't have worried and his fans could also breathe a sigh of relief for on 8 June 1992 the most popular Isle of Man TT rider in history finally did the trick and equalled the record by winning the 125cc class, beating his brother Robert into second place.

It was a complete reversal of the previous year's race when Joey had lost because of a bad pit stop. This time Robert lost ground in similar circumstances and after that Joey just went further and further away although it was tight enough at the finish with Robert launching a last lap counter attack which just failed to pay off by nine seconds. Joey said afterwards: 'I'm glad to get that over. Maybe this will keep a lot of the critics quiet. It was very tight and I started to get tired during that last lap. I was also beginning to worry and I felt I might not make it but the bike was going great and I just managed to hold on. I have been trying for four years to equal Hailwood's record of 14 wins and now I'm so tired I'm just ready to go home. It's a wonderful feeling.'

Joey led by three seconds early on and increased this to nine at the halfway mark. Then, as both riders came in for petrol, Robert had cut the lead back to one second and it all depended on that fuel stop. Robert's Honda failed to start on time after the refuel. Joey took advantage and was 17 seconds ahead by the time the riders had reached Glen Helen on lap three. After that it was only a matter of Joey holding on and maintaining his advantage which he did until the end. There were some who said at the time that Robert had deliberately stalled in the pits to allow Joey to win. But knowing Robert, I find that hard to believe.

When Joey arrived in the winner's enclosure he was greeted with a tumultuous cheer which made Brian Reid, Philip McCallen and Steve Linsdell, who were already on the rostrum for the 400cc ceremony, almost dive for cover! The moment Dunlop appeared Reid, McCallen and Linsdell were totally ignored as Press and public howled for Joey. One of the first to congratulate him was Robert. Joey said: 'Being mentioned in the same breath as Mike Hailwood is something special. It's also marvellous to win my first 125cc race here. It was a personal ambition. It was the one I hadn't won.'

There was even more pandemonium at the awards ceremony in the Villa Marina that evening. Chants of 'Joey, Joey, Joey,' greeted

Dunlop and the efforts of compere John Brown to announce him were drowned out. Once Brown made the announcement Joey received a standing and thunderous ovation which lasted for over five minutes before the presentation could be made. Earlier in the afternoon his father Willie, anticipating the reception his son would get, had asked: 'I wonder who they will get to put the roof back on the Villa Marina after tonight?' And he was right.

Bob McMillan, who presented the manufacturer's award, said: 'This is the greatest night I have ever seen here. We have never witnessed anything like it and probably never will again.'

Following the Isle of Man triumph Joey continued in winning mood, scoring a double in the Steam Packet road racing at Billown near Castletown on the Saturday night after the TT. He won the 125cc and 750cc races, and in the big bike category he pushed the lap record up to 104.65mph to beat McCallen with Welshman Jason Griffiths third. Next stop was the Ulster Grand Prix where Joey repeated his 125cc success, beating Mick Lofthouse and Ian Lougher. But it was Robert who stole the show that day when he won both the Superbike races on the Norton.

But there was no respite for Joey in 1993. Having equalled the TT record he hungered after a new goal – beating it outright. With 14 wins now under his belt Joey saw no reason why he couldn't make it 15.

At the beginning of the season it was announced that he would have the full backing of Castrol Honda Britain. They said they would support him with an improved 750cc bike and for the first time would back him on a 250cc. In what was hinted as perhaps his final season, Dunlop was also scheduled to ride privately-sponsored 125cc and 600cc machines. He was to join fellow Honda riders McCallen and Hislop but while this pair would concentrate on the British championships, Dunlop would be riding only in Irish races apart from the TT.

Joey quickly moved into top gear that season when he delighted a huge crowd by scoring a hat trick in the Tandragee 100 in early May. At the age of 41 the Ballymoney maestro began his string of successes with a superb victory in the 250cc race, beating Brian Reid and newcomer James Courtney. He then followed this up with a heart-stopping ride in the Regal 600, which he led from start to finish to beat Ian King and Johnnie Rea, son of the John Rea who had sponsored Joey all those years earlier. Joey's treble was completed in the Open 1000cc race; he led from the start to power his big Castrol Honda to an easy win over Derek Young and Alan Irwin.

Joey was now back with a bang. After two meetings that season he had knocked out five wins. His other two successes were gained in the earlier Cookstown 100. What a turnaround! With many writing Joey's racing obituary in 1989 after his Brands crash now, only four years later, he was on the brink of something very special. It certainly seemed to be the most celebrated renaissance in any sport in my time – at an Ulster level at any rate.

At the end of the previous year Joey had received a special award from the Motor Cycle Union of Ireland. President Drew Armstrong had astonished Joey by telling him that they were making a presentation to him in view of his record-equalling performance in the TT and also to acknowledge the many years he had ruled the sport. Joey appeared somewhat taken aback by the presentation and obviously felt that he was getting a broad hint to retire. In receiving the award he said quite forcibly that he had no intention of giving up racing just yet but many of us still doubted whether he had another year at the top in him.

We couldn't have been more wrong. Joey suddenly began to turn the clock back and with the aid of that new Honda machinery he saw off his hottest pursuers.

The next stage in 1993 was the Isle of Man TT, the Holy Grail, and the all-time TT record. Would Joey make it? That was the question on everyone's lips as the rider who had become a living legend wheeled his bike to the starting line with his customary air of studied disinterest.

Once again it was the 125cc class which saw history made, further justifying Joey's decision to move down the classes. Riding a Honda with an engine flown in at the last minute for the race, Joey was never seriously challenged and, after taking the lead shortly after Glen Helen, he increased the pace steadily. The engine which Joey used was loaned to him by James Courtney who was unable to ride because of a crash in the North West 200. A delighted Dunlop told me afterwards: 'What a day. I will always remember it and I want to thank Jim for that engine. It made all the difference. Now the pressure is off me and I can enjoy myself for the rest of the week.'

Riding with tremendous style Joey gave a vintage display and although Robert cut the deficit to eight seconds at one stage, Joey always appeared to be in command. There was a last minute hiccup when the clock which indicates a rider's arrival at the Bungalow failed to operate on the last lap and it appeared as though Joey had gone missing. With the light over Robert's number at Signpost Corner things looked gloomy for Joey's fans. But it was only a technical hitch for very soon afterwards the light came on over Joey's number and he screeched into sight to a crescendo of cheering.

What a night it was for Joey and the whole Dunlop family to remember. Needless to say the Villa Marina was packed to capacity once again. These were halcyon days for Joey. But was the night of 7 June 1993 a night which Joey never thought would happen?

'Ach, I suppose you could say that,' he conceded. 'I had a lot of trouble over the last few years with my leg and my arm broken and then Robert beating me two years ago. I always thought to myself that I wouldn't stick my neck out any more to get records. But the chance came along and I just took it.

'Someone once said to me when you win one TT, the second one is much easier. Well, once I had equalled the record the pressure was off me. It was a bit like winning that first TT. I was able to ride in the race and feel normal again. For a couple of years I was under a lot of pressure. Some people wanted me to beat Hailwood's record. Others didn't. At times I thought I could beat it but then I felt if I did a lot of folk would turn against me and that my career would go sour.

'In the end I was glad the way people took it. I know Mike was a legend here. I remember coming here at the time of Mike's come-back. That was in 1978 and I had two really good laps with him on the Yamaha. He was teaching me then and I followed him round. I kept him in sight the whole way and I knew that if he was just in front of me at the finishing line I would have beaten the great Mike Hailwood round the TT course. At that time I was a lot younger and that's the way I thought. I was really keen to win and especially to beat someone with a name like Hailwood. Mike will never be for-gotten because he won at the Isle of Man on all types of bikes. He was the greatest.'

Joey was asked that evening if he was intending to carry on or was he happy to pull the plug after 15 TTs. He thought for a moment before saying: 'I couldn't really answer to tell you the truth. I said this year I probably wouldn't do the TT because I would rather come back and ride classic bikes than come back and ride bikes that weren't competitive. But I'm riding hard enough now to still win a TT, so I'll probably come back. You know I still get the same feeling competing in the TT as I did almost 20 years ago. It's something special when you are lining up to go out there. It would have to be or I wouldn't be here.

'It is always disappointing when something goes wrong but then I do most of my own work and I like to prepare the bikes my own way so if there is a problem I can always blame myself. If I have a bad TT and retire or fall off that's all part of the game. It has never prevented my enjoyment of these superb races. Yes, I'll definitely be back.'

And of course he was.

CHAPTER 14

JOURNEY INTO THE UNKNOWN

F or it's a long, long time from May to December, and the days grow short when you reach September.'

Joey Dunlop fans may not have been music critics, but the words of this nostalgic song aptly summed up the stage which Joey had reached by the time 1994 dawned. He had beaten Mike Hailwood's TT record; there was no longer a world championship on pure roads to become involved in and, at 42 years of age, Joey had nothing left to prove. So why go on? Well, as Joey once said to Brian Reid: 'What else would I do?'

You could understand Joey easing down if he was by now a back number. But the opposite was the case. He was highly popular, so much so that he topped the poll at the end of 1993 for the leading personality in Ulster sport. The voting was organised by the *Belfast Telegraph* newspaper and a firm of jewellers – and Joey won by a distance.

After recovering from a severe bout of 'flu which came at just the wrong time, Joey was presented with a £2,000 Rolex watch and was totally stunned by all the fuss. 'I thought somebody was having me on when I was told I was a winner,' said the unbelievably modest Dunlop. 'I just didn't believe it. Winning my 15th TT meant a great deal to me personally but I didn't realise it was so important to so many people.'

One could almost say that at his stage in his career Joey Dunlop was the best known Irish sports personality on the planet and it seemed at the time as though he would continue to hold centre stage for as long as he liked. But the sands of fate have a habit of shifting and before very long as far as headlines were concerned, Joey was again taking a back seat to brother Robert although this time it wasn't because of Robert's successes on the track. It was as a result of an horrific accident which Robert was involved in at the Formula One TT.

Robert, who had now switched to Hondas, looked like taking over the Superbike throne which had for so long been occupied by his elder brother. He hammered out a memorable double at the North West 200 in May 1994, making himself one of the favourites for the TT the following month.

Then it all went wrong.

Sunday 5 June 1994 is a date which will always be remembered by the Dunlop family, for that was the day when Robert's career nearly ended as he lay in a heap beside a stone wall on the unforgiving TT Mountain circuit. Robert had been in contention for the lead in the Formula One race when suddenly at a bend shortly after Ballaugh Bridge the back wheel of his Honda appeared to disintegrate; he hurtled across the road and hit a nearby wall before coming to rest like a crumpled rag doll.

Was it the end for Robert Dunlop? Well this gritty little rider always appeared to have the last laugh and although at the time it seemed that he would race no more, he fought his way back and by the time it came to 1996 he was racing once again. But in those two years he suffered a lot of pain and misery as he contemplated what was left of his career. I used to visit him at the Ulster Hospital in Belfast and we chatted about what he would do in the future. He always insisted that he would race again, but personally I had my doubts. As I looked at his battered body which was covered in scars and breakages, I just wondered what drove a man like this to virtual self destruction.

But the Dunlop family are unique. Like brother Joey, Robert

would have no other life except road racing and, as weeks became months and then years, he gradually regained his strength although he was never going to be a Superbike rider again. Robert, wisely in my view, decided to stick to 125cc machinery when he made his comeback in 1996.

But what was happening to Joey while Robert was reconsidering his future? Obviously he had been greatly affected by his brother's crash but the single-mindedness which had distinguished Joey Dunlop's life from the start soon reasserted itself and he continued to win TTs in much the same way as morning follows night.

Win number 16 came along only two days after Robert's crash. Many a rider would have stepped aside and not raced that week but the Dunlops are a rare breed. Joey decided that it would be best for all concerned that he raced and after being reassured that Robert was recovering in hospital he went to the line for the 125cc TT and duly won again. It was one of Joey's easiest successes and he admitted afterwards: 'I missed racing against Robert.' Whether this meant he missed his brother's presence or his opposition remained in doubt for Joey had an enigmatic way of handling questions.

Joey had been in a sombre mood before the race but he brightened up considerably when he was informed afterwards that Robert was on the mend and this, together with his success, put him in a more positive frame of mind for the rest of the week. He was never in any sweat, leading from start to finish and ending up over one and a half minutes in front of the second place man Denis McCullough, nephew of Ray McCullough who had given Joey all those close calls 20 years earlier.

Although Joey was racing against a new generation he still proved that he had what it took to succeed and later in the week he made it a TT double and number 17 of his career when he achieved a dramatic last lap victory in the 250cc race. The race had looked all over in favour of McCallen, who was fast becoming the rider to beat. McCallen had a 15 second lead at Ramsey on the final lap, having been in front for most of the race, but then came the news that he was touring on his Honda between the Bungalow and Brandywell and as a result he was out of contention.

Dunlop, who had been lying in second place throughout, now had no pressure on him and when the light went up over his name stating that he was within sight of Signpost Corner and almost at the finish a huge Dunlop cheer erupted from the Grandstand as his fans realised yet again that Joey was 'The Man'. Joey roared across the line and afterwards said: 'I thought that I would be second for Phillip was well ahead of me. I don't know what happened to him but I had my own problems for the footrest broke off at Ramsey on the first lap and I had to rest my foot on the exhaust pipe at times.'

The ever present Davy Wood added: 'At least we put enough fuel in to finish the race. Phillip must have cut it too fine.'

And of course Davy was spot on.

A rueful McCallen said afterwards that he had made a monumental blunder as a result of which he had run out of fuel on that vital last lap. McCallen had tried to pull a fast one earlier in the race when the riders came in to refuel at the half distance. Phillip turned a nine second lead over Dunlop into a whopping 20 second advantage; he was literally into the pits and out again in the shortest possible time but sadly for McCallen he had to pay the penalty for not taking enough fuel on board. This mistake was something which rarely failed to appear in conversation when McCallen discussed his TT career. It was obvious to me that this misjudgement had haunted him for a long time, for Phillip never liked to contemplate defeat.

Still, it was another win for Joey. And he went on to score a record-breaking four-timer in the Southern 100 road races over the Castletown circuit in the southern tip of the Isle of Man the following month.

Could nobody stop Joey? Well McCallen obviously thought he could and most fans believed that the talented Co Armagh rider was the only one around with the flair and the ability to take Dunlop on, especially at a meeting like the Ulster Grand Prix, which loomed up again in August. McCallen predicted that he had a great chance in every race and he nearly made it a full house. He picked up four wins and would have had a five-timer – unheard of in those days – but for that man Dunlop who won the opening Superbike race after a nerve-racking battle.

In his autobiography McCallen described this race as 'an absolute classic.' And no one who was there that day would argue. Welshman Jason Griffiths exploded into action by leading the field early on with McCallen and Dunlop close behind. Then the race was suddenly stopped because a car had tried to get on to the course at the Hairpin bend! The race was restarted over the full distance and McCallen took the lead this time with Griffiths and Dunlop in tow. But Joey came storming past at the Deer's Leap, missing an oil flag and ending up on a slip road.

Joey soon resumed the chase however and with a lap record of 123.75mph he caught up with Griffiths and the pace got hotter and hotter. Joey raised the tempo again and passed Griffiths to get on McCallen's tail before overtaking him on lap five. McCallen stuck with him, hoping to slipstream at the end of the race, and the riders were side by side at the Quarry Bends on the final lap when incredibly they banged into each other. Fortunately no one fell off; Joey held McCallen at bay and in a heart-stopping finish got past a couple of slower riders at the end to win by one fifth of a second.

The crowd had been going wild throughout and you can guess what their reaction was when Joey took the flag. This was one of those special occasions when Joey raised his game and put on his 'race face', as his supporters used to call it. They reckoned – and I was inclined to agree – that at this stage of his career Joey only raced to win when he felt like it. On other occasions he was content to sit it out. That Superbike race of 1994 will always be remembered as one of those occasions. Joey really didn't need to race his guts out, but when Joey felt 'the call' there was no stopping him.

Later that year Joey headed a party of riders who flew to New Zealand for a series of road races under the leadership of entrepreneur Billy Nutt. Billy had transformed the North West 200 into one of the sport's major international road races and he was intending to do the same for the Ulster Grand Prix, which he had organised for the first time in 1994. Nutt was hoping that with Joey in the van-guard, the Irish party would attract the attention of New Zealand competitors who would in turn travel over for the following year's Ulster. Well it didn't quite turn out that way, but the New Zealand trip established a link between Nutt and Dunlop which was to last until Joey's death.

Billy reminded me of that trip some years later when he said: 'Joey was always his own man. In New Zealand, although we had booked accommodation Joey felt much more at home getting into a van and sleeping on a mattress. He would then take off into the country but we knew he would turn up for the next race meeting and sure enough just before the start Joey arrived as usual!'

The following year Nutt and Dunlop joined in an attempt to run a new road racing championship over circuits in eastern Europe. This was the start of Joey's travels to Estonia and Latvia which ended up in such tragic circumstances five years later. Nutt contin-ued: 'The idea had come to my mind when I had been attending a congress of the FIM, the controlling body of the sport. After chat-ting with Jo Sigward, one of the FIM representatives, I thought it would be a good idea to establish a championship on purely road circuits. This series would take in the Ulster Grand Prix and the Isle of Man TT.

'I met with John Shand, a New Zealand representative, and he appeared to be keen for us to race in his country,' said Nutt. 'Things moved along slowly but we never really got it off the ground. I remember Joey and I visiting several road racing countries including Russia to see if we could whip up some interest but it was hard going. Eventually we managed to launch a series consisting of races in Germany, Belgium, Ireland, Latvia and Estonia. Joey told me at the time that he always liked to travel and would be keen to make an appearance at all these meetings.

'We first went to Estonia in 1995 and Joey liked what he saw. He was also in cracking form for he won four races – 125cc, 250cc, and the two Superbikes. Afterwards the prizegiving was done at the side of the road and Joey told me later: "The cups were filled with pure vodka. It was the real thing. I want to race here more often!"

'My memory of the track was that it was used for heavy traffic all the year round and as a result was most certainly a natural circuit! It was about four miles round and the only thing I wasn't keen on were the trees which were close to the course. Admittedly we had plenty of trees on our home tracks but I just had a feeling at the time that the wooded area would cause problems.'

Nutt wasn't to know how prophetic those fears would be, for five years later Joey Dunlop would end his life by crashing into those same woods.

Billy was full of praise for the Estonians: 'They couldn't have been more hospitable. They really took to Joey and were fascinated by the fact that he had travelled there on his own. I met him in Estonia while Joey drove there in his van. We used to sit out at night at the camp site eating and chatting about the sport. The local fans loved to listen to Joey's stories and they seemed to be able to understand him reasonably well. In addition the Estonian television people really lapped him up and he was rarely off their screens. Joey was to many an honorary Estonian!'

Joey's activities in eastern Europe formed a backdrop in 1995 to yet another double success at the Isle of Man TT. It had got to the point where few were really counting his TT wins and you sometimes had difficulty remembering how many he had totted up.

Just for the record he went into the 1995 meeting with 17 successes – a breathtaking achievement – and in his 25th year in road racing he headed a three-man Castrol Honda team. Bob McMillan visited Joey at his home and struck a deal whereby Joey headed an outfit which was completed by Nick Jefferies and Stephen Ward in the TT and the Ulster Grand Prix, while Mike Edwards was set to replace Ward in the North West 200.

There had been rumours yet again that Joey was set to quit his long and illustrious career but Davy Wood informed those who thought otherwise that Joey was as keen as ever and that this new deal would give him the incentive he needed. 'Honda have always thought highly of Joey and all his involvement with them has been on a personal level,' said Davy. And Honda's confidence was proved well founded yet again when Joey thumped out an amazing 18th TT victory by winning the 250cc race.

This was a class for which he had really got a taste for success. After winning it in 1994 he continued his string of successes until 1999, when he drew a blank before resuming with a win in the year 2000. Six successes out of seven starts in the one class. How do you beat that!

The 1995 win was contemptuously easy. Joey made up for the disappointment of retiring after only six miles in the 125cc race – the one he was expected to win – and knuckled down to a determined effort in the 250cc which saw him take a quick lead after which he never looked like being caught. 'I was disappointed with that 125cc retirement but it made me all the more determined to win the 250,' he said. 'Once I had settled into an early lead I felt fairly comfortable.'

Not only did Joey win the race by 25 seconds from fellow Ulsterman James Courtney, he set a record race average of 115.68mph despite not having had any real pressure put on him. McCallen, who had been regarded as a hot favourite, drew a blank, finishing a disappointing fourth. It was to be a patchy TT week for the Portadown rider. In view of the fact that he was taking part in the new Thunderbike series on the Continent it meant that he had to miss the Senior TT at the end of the week and race in Italy instead. And who stepped in to replace him at the top of the rostrum? You've got it – Joey again!

This was Joey's 19th TT success but more importantly it was his first Senior race win since 1988. Joey was in tremendous form and finished 41 seconds ahead of Scots rider Iain Duffus, with third place going to Stephen Ward. He said afterwards in typical understatement: 'I'm a bit tired. I will have to get used to riding these big bikes again!'

McCallen was still an absentee when the Ulster Grand Prix came along and once again Dunlop took advantage by recording his first hat trick at the meeting since 1985. He won both 250cc races and also one of the Superbike contests, the other going to New Zealander Robert Holden, who was to end his career in tragedy at the following year's TT.

Meanwhile, the honours hadn't dried up and after having been awarded the MBE for services to motorcycling in 1986, Dunlop had double delight when it was announced in the New Year's Honours List for 1996 that he had received an OBE for 'services to the sport and humanitarian deeds'. This meant that Ulster's most enduring sporting personality would be the only motorcyclist in the British Isles ever to have received two decorations from Buckingham Palace.

The words 'humanitarian deeds' may have confused many of Joey's fans, for they were unaware that he did anything other than race motorcycles. However there was another side to Joey Dunlop's complex personality. It involved compassion and it tied in comfortably with his self styled image as a lone ranger.

One of the most outstanding qualities which Joey possessed, in addition to his racing and mechanical skills, was his love for children. This caring attitude, of which he was not ashamed, did not end with his own family, but included the many thousands of orphans in Eastern European countries. He was first alerted to their plight when visiting these countries with Billy Nutt in 1995.

It was his wish to help these children that took Joey on a number of mercy missions to Romania, Bosnia and Albania. On these trips Joey, true to his own tradition, travelled alone, for between three and six weeks, through unknown territory, and in many instances he met with hostile personnel both on the ground and administratively.

It all began when a young nurse from Portglenone, Co Antrim called Siobhan Lagan, who was working in a Romanian orphanage, requested food from home to be sent out. The children in the orphanage were having to live on a ghastly ration of gruel, which was life-sustaining and no more.

When it was discovered that posting a parcel of food to Romania would cost £40, a friend and neighbour of Joey's, Lexie Kerr, approached him to see if he would make a trip to Romania. Joey was more than willing but replied that it would have to be pretty soon as the racing season was fast approaching.

When it became known that Joey was going to make the trip, foodstuffs and other essential goods poured in, necessitating the use of a large van and trailer to hold everything that had been donated.

Unaware of what lay ahead of him he set off for Romania in the dead of winter, all alone, an expedition that only Joey would have tackled. As was his wont, Joey drove, ate and slept in the van, despite the extremely low temperatures, which were estimated to be 30 degrees below zero in places. When he stopped to rest for the night, it was so cold that the diesel fuel in the van froze, and also the fuel in his cigarette lighter. All he could do was huddle up in his sleeping bag and try to keep as warm as possible.

Joey was very aware of the importance of the trips. He always gave himself plenty of time, so that he would not have to drive too fast. After one mission he said: 'It is a very long run, and I had a good load, so I took my time. I could not afford to have a break-down. Not only would it be impossible to get anything fixed, but if you had to leave the van, everything would be stolen by the time you got back. The only thing to do was to get there without any mishaps.'

This braving of the elements took its toll on the hardy Joey. When he arrived at the orphanage in Ungureni, Siobhan Lagan admitted that he was suffering from mild hypothermia, so the first thing they did was get him warmed up. The goods and food which he was carrying had to be hidden in one of the little bunga-lows used by the staff in the grounds of the orphanage. Joey again explained: 'They could not leave the food and stuff in the orphanage as it was likely to be stolen so they put it in through the windows in the wee flats that the nurses lived in and hid it there.'

Joey was very touched by what he saw in the orphanage, but did not talk a lot about it. However his good friend John Harris, whom he visited on the way back home to collect a bike, admitted that it was very obvious by the expression on his face and the tone of his voice that it had not been a pleasant experience.

Many a lesser man would have decided that he had done his bit and left it at that, but such was the quality and humanity of the man that he made further missions to Bosnia and Albania.

Travel weariness and the intense cold were not the only problems on these frequent excursions to Eastern Europe. There were scary episodes as well. 'On the way back from Albania I was arrested at gunpoint for not having the correct documents,' Joey recalled. 'They wanted £25 for me to cross the checkpoint but I wouldn't pay.'

Border guards in those parts expected to be bribed into allowing strangers to cross into a country. Mostly they wanted cigarettes or food but Joey tried to explain to them who he was and what he was doing.

Seemingly he was not making much progress until one of the guards spotted a copy of *Motor Cycle News* with Joey's photograph on the front lying on the dashboard of the van. When the guard saw this and was convinced that it really was Joey Dunlop in the flesh, he contacted the chief of police who provided Joey with a letter which he produced every time he was stopped. According to Joey this letter worked wonders and he had very few problems from then on. As we all know, and as Raido Ruutel from the Estonian Motor Cycle Federation said at Joey's funeral, he was an even bigger man abroad than he was at home.

The true value of Joey's mercy missions could only be truly calculated by someone like Siobhan Lagan and her fellow nurses or the children in the orphanages. The physical and psychological cost to Joey Dunlop will never be known, as he rarely spoke about these courageous trips.

However, his exploits and the sacrifices he made did not go unnoticed. In 1996 when he was called to Buckingham Palace to be presented with his OBE he said to reporters and cameramen: 'This means more to me than winning any motorbike race.' There lies a statement which sums up the truly genuine caring nature of Joey Dunlop. He was a rider with nerves of steel and a heart as big as the racing world which he dominated.

CHAPTER 15

HAND OF FATE

Joey Dunlop could have rested on his laurels at the start of 1996 secure in the knowledge that his place in sporting history was assured. But Joey was never one to think in those terms. Competition was what life was all about even at the age of 44 and he still had a thirst for victory at the TT which was never sated.

In June of that year he travelled to the island looking for his 20th victory. Needless to say he not only achieved his goal but added one more win for good measure. The previous year Joey had given up smoking after a lifetime on the weed. How he did it I will never know but it didn't seem to upset his concentration or his courage. No longer was he 'Smoking Joe' but the new look Joey was still as effective and he opened his account during TT week by winning the 250cc class – a race which he could now virtually call his own.

He snatched victory by just six seconds from Scot Jim Moodie after a dramatic last lap when Dunlop led Moodie by 11 seconds at Ramsey only to find on the run down the final Mountain stretch that the Scot was clawing back the time difference. Moodie eventually cut the gap in half but he still wasn't able to stop Joey from recording that landmark 20th success.

Joey had taken the lead at the halfway mark following pit stops which saw him exit sharply while the leader at that stage, Phillip McCallen, made a mess of things. From being three seconds ahead

McCallen ended up 14 seconds behind, then ran into more trouble when the exhaust pipe came loose on his Honda on the third lap and he dropped behind Moodie.

At Ramsey, Dunlop led Moodie by 18 seconds but this was reduced to 11 seconds at the end of the lap and at Glen Helen on the final circuit Dunlop's lead was down to only eight seconds. Then Joey increased this to 11 seconds at Ramsey and looked assured of victory until Moodie mounted that late charge down the Mountain.

With yet another victory in the bag Joey was looking for a treble that TT week and he made it win number 21 when he landed the 125cc class the day after his 250cc success. He had to wait for over six hours before the 125cc class was started and then it was reduced to only two laps because of the poor weather.

The race turned into a close run thing, for Gavin Lee took the lead at halfway and was still two seconds up on Joey on the last lap as the pair headed towards Ramsey. It looked as though the Dunlop success streak had come to an end but Joey levelled the issue at the beginning of the Mountain section and his experience told on the run in as he came home to win by five seconds.

Accepting the cheering of the crowd who had waited all day in pouring rain and thick mist to see him, Dunlop said: 'I got stuck in traffic in the first lap and lost the lead. I didn't think I was going to win. In fact coming over the Mountain on the last lap I was convinced that I would only be second.'

Joey didn't achieve the treble. He had to settle for second place in the Senior to McCallen but he did achieve a race average of 118.50mph.

In July Joey paid yet another visit to Eastern Europe, this time for the races in Latvia, next door to Estonia. It proved to be a watershed trip and one which almost ended Joey's career. Joey was accompanied by a Belfast TV crew who were able to capture for home consumption his crash on the fifth lap of the 250cc race which he was leading. He came home for treatment to injuries which included damage to the little finger of his left hand.

Joey had earlier put in two fine performances by winning the Senior race and the 125cc. He finished ahead of Raimo Kesseli in the Senior race and in the 125cc he beat Latvian rider Karlis Zarins.

Joey's injuries didn't appear at first to be all that serious but when he arrived home he found himself in a battle to be fit in time for the Ulster Grand Prix which was due to take place the following month. In addition to the injury to his left hand he had also banged his shoulder, but Joey was mainly concerned about the finger and visited a specialist on the first day of practice for the Ulster.

The news wasn't encouraging and it appeared at the time that there would only be a 50 per cent chance of Joey riding at Dundrod. He underwent plastic surgery on the little finger which had lost most of the skin as a result of being scraped along the road under the fairing of his bike. He was comfortable in hospital but was told he would have to rest; they weren't the words he wanted to hear.

The fans were in a state of confusion. The legion of Joey Dunlop followers who were hooked on their annual 'fix' at the Ulster couldn't take in the fact that their hero would be absent. Withdrawal symptoms were obvious everywhere as practice was dominated by rumour and counter rumour. 'Will Joey be fit?' This was the question I was asked throughout the two practice evenings. At that time an Ulster Grand Prix without Joey Dunlop was like a gin and tonic without the gin!

Davy Wood brought Joey's big Honda machines up for the practice sessions but they lay there unattended as the great man failed to appear. Linda said during practice: 'The injuries are healing but Joey isn't fully committed to racing on Saturday. It will be late in the day before he makes any decision, but he doesn't appear to be in the right frame of mind.'

Wood was equally cautious: 'I'm in the dark about Joey. But you know he has always been his own man,' he said. 'I brought his bikes up for the first practice session and he failed to appear. I was hoping he would turn up for the second session but as you know Joey is totally unpredictable.'

As it turned out, to the disappointment of thousands of Joey worshippers, Dunlop didn't appear and the meeting lost its sting. With Joey's absence McCallen had a free run and created history by winning five times out of five which equalled his five-timer at the 1992 North West 200.

The strange thing about meetings between Dunlop and McCallen during the 1990s is that they were few and far between at Dundrod. Joey certainly had the edge and scored those two epic Superbike wins in 1991. However, in 1992 McCallen was injured in a first race crash and missed the rest of the meeting, then he beat Joey in the Superbike the following year before the epic Superbike clash of 1994 came along. In 1995 McCallen was an absentee; in 1996 it was Joey who didn't appear; then in 1997 McCallen again crashed in the first race and that was his last appearance at the Ulster. So Ulster's two greatest riders of that period on public roads didn't meet as often to settle their differences as everyone imagines.

It was also during 1996 that I became very aware of the fact that Joey Dunlop, at that stage in his career, was above criticism, at least as far as his fans were concerned. Most idols have Achilles' heels but Joey didn't appear to have any – until I spotted the fact that he had appeared to make a double entry at the end of the season.

His name was on the entry list for the Carrowdore 100 in Co Down, which was due to take place in early September. This would be his first race since Latvia. But he was also booked to race in Germany so, naturally, I wondered what the score was. Riders doubling up entries are not regarded favourably by either officials or fans and when Joey failed to turn up at the Carrowdore, despite the fact that his name was on the programme, I felt it was time to air my views as forcibly as I knew how.

I wrote that in my view Joey had let the public down by entering for a meeting where he had no intention of riding. 'What was he doing in East Germany when he was entered at Carrowdore the same weekend?' I questioned. 'This coming on top of the fact that we only learned about his Ulster Grand Prix non-appearance through the grapevine gives me the impression that Joey is playing ducks and drakes with the public.' In other words he was leaving his options open until the last moment. Not a very satisfactory state of affairs, especially when his appearance at Carrowdore had been trumpeted on television virtually every night during the run up to the Ulster race.

I felt at the time that my article was fair and to the point. I wasn't aware that I would be disturbing a hornets' nest.

Letters defending Joey came into the *Belfast Telegraph* office thick and fast, all supporting Joey needless to say. 'Joey can do as he likes' was the general impression I got. So that was me put in my place.

One particular letter, which was signed by Linda Dunlop and Andy McMenemy, Joey's 125 sponsor, summed it all up. The letter said:

'We feel that the article by Jimmy Walker was a blatant attempt to deface the reputation of a man who has given 26 years of his life to motorcycle racing.

'This view has been supported by the many callers from the world of bike racing who have contacted us since the article appeared. Mr Walker would do well to remember that Joey is held in the highest regard, not only in NI but throughout the world as an outstanding sportsman and a legend in motor-cycle racing circles.

'We would like to set the record straight on two of the points mentioned. First Joey's bikes were at Dundrod during practice weeks, as stated. But he didn't compete on medical grounds having been advised just beforehand that racing at that time would set back his recovery. The organisers were of course aware of the situation.

'While Joey was provisionally entered for Carrowdore it was no secret that he was not going to compete for it was announced on television on Tuesday night that he would not be racing there.

'Mr Walker should know by now that Joey Dunlop has never gone out of his way to seek publicity; in fact the opposite is probably the case. Despite the fact that he is recognised world-wide he has no publicity machine to promote his activities, unlike many sportsmen today.

'It's unlikely that he will start now and journalists who want to keep up to date and write factual articles will have to make a bit of an effort to get their facts straight.'

Phew!!

Shortly afterwards the Sunflower Trophy international meeting took place at Bishopcourt in Co Down and during the practice session I was sitting in the double-decker bus which was used to house the timekeepers and the Press (reporting facilities for motor-cycling in Northern Ireland are still pretty basic). Into the bus strode an irate McMenemy who tackled me aggressively and said: 'What have you got against Joey Dunlop?' The blood started to drain from me as I realised the exit from the bus was blocked. However after some verbal sparring I eventually squeezed past the ruffled Andy and made my way out into the paddock where I met Davy Wood.

'I'm in trouble Davy,' I said. 'Andy McMenemy is blowing fuses about my article on Joey after the Carrowdore.'

Wood looked at me reassuringly and said: 'Never mind pal. I made those entries for Joey at Carrowdore. He didn't tell me what he was doing and I'm his manager. There will be nothing further said.' And of course he was right.

Andy and I became great friends afterwards and Joey, as far as I'm aware, never held my critical comments against me.

Meanwhile, Billy Nutt, who had organised the German trip, said to me: 'What was all the fuss about? Joey was always going to race at Fromberg. I don't know how he became involved with the Carrowdore on the same weekend.'

The mystery remains to this day.

Joey, who was coming back after a nine-week lay off following that Latvian crash, claimed sixth place in Germany in the 250cc class, although he said afterwards that he was still bothered slightly by the finger injury and found it difficult to work the clutch lever. Anyway, as far as the fans were concerned, Joey was back and that was the main thing. Life as we knew it would not end in 1996.

That year also saw Joey's brother Robert involved in a storm with officialdom which took a long time to blow over. Robert had been out of action since the Isle of Man crash in 1994 but had been cleared by the doctors to come back and had a 125cc machine adapted to his particular requirements. This meant that he had a thumb brake on the left-hand side of the bike as opposed to having a brake on the right, as is normal.

There were many officials and fans who felt that Robert was taking a chance with such a radical move. His right wrist, it was argued, had still not fully recovered and what would happen in a panic situation if Dunlop, acting on instinct, grabbed for a right-hand brake which was not there?

Billy Nutt brought the whole affair to light when he dropped a bombshell in April of that year by telling Robert that he would not be allowed to race at the North West 200. A storm erupted and there were many in the North West area who felt aggrieved that Robert had been picked on as an 'example' for those who might be tempted to take chances with their machinery and fitness in major races.

Patsy O'Kane was incensed and took the trouble to come to my house to explain the situation. 'I'm pulling out all sponsorship at the North West 200,' he told me. 'What Nutt has done is a disgrace. I have a bungalow on the course and I'm not even going to use it during race week. I am disgusted.'

Robert began to appear on television almost as many times as the Nine O'Clock News. He gave his version of what he thought should be allowed and of course Nutt also said his piece. The matter was going nowhere and as the year went on Robert had to fight a battle to take part in every race. He even had a solicitor on the case. It was all happening.

But while this maelstrom surrounding Robert showed no signs of going away, Joey remained totally unaffected. At least that is what it seemed. He was never drawn on the matter, never publicly anyway. And the added irony was that he was spearheading Nutt's road racing series in Europe at the same time as Nutt was preventing his brother from racing in Ireland! All very unusual and I often wondered what the two brothers said to each other in private. Joey never admitted to having any views on Robert's dilemma while Robert did say to me once: 'Joey is his own man. He doesn't get involved with what I do but he did tell me that perhaps I opened my mouth too much to the Press.'

Robert eventually won his battle with officialdom and although Nutt barred him again from the 1997 North West, Robert proved his point by winning at the TT and the Ulster Grand Prix in 1998.

The 1997 season was a quiet one as far as Joey was concerned. Once again the TT was the centrepiece and early in the season Joey took delivery of a new 500cc VTwin Honda.

Off the track, however, Joey made news when he passed his motorcycle learning test! He admitted: 'I was more nervous doing the test than I had ever been during a race.' The 21 times TT winner had, by 1997, not ridden a bike on public roads since those early days as a teenager – but he decided that it was about time to learn again. 'I am coming to the end of my racing career and I thought it was time to get my licence so that I could go out for recreational purposes,' he said. 'Now if someone offers me a run on a road bike I will be able to say yes. I had to get used to the traffic and it is difficult concentrating on riding on one side of the road.'

He didn't take any lessons while waiting for the test date but a friend loaned him a bike and the examiner – from Coleraine Driving Test Centre – was not overawed by having such a prestigious learner in front of him. To the examiner, Joey was just the same as anyone else. Afterwards Joey added: 'You may see me riding along at a sedate pace below the speed limit around Coleraine but I think I will keep off the streets of Belfast until I get used to it!'

Joey certainly had no problem with the roads in the Isle of Man and he went there in June 1997 looking for his 22nd TT win. He had the usual maximum number of entries but this time only one victory. Once again it was the 'old favourite', the 250cc class which he lifted for the fourth year in a row. Joey won by almost a minute from Ian Lougher and John McGuinness, averaging 115.59mph for the four laps. But Joey would be the first to admit that his victory had a hollow ring about it for McCallen fell off at Quarry Bends on the third lap. Fortunately he was uninjured and later ran up a treble that week.

In many ways McCallen handed the 250cc race to Joey for he was leading by three seconds at Ramsey on lap two after which the riders came in for their pit stop. Dunlop had a smooth changeover and was out in 25 seconds but for some reason McCallen decided to change the rear wheel and this led to problems. By the time he had got going again, he had allowed Dunlop to lead the race by 18 seconds and he fell off while trying to make up the lost time. For McCallen this was bad luck for the fourth time in what had become his jinxed Isle of Man race.

In February 1998 Joey reached 46 years of age and to mark the occasion Linda bought him an unusual birthday present – a trip to Australia. This holiday jaunt, which he made on his own, was to add further lustre to the legend and also give birth to the most famous Joey Dunlop story of them all.

While staying in Queensland Joey took out a friend's bike for a test ride. He had edged five miles an hour over the speed limit when he was flagged down by a highway patrol police officer. Approaching Joey the officer asked sarcastically: 'Who do you think you are, Joey Dunlop?' When Joey confirmed that he was in fact that same person, the stunned patrolman speedily withdrew the penalty ticket and replaced it with a request for an autograph!

On returning to his hotel room, Joey was surprised to find a message asking him to report to the local police station. 'When I got the call to go to the station the next day, I thought they were going to book me,' he said. Joey arrived to find instead a full house with local policemen waiting for him with autograph books and cameras. After a short 'detention' during which Joey signed autographs he was finally released!

Apart from expanding his world-wide fame, that Australian trip charged Joey's batteries for yet another season – in which he hoped to add to his seemingly unending list of TT successes. Honda again supplied him with a new 500cc bike for the Cookstown 100 – the first race of the new season on 25 April. But it was the Tandragee 100 in May of that year which pushed Joey back on to the front pages. Once again he was involved in a shattering crash which many thought would signal the end of his career.

While riding in the 125cc race and lying in third place behind Owen McNally and his brother Robert, he parted company with his Honda on a series of bumps between Castle Corner and Cooley Hill, halfway round the circuit. The race was immediately stopped while Dunlop was attended to by course medical officials and was then sent to hospital. But the rumours had already started.

'Joey's dead.' This was what we heard in an otherwise hushed paddock and it was then that a youngster blurted out: 'He can't be dead – he's Joey Dunlop.'

Robert meanwhile was able to give an eye witness view of what had happened: 'The first I knew about it was when I saw Joey's bike career past me into the side of the road,' he said. 'Later when I came round on the slowing down lap after the race was stopped I saw Joey on the side of the road and immediately went over to find out what had happened. He seemed to be in good spirits but in great pain and it looked as though both his hands were broken.'

It gradually began to emerge that Joey had suffered major injury and was lucky to have avoided being killed. Had he hit a wall or a tree instead of bouncing down the road the crash would almost certainly have been fatal. But Joey's luck was in.

Later in hospital Joey revealed that he had lost the top of the ring finger of his left hand. Just hours after surgeons had operated on his wedding ring finger he said: 'I am very sore at the moment. I have lost the point of the finger but I'm not sure how much. From what I have been told, the operation went well.' Joey, who also suffered pelvic injuries and a broken collar bone, added that he was very lucky to be alive.

As for the future, well obviously the North West 200 was out of the question and even the Isle of Man TT looked doubtful. As Linda stayed by his bedside at the Ulster Hospital, which specialises in micro-surgery, doctors were assessing the extent of his injuries. He was eventually told he was on the mend, but the resumption of his racing career appeared to be non-existent.

But Joey was unstoppable when he had his mind made up – and he was determined that he wouldn't miss another TT. So he sat out the North West 200 and concentrated on the one meeting which by now had become his sole reason for continuing to road race. Once again it was a haggard-looking Joey who made his way to the medical centre in Douglas just as he had done in 1989. However this time there was a happier ending. He was given the all clear and incredibly he added a 23rd TT victory to his list when winning the 250cc class for the fifth year in a row.

This was one of the great races of Dunlop's career for here was a man whom some would have said shouldn't have been racing at all on what many regarded as the most dangerous circuit in the world. In addition the race was totally wrecked by the conditions. Lashing rain made it seem impossible that riders would be allowed on to this unforgiving circuit. But eventually the decision was made to start, with the race trimmed from four laps to three.

With the rain pelting down it soon became obvious that even three laps would be stretching the endurance level of the riders and halfway through the second lap it was announced that the race would be stopped after that lap. This suited the 'old fox' Joey Dunlop right down to the ground. He had known inherently that the race would not go full distance so he set out to take the lead right from the start in the hope that the race would soon be short-ened and he would be in front at that time.

Joey chose the right set of tyres and at the end of the first lap, while others pulled into the pits, the wily Joey went straight on. This move paid off for he had soon built up an unassailable advan-tage. This could have backfired on him had the race gone the full distance, but when the officials decided to stop it at the end of lap two Joey was home and dry – figuratively speaking – for in practical terms he was soaked to the skin!

Joey said afterwards: 'Had it been a full four-lap race on dry roads I might not have stuck the race because of my recent injuries. I had a feeling the race would only go two laps but I told the boys in the pits to get ready to refuel after lap one. Then I made the decision to go straight through and it paid off. At the beginning of the race I felt I was too old for this sort of thing, but I can tell you I feel a lot younger now!'

History was made when Robert won the 125cc class. Despite their many successes over the years, this was the first time that both brothers had scored TT wins in the same week. Robert had won four times previously but that 1998 success was surely his most memorable. After four years of battling against injury the man they called 'Micro Dunlop' had at last made it back to the podium in Douglas.

Robert was emotional and choked back the tears as he told a packed audience at the Villa Marina prizegiving that evening: 'This is the best TT I have ever won. Psychologically and physically I will always remember it and I will never forget my friends.' Second placed man Ian Lougher paid tribute to Robert's resilience when he said: 'The best 125cc rider in the country won out there today.' And this was cheered to the echo by the packed hall.

Meanwhile Joey, who had finished a lowly ninth in the race, said that he intended to rest because there were still pains in his hands following his crash at Tandragee. Later that year, although he rode in the Ulster Grand Prix, it was brother Robert who again stole the show when winning the 125cc race to seal a memorable comeback year.

With the year 2000 looming there was no sign of any let-up in Joey Dunlop's hunger for the sport and although he had no TT successes in 1999, he still produced a race for the history books. The Ulster Grand Prix was the occasion and I will never forget the sight of Joey charging past David Jefferies on the run to the finish of the final Superbike race to give 50,000 fans at Dundrod an experience they will remember for many years to come. Joey also lapped his favourite track faster than at any time in his career. A speed of 126.84mph at 47 years of age!

But death is never far away from this most demanding and exhil-arating of sports and tragedy struck in the very last race when Owen McNally, one of Joey's closest friends, crashed into a ditch on the final bend of the 250cc class. He died shortly afterwards.

It was a loss which Ulster motorcycling felt in many ways repre-sented the final straw. For many years riders who had been house-hold names had been killed either on Ulster roads or on the Isle of Man and after McNally's crash, which was seen by millions on tele-vison, it was agreed that the time had to come to make greater efforts for safety.

Chicanes, which brought riders to a virtual halt, were thought of as the answer – or at least part of the answer – to making courses much safer. But ironically Joey was one of those who fought this idea. 'I think they do nothing for road racing,' he told me. He was certainly not a happy man at the new moves; Joey was a traditional-ist through and through.

But the safety of Ulster circuits and the controversy which these changes aroused were still to come in the year 2000. Before then Joey received an unexpected £500,000 Christmas present when his old friend, Honda Chief Bob McMillan, gave him the RC45 Honda which had brought Joey such success in 1999. McMillan said at the time: 'Joey is the longest contracted rider with Honda and they thought it would be marvellous to give him this bike. He can keep it or put it in a museum.'

A short time later, at the beginning of the 2000 season, McMillan is reported to have gone further in his admiration for Dunlop when he told a friend: 'I am advocating that if Joey retires he should receive a lifetime job from Honda for he has been our standard bearer over many years. I would like to see him retire now when he is at the top and has done everything. We owe him so much. We can never repay him.'

Sadly, for everyone connected with motorcycle racing the world over, Joey had other ideas.

CHAPTER 16

A WORLD IN MOURNING

At 4am on the morning of Tuesday 20 June 2000 Joey Dunlop, living legend, got into his van alone and drove to Eastern Europe in order to ride in a road racing event in Estonia. His family and friends never heard from him again . . .

I suppose you could say this was pure theatre or, if you like, something out of a Hollywood film script. It was the big exit. John Wayne walking off into the mist at the end of one of his classic movies. Of course Joey Dunlop didn't intend to go out like this but then there are those of us who would say that it was bound to happen some time. Could you really imagine Joey turning up as a pensioner and reminiscing about the old days? It just wasn't his style. He liked to do things his own way and usually unescorted.

That was the case during a week in June when he reached the pinnacle with that glorious treble at the TT. His exploits on the track during that TT week have been well recorded but even when not racing Joey was making a name for himself. Very few people are aware that he was elected president of the TT Riders' Association the night before he clinched the treble in the 125cc TT.

Former road racer Tommy Robb, who has had a long association with the TT, told me: 'I had the privilege of getting to know the great man more closely over the final few years of his career than I had at any time in the previous 30. The reason for this was that the

TT Riders' Association had agreed during my own year in office as president that it would be appropriate to have someone 'extra special' in the chair for the Millennium Year 2000.

'A unanimous decision was taken that there was only one man who could fill that position and it was 'Yer Maun'. Knowing what a shy person Joey was, and that he was renowned for shunning the limelight, we realised it was going to be no easy task to get him into the presidential chair.

'I am delighted to say that we managed to get Jim Geddis, who had assisted Joey during part of his career, to persuade him to say 'yes' in time for the 2000 TTRA annual meeting at Tremode Cricket Club near the bottom of Bray Hill.

'That night Joey, in front of a large number of former 'TT' riders and their guests, was installed as our president and was also adorned with the presidential chain around his neck.

'Joey also delighted everyone in the room by making a wonderful acceptance speech (contrary to his dislike of public speaking). But then he had to be excused early as he dashed off to get out of his suit and tie at 8pm to get back into his overalls to finish preparing his bikes for Wednesday's races.

'I remember that night well because Joey told me he was more worried about his speech, that as the new president he would have to make later in the year at the annual dinner of the TTRA in the Motorcycle Museum, than he was about the races in which he was about to participate for the rest of TT week. That was Joey. Uppermost on his mind was racing. He had little time for anything else.'

Joey of course completed his treble but even then he showed his anxiety to be elsewhere once the job was done. Throughout his career Joey loved to get there, win his races, then get home as quickly as possible. It was though he never liked to join in the celebrations which others expected of him. In fact when one of my friends, Willis Marshall, Press Officer for former Robert Dunlop sponsor Patsy O'Kane, approached Joey immediately after his 125cc win he asked him: 'I suppose you will go out and celebrate now.' To which Joey replied as he pushed his machine away from the start-ing area: 'To tell you the truth I'd rather be back home in Ballymoney.'

Not long after the congratulations had been exhausted Joey did get his wish to travel home again but sadly, and perhaps more than any of us will know, he was struck by the news that his friend and long time sponsor Andy McMenemy had taken his own life. This was a shattering blow, not only to Joey, but to everyone else in motorcycling.

McMenemy's death took place only four days after the Senior TT – the final race on the Saturday – and I will never forget how I learned of the news. I had been speaking to Andy on the Saturday and he seemed quite chirpy and self confident as usual, predicting a Joey win. Then on the Wednesday my telephone rang at home and it was Harold Crooks to tell me that Andy was dead. His death had taken place on the same night that Joey was awarded the freedom of the town of Ballymoney - a function which Andy had decided not to attend.

Shortly after the funeral, which naturally Joey attended, the word was out that the great man was about to retire from the road racing scene. I was pursued by the Ulster broadcasting media to find out the answer but Joey hadn't turned up at practice for the Dundrod 150 which was taking place that Saturday and his brother Robert confided in me: 'I don't know what the future holds. He has been upset as you know and a lot of the gloss has been taken off that TT treble. I can't tell you whether or not Joey will pack it in. Only he will make that decision at a time which suits himself.'

Needless to say Joey didn't ride in the Dundrod 150 and it seemed to me as though his season has gone on 'hold' after which he would come back, as he always did, and ride in the Ulster Grand Prix.

That was the scenario as I saw it but there is always a twist.

A few nights later I was attending a press conference at the Temple Golf and Country Club in Co Down. The meeting had been called to promote a motocross event. At some point during the evening Jim Cray, President of the Motor Cycle Union of Ireland, told me that Joey had applied for insurance cover to race in Russia.

'In Russia?' I said.

'Well I think that's the case,' replied Jim. 'My wife has the details, I will give her a ring.'

So we left the press conference, Jim rang home and afterwards told me: 'It's not Russia. Apparently it's Latvia.'

Determined to establish exactly what was happening I drove home and rang Linda. She told me that Joey had already gone, as far as she was aware, to Latvia. The next day a further twist. I spoke to Billy Nutt and although he wasn't sure of the arrangements he thought Joey was riding in Estonia; apparently he had been invited there by the Estonian Motor Cycling Federation.

So that was it. Life went on until that never to be forgotten day on Sunday 2 July 2000 when the word came through that Joey had crashed and been killed. The news came to me via a phone call from Willis Marshall. I was at the Curragh race course at the time covering the Irish Derby and you can imagine my reaction when I heard the news about Joey on my mobile phone. I just didn't believe it, but I contacted Downtown radio station near Belfast and told them of what I had heard. It came as a bombshell to them but they did their checks and called me back to say that it was true.

After that, the world turned upside-down as far as I was concerned. I broadcast an immediate appreciation of Joey and then wrote numerous other articles off the cuff that afternoon for various newspapers while covering the Irish Derby as well. Needless to say, my mind was in a whirl when I came home.

So what actually had happened to Joey? What were the circumstances surrounding his accident? The news we had received was that he had crashed into a clump of trees during the 125cc race, which was held in heavy rain.

I phoned Billy Nutt's wife Isobel to try to piece together more details, for I knew that Nutt would have the key to some of the questions. Nutt learned of Joey's death from John Caffrey, a fellow road racer and the only other British rider with Joey at the Estonia meeting. Billy was at a meeting at Silverstone with his son Marty at the time so Caffrey spoke to Isobel.

'I couldn't believe the news,' said Isobel. 'I rang Billy and told him what had happened. Billy asked me was I sure that it was Caffrey on the phone and I said I was. Billy couldn't take in that Joey was dead either. My son Marty was with Billy. He had been competing at Silverstone and had fallen off but, believe it or not, I was so shocked by Joey Dunlop's death that I forgot to ask about my own son.'

Billy takes up the story from there. 'When I received the call it was like the ground had opened up underneath me,' he said. 'My first thought was, "Is this true and if so how am I going to tell Joey's family?" Eventually I contacted Jim Archibald, who was one of Dunlop's closest friends and the father of road racer Adrian Archibald. I asked Jim if he would go round to Linda and break the news. Linda rang me back and told me she didn't believe it; eventually her daughter Donna came on the phone and I told her. It was a terrible day.'

Meanwhile Patsy O'Kane had been sitting at home when he received a phone call from Robert Dunlop's mechanic Liam Beckett. 'Joey's son Richard was staying with Liam for Richard was a good friend of Liam's son,' Patsy said. 'In the early afternoon Joey's daughter Julie came to the door looking for Richard and told him about the news of their father. Beckett phoned me and alerted me as to what had happened. "Are you sure?" I said. Liam replied "Sadly I am. The two kids are standing here crying in my house."'

O'Kane then phoned Marshall, who contacted me, and the world was soon to know that the legend that was Joey Dunlop was no longer.

So what did happen to Joey in Estonia? In order to get to the bottom of it I contacted John Caffrey and he told me of Joey's final hours. In many ways they are poignant and say a lot about the personality of this great rider.

'I met Joey at the circuit at Tallinn shortly before racing began on the Saturday,' John told me. 'It had been raining heavily and was still raining when we went out to ride in the 600cc class. Joey led for a while and then I passed him and felt quite pleased to do so. There was a lot of heavy traffic on the course and it was difficult to get past some of the tailenders but I managed to finish in second place and I can tell you I was really chuffed. Joey and I were great friends and the fact that he was out in Estonia perked me up no end.

'I was looking forward to standing on the podium with him the next day which was the Sunday. It's not often you can say that you are up there with Joey Dunlop.

'We went for a meal that night and we talked about the old days, reminiscing about a lot of the races we had been involved in. Joey was of my era and he knew many of the people whom I had competed against. I was never going to be of the class of Joey Dunlop but that didn't matter to Joey. He regarded me as a friend and a long time campaigner whom he obviously felt at ease with. We chatted about different things and about an accident we recalled in Sicily. To be honest I had never seen Joey so relaxed as he was that night. At the time of the TT I thought he had looked stressed but this wasn't the case in Tallinn. He was sitting back and laughing. It was just the old Joey of many years earlier and he told me that he loved Eastern Europe and would like to race there again the following year.

'Eventually we finished our meal and went back to the camp where the riders were staying. As I was about to nod off to sleep Joey wakened me and said that he couldn't settle and that he was going back to his van and into his sleeping bag. So, on what turned out to be his last night alive, Joey Dunlop spent it as he had done so many times sleeping in his van.

'The following morning Joey won the Superbike race. To be honest I don't know where I finished, but after I came in I put my bike on the stand and then was rather amazed to see Joey change my front wheel. "That's what you need for the next Superbike race," he told me. "You'll not get any grip with what you had in that first race."

'Joey was then set to compete in the 125cc race, after which he and I would ride again in the second Superbike. He asked me to hold up his 125cc front wheel and I did so but I don't know what tyre he put on. At the same time I was busy getting my bike ready for the Superbike. Anyway, the 125cc race went off and after a short time I was aware of a great silence. There was the lone sound of a woman screaming and that was all. I realised that something terrible had happened.

'I am an ex-policeman and I dashed to the scene of the accident and sure enough it was Joey Dunlop who had been involved. I helped the officials at the accident and attended to Joey's bike which was badly damaged. He had a full wet tyre on the front and an intermediate on the back and I wondered why he had chosen that combination. It was so unlike Joey. It was obvious to me that the back end of the bike would swing out of control in any emergency given this choice of tyres.

'Ironically the corner where Joey crashed was one which I had wanted resurfaced before the meeting. The Estonians couldn't have been more helpful and I arrived at the meeting thinking that they had done what I had asked. But they had got it wrong and resurfaced the wrong corner. I had a look at the corner where Joey was later to crash and it was full of deep ruts, the result of years of heavy traffic moving along this road. After all, we were using the public highway.

'I could see that rain had fallen into the grooves which had been made by trucks and I pointed this out to Joey during practice. I told him that a bike would weave about if it hit any of those ruts and that the water would make it worse. But Joey laughed it off and said that we were used to racing in these conditions and what of it. We would be OK.

'This was a fast left-hander, about 120–125mph, so we were talking about a major part of the course. Well, Joey went on and raced as you know and the only conclusion I could come to regarding his accident was that the back end had stepped out and he had lost control. What is not generally known was that he hit a woman and a child before he struck the tree. He was obviously trying to avoid them but he was killed instantly.

'The Eastern Europeans have a different view of death than we have in the West. While we would be more respectful of anyone who has been killed, they were dashing about photographing Joey's body from all directions. I couldn't really apportion blame to them for that is their way of life but I didn't like it at the time.'

John also revealed that Joey's body was discovered without a good luck pendant from Linda which he usually wore in a race. 'Despite the use of metal detectors we just couldn't find it,' Caffrey said. 'I can only come to the conclusion that it was either stolen by someone as Joey's body lay there or that Joey didn't wear it at all. I honestly don't know.'

Linda was not only devastated by Joey's death but in anguish because of the keepsake which had been lost. In an interview in the *Daily Mirror* a few weeks after Joey's death she said 'This was a gold chain and medallion which Joey always wore. It was not expensive but it was a special thing, something which Joey never took off. I would love to have it back.'

Joey bought the medallion in Japan and Linda bought him the gold chain so that he could always wear it. Needless to say Linda's reaction to the whole affair was, in her grief, to lash out at the fact that the race was held at all. In the same *Daily Mirror* interview she said: 'I hate the way it has ended. I despise Estonia, the country – not the people – for taking Joey away from me. I know nothing about the place but that is where it happened – it's where half of my life closed down. But to be honest if it was going to happen it is so much better that it happened there rather than at home.

'For Joey to be killed on his home ground would have been harder for me to cope with. I would have been driving past the place and I would have hated it and anything associated with it. And I would probably, along with the rest of my family, have grown to detest the people who ran the race and they wouldn't have deserved that. So it's easy for me to hate Estonia because I never have to see it. I have no memories of it – and I can blank it out.'

Public shock at the death of Joey was enormous in Northern Ireland; sadly it came at a time when the Province was going through one of its periods of civil unrest. Joey's body had to be brought home and the only person out in Estonia, other than Caffrey, who was involved with Joey was sponsor John Harris, who had arrived at the weekend to see Joey race. It was obvious that one of the Honda big guns was needed to sort out the red tape and Bob McMillan flew out to Tallinn to organise the despatch of the body back home to Ulster.

Ironically the body had to be flown to Dublin and from there it received a motorcycle escort all the way to the Irish border. By this time it was nearly midnight and Ulster had not yet settled down after another day of violence which had included hijacked cars and burning barricades. It was totally the worst time to bring a body home by road along the dark roads of South Down and South Armagh.

As it turned out the vehicle carrying the body had to make a few diversions in order to bring it home to Ballymoney but eventually they did so in the early hours of the morning. However, the trouble which they had encountered was not lost on Robert Dunlop, who made a plea on television to the people of the Province asking them to allow his brother to be buried in peace without any obstructions on the roads. And this is exactly what happened.

Northern Ireland is a strange place as we all know. It can switch on and it can also switch off virtually on cue. After Robert's impassioned pleas, the day of Joey's funeral went off not only smoothly but one might say superbly – if that is the right word to use for such a tragic occasion.

Linda had said that she had expected a crowd of about 3,000 at the funeral. But nearly 60,000 turned up. As far as I was concerned I parked along with Willis Marshall as near as I could get – or thought I could get – to Garryduff Presbyterian Church where Joey was to be buried. But it was a long walk from where we parked to the graveyard.

I must have walked the best part of four miles along roads which were teeming with fans and people who simply regarded Joey as their idol. It hadn't yet sunk in that Joey was dead and it seemed as though most of Ulster had to be there to witness the evidence with their own eyes. Joey's daughter Donna touched everyone's feelings when she read out a poem she had written about her father. Tributes poured into the radio, television and the press. There were also tribute sites posted on the internet so that fans throughout the world could pay their respects.

In addition to his supporters from around the Province the Manx Radio broadcasters also arrived on the scene to pay their own tribute. Peter Kneale told me when I eventually arrived – half exhausted – at the burial point: 'We'll never see the like of this man again. As far as I'm concerned he made the TT and was the reason for keeping it going over the past two decades. I am honoured to have known him.'

Geoff Cannell of 'Gasoline Alley' was also there along with other broadcasters; from the political world the Rev. Ian Paisley, MP for North Antrim where Joey lived, also paid his tribute as did Kate Hoey, Minister for Sport at Westminster. Ms Hoey is of Ulster extraction and had been at the TT only weeks earlier to witness Joey's success.

She said: 'Joey was a wonderful ambassador and I am particularly upset after having presented him with his prizes at the TT garlanding ceremony last month. This is terribly sad news and I am just so shocked. He was a wonderful ambassador for Northern Ireland and for his sport and truly showed dedication and commitment. I extend my deepest sympathy to his family. I enjoyed his company on the Isle of Man and it was so thrilling to see him win there. His loss is a huge one to the sport of motorcycle racing. He will be missed throughout the world.'

Rev. Ian Paisley added: 'I happened to be in North Antrim when I heard the news of the champion's death. It has cast a dark shadow over us all. North Antrim has lost one of its most prominent citizens in the field of sport. The whole of the county as well as the rest of Northern Ireland will mourn his loss.'

The then Secretary of State for Northern Ireland, Peter Mandelson, said: 'There are few sportsmen who are acknowledged by the world as masters of their craft. Joey Dunlop undisputedly was one. As such, in his unassuming way, he brought immense honour to Northern Ireland and rightly was a source of pride for many in that country, both fans of motorcycling and those who were not.'

Joey's old rival Phillip McCallen was in a sombre mood. 'It is unbelievable that Joey Dunlop is no more. As you know I retired from the sport this year and I had tinkered with the thought of making a comeback. In fact, at the Skerries 100 [in Co Dublin] I did a few parade laps and I enjoyed myself but the day afterwards when I heard of Joey's death my mind was settled. Take it from me I could never race again.

'Joey was the sort of rider who could do anything. If he felt like it he would win. If he didn't he would be content to finish down the field. I could never do that. I was always a win or bust man. That's why I admired Joey so much because of the way he was in control. There were days when I rode as fast as I could but when Joey was in the mood he would always beat me. He just had that edge.

'There were many who felt he should have retired but I'm not one of them. After all he was still winning so why give up so soon? It would have been different if he had been tailed off in every race. He had great fun for 20 years and I can see his point in continuing. He was going better than ever at the time he died.

'Racing will miss him enormously. The problem is that we all thought that Joey Dunlop would live forever. There will certainly never be a rider like him.'

Billy Nutt said: 'Joey did everything his own way. He just decided to drive to Estonia on his own and that was that. It is a great tragedy that his career has come to such a terrible end. He was an ambassador for the sport everywhere but no one ever really got close to him. Of course motorcycling will continue but nothing will ever be the same.'

The people of the Isle of Man paid their own tribute on 26 August when former Honda team-mate Ron Haslam led a special cavalcade of bikers with Joey's son Gary on the pillion of the SP-1 Honda on which Joey had won the Formula One race in June. Over 5,000 bikers from all over the world were in the parade and Haslam said: 'It's an honour to be asked to lead it. Joey and I had some battles at the TT as well as at the Ulster Grand Prix and his career will be remembered for as long as there is road racing.'

Included in the cavalcade were not only road bikes but scooters and trial machines. According to Peter Kneale, the bikes were crossing the line at the Grandstand at around 180 per minute. 'It was truly amazing,' he said.

In addition to the bikers' parade a commemorative stone plaque of Joey was cemented into the wall at the TT start alongside that of Mike Hailwood. Both memorials are next to the timing box. Included in the inscription are the words 'From the people and Government of the Isle of Man'.

In September, with Joey's death still raw, Joey's father and mother Willie and May were interviewed by Gail Walker in the *Belfast Telegraph*. Of course, it was a time for reminiscing. 'Joey loved travelling but he also missed his home,' his father said. 'He would call round here for a cup of tea and on other occasions he would just say "Come on dad and we'll head off and look at the bikes".'

Joey's father loved to recall the story of Joey being stopped for speeding by the Australian patrolman and speeding offences appeared to have been a recurring hazard where Joey was concerned.

His mother recalled how a few years earlier she was asked to be an audience member of Ulster Television's *Kelly Show*. It was a special Mother's Day edition and as a surprise Joey was to walk on to the set bearing a large bouquet of flowers for his mother. May said: 'He came on stage towards me looking a bit flustered. "Mum I'm lucky to have got here at all," he told me. "I was coming back through England and I thought I was going to miss the boat. I was going that hard I ended up getting another speeding ticket." That was Joey for you.'

The week leading up to Joey's funeral as his remains were

brought home from Tallinn was agonisingly long. May said that she will never know where she and her husband found the strength to get out of bed, get dressed and get through the service and the burial. They were astonished by the tens of thousands of mourners although they were glad that everyone who wanted to attend was able to do so.

They say that time heals all wounds and eventually Joey's parents began to smile again, although the thought of him will never leave their minds. In many ways Joey's father appeared to feel relieved that his son's career had ended in such a manner. Many of us are of the opinion that he would not have liked to have seen Joey turning up at motorcycle functions as someone from the past. They were not going to say so but his parents are obviously proud of the way he lived and died.

Still, world motorcycling has found it difficult to come to terms with such a sudden and dramatic end to an era. As a friend of George Gershwin said at the funeral of the great composer of the 1920s and 30s: 'I don't have to believe it if I don't want to – and I don't want to.' That's the way most people in motorcycle road racing have felt since Joey's death. Sure, there will be more champions, but there will never be another with such a grip on the public's affection.

Quite simply, we'll never see his like again.

CAREER STATISTICS

Main Road Race wins

Isle of Man TT	26 wins
Formula One world championship title	5 wins
North West 200	13 wins
Ulster Grand Prix	24 wins
Southern 100 (Isle of Man)	31 wins
Isle of Man Steam Packet Co. Races	11 wins

Irish National Road Races – 117 wins

Temple 100	5
Mid-Antrim 150	15
Killalane	6
Kells	2
Carrowdore 100	8
Skerries	17
Killinchy 150	22
Dundrod 150	2
Monaghan	1
Tandragee 100	17
Cookstown 100	11
Fore	6
Munster 100	1
Dundalk	4

Isle of Man TT wins

Joey Dunlop made his Isle of Man TT debut in 1976, finishing 16th in the Junior and 18th in the Senior races.

1977	Jubilee TT	Yamaha	108.86mph
1980	Classic TT	Yamaha	112.72mph
1983	Formula One TT	Honda	114.03mph
1984	Formula One TT	Honda	111.68mph
1985	Formula One TT	Honda	113.95mph
	Junior TT	Honda	109.91mph
	Senior TT	Honda	113.69mph
1986	Formula One TT	Honda	112.96mph
1987	Formula One TT	Honda	115.03mph
	Senior TT	Honda	99.85mph
1988	Formula One TT	Honda	116.25mph
	Junior TT	Honda	111.87mph
	Senior TT	Honda	117.38mph
1992	125cc TT	Honda	106.49mph
1993	125cc TT	Honda	107.26mph
1994	125cc TT	Honda	105.74mph
	Junior TT	Honda	114.67mph
1995	Lightweight TT	Honda	115.68mph
	Senior TT	Honda	119.11mph
1996	125cc TT	Honda	106.33mph
	250cc TT	Honda	115.31mph
1997	250cc TT	Honda	115.59mph
1998	250cc TT	Honda	96.61mph
2000	Formula One TT	Honda	120.99mph
	250cc TT	Honda	116.01mph
	125cc TT	Honda	107.14mph

Joey Dunlop's fastest ever TT lap was set in the Senior race on Saturday 10 June, 2000 – 123.87mph – on his way to third place behind David Jefferies and Michael Rutter.

TT Formula One world championship results

1980

1.	Graeme Crosby (New Zealand)	Suzuki	27 points
2.	Mick Grant (GB)	Honda	25
3.	Joey Dunlop (Ireland)	Honda	12

1981

1.	Graeme Crosby (New Zealand)	Suzuki	27
2.	Ron Haslam (GB)	Honda	27
3.	Joey Dunlop (Ireland)	Honda	16

1982

1.	Joey Dunlop (Ireland)	Honda	36
2.	Ron Haslam (GB)	Suzuki	30
3.	Dave Hiscock (New Zealand)	Suzuki	26

1983

1.	Joey Dunlop (Ireland)	Honda	42
2.	Rob McElnea (GB)	Suzuki	35
3.	Roger Marshall (GB)	Honda	26

1984

1.	Joey Dunlop (Ireland)	Honda	66
2.	Roger Marshall (GB)	Honda	54
3.	Tony Rutter (GB)	Ducati	36

1985

1.	Joey Dunlop (Ireland)	Honda	90
2.	Mick Grant (GB)	Suzuki	40
3.	Graeme McGregor (Australia)	Suzuki	32

1986

1.	Joey Dunlop (Ireland)	Honda	93
2.	Paul Iddon (GB)	Suzuki	61
3.	Anders Andersson (Sweden)	Suzuki	58

1987

1.	Virginio Ferrari (Italy)	Bimota	49
2.	Joey Dunlop (Ireland)	Honda	46
3.	Paul Iddon (GB)	Suzuki	43

1988

1.	Carl Fogarty (GB)	Honda	84
2.	Joey Dunlop (GB)	Honda	63.5
3.	Roger Burnett (GB)	Honda	62

1989
Joey Dunlop was injured in an accident at Brands Hatch early in the year and missed the Formula One world championship of 1989. He rode in the Ulster Grand Prix in August, finishing 20th in the Formula One race.

1990 FIM TT Cup (the Formula One title was dropped for 1990)

1.	Carl Fogarty (GB)	Honda	71
2.	Joey Dunlop (Ireland)	Honda	54
3.	Robert Dunlop (Ireland)	Norton	49

Machines ridden by Joey:
Triumph, Suzuki, Aermacchi, Yamaha, Benelli, Honda

British Championship rounds
1980
Forward Trust/Motor Cycle Weekly TT Formula One
    championship:
Winner – Mick Grant (Suzuki)
7th – Joey Dunlop (Suzuki)

1981
Marlboro Transatlantic Trophy – Individual riders' scores:
Winner – John Newbold (Suzuki)
14th – Joey Dunlop (Honda)

Forward Trust/Motor Cycle Weekly TT Formula One
   championship
Winner – Graeme Crosby (Suzuki)
6th – Joey Dunlop (Honda)

Motor Cycle News/Shell Streetbike championship
Winner – Ron Haslam (Honda)
6th – Joey Dunlop (Honda)

1982
British TT Formula One championship
Winner – Roger Marshall (Suzuki)
6th – Joey Dunlop (Honda)

Motor Cycle News Superbike championship
Winner – Roger Marshall (Suzuki)
15th – Joey Dunlop (Honda)

Motor Cycle News/Shell Streetbike championship
Winner (tie) – Wayne Gardner (Honda) / Ron Haslam (Honda)
2nd – Joey Dunlop (Honda)

1983
Motor Cycle News Masters championship
Winner – Keith Huewen (Suzuki)
10th – Joey Dunlop (Honda)

ACU Shell Oils TT Formula One championship
Winner – Wayne Gardner (Honda)
5th – Joey Dunlop (Honda)

1984
ITV World of Sport Superbike Challenge
Winner – Ron Haslam (Honda)
15th – Joey Dunlop (Honda)

Shell Oils TT Formula One championship
Winner – Wayne Gardner (Honda)
5th – Joey Dunlop (Honda)

1985
ITV World of Sport Superbike Challenge
Winner – Wayne Gardner (Honda)
17th – Joey Dunlop (Honda)

British Grand Prix
Winner – A. Mang (Honda)
10th – Joey Dunlop (Honda)

Macau Grand Prix
1982

1.	Ron Haslam (GB)	Honda	84.98mph
2.	Mick Grant (GB)	Suzuki	
3.	Joey Dunlop (Ireland)	Honda	

1983

1.	Ron Haslam (GB)	Honda	85.93mph
2.	Joey Dunlop (Ireland)	Honda	
3.	Roger Marshall (GB)	Honda	

INDEX

#KillChalk